P9-BJB-708

DATE DUE

MY15 '89		

362.292 CAH
Cahalan, Don.
Understanding America's
 drinking problem

BRENTWOOD SCHOOL LIBRARY
155 SOUTH LAYTON DRIVE
LOS ANGELES, CALIFORNIA 90049
(213) 476-9633

T 21373

EX LIBRIS

BRENTWOOD SCHOOL
DONATED BY:

Peter Sather

Brentwood School Library
155 S. Layton Drive
Los Angeles, CA 90049
(213) 476-9633

Understanding
America's Drinking Problem

Don Cahalan

Understanding
America's Drinking Problem

*How to Combat the
Hazards of Alcohol*

Jossey-Bass Publishers
San Francisco • London • 1987

UNDERSTANDING AMERICA'S DRINKING PROBLEM
How to Combat the Hazards of Alcohol
   by Don Cahalan

Copyright © 1987 by: Jossey-Bass Inc., Publishers
                      433 California Street
                      San Francisco, California 94104

                            &

                      Jossey-Bass Limited
                      28 Banner Street
                      London EC1Y 8QE

Copyright under International, Pan American, and Universal Copyright
Conventions. All rights reserved. No part of this book may be reproduced in any
form—except for brief quotation (not to exceed 1,000 words) in a review or
professional work—without permission in writing from the publishers.

Excerpts from the paper "Alcohol Studies in Social Perspective" by R. Straus
delivered at the meeting of the Research Society on Alcoholism and the Medical
Society on Alcoholism, San Francisco, April 21, 1986, are reprinted with the
permission of the author.

Excerpts from *The Booze Merchants: The Inebriating of America* by M. Jacobson,
R. Atkins, and G. Hacker are reprinted with the permission of the Center for
Science in the Public Interest, Washington, D.C., copyright © 1983.

Excerpts from the article "The Problem of Alcohol Advertisements in College
Newspapers" by J. De Foe and W. Breed are taken from the *Journal of the
American College Health Association, 27,* 195–199, February 1979. Reprinted with
permission of the Helen Dwight Reid Educational Foundation. Published by
Heldref Publications, 4000 Albemarle St., N.W., Washington, D.C. 20016.
Copyright © 1979.

Library of Congress Cataloging-in-Publication Data

Cahalan, Don.
   Understanding America's drinking problem.

   (A Joint publication in the Jossey-Bass social and
behavioral science series and the Jossey-Bass health
series)
   Bibliography: p.
   Includes index.
   1. Alcoholism—United States.   2. Alcoholism—United
States—Prevention.   3. Alcoholism—Treatment—United
States.   I. Title.   II. Series: The Jossey-Bass social
and behavioral science series.   III. Series: Jossey-
Bass health series.   [DNLM: 1. Alcohol Drinking.
2. Alcoholism—Occurrence—United States.   3. Alcoholism
—prevention & control—United States.   WM 274 C132u]
HV5292.C337   1987   362.2'928   87-45418
ISBN 1-55542-057-5 (alk. paper)

Manufactured in the United States of America

JACKET DESIGN BY WILLI BAUM

FIRST EDITION

Code 8725

A joint publication in
The Jossey-Bass
Social and Behavioral Science Series
and
The Jossey-Bass Health Series

Contents

Preface

Throughout the last generation, public and private agencies have exerted much earnest effort to reduce the growing prevalence of American drinking problems reported in *Problem Drinkers* in 1970. The National Institute on Alcohol Abuse and Alcoholism came into being the next year, and a vast assortment of public and private alcoholism treatment clinics, think-tanks, and administrative agencies mushroomed as soon as federal funds became available. Since then, hundreds of millions of dollars have been spent to bring alcoholics into treatment and devise alcohol education programs to cope with alcohol problems. Yet today there are even more alcoholics than there were a generation ago; and the percentage of people with severe drinking problems has hardly diminished at all. Clearly, something is wrong. The big questions are: *Why?* and *What can be done?*

This book describes the major successes and failures of governmental and private efforts to control alcohol problems during our recent history and also offers some remedial proposals. It is designed to help those with responsibilities for coping with alcohol problems in society, either as practitioners or as administrators. Since alcohol problems interact with a great many health and social problems, I have attempted to provide information and perspectives of interest to those whose work involves them in alcohol-related issues: administrators of alcohol-problem prevention or treatment programs or employee assistance programs;

physicians, psychologists, nurses, social workers, behavioral scientists, and public health and social policy professionals; teachers and planners; pastoral counselors; paraprofessionals and volunteer workers in prevention or treatment programs; legislators or others who deal with the funding of alcohol programs; and jurists or others involved in the criminal justice aspects of alcohol problems.

Understanding America's Drinking Problem does not attempt to provide easy answers to the difficult questions of how to control alcohol problems. Instead, it raises even more questions—about the things we don't understand and don't realize that we don't understand. Nor does it provide all the details of the major developments since the 1960s in the alcohol field. However, I have attempted to document my personal opinions and conclusions by citations to the research and reviews of specialists whose works can be consulted for further details.

From twenty-five years of studying American drinking practices and politics, I have drawn this general conclusion—admittedly a controversial one: Most of those involved in the control of alcohol problems during that time have been witting or unwitting coconspirators in a gigantic shell game. A visitor from another planet would be amazed to see how much alcoholic beverages are prized in our society, even though alcohol is responsible for far more deaths and social, economic, and health damage than most of the other psychedelic drugs that are absolutely forbidden in America. We have had bitter experiences with prohibition, which we do not want to repeat; so, not knowing what to do about alcohol problems, we are unwilling to take any decisive steps. Meanwhile, the alcohol industry protests that it is dedicated to "moderate" consumption while at the same time aggressively promoting increases in consumption, which in turn create more drinking problems. Congress and the White House decry drunken driving but provide little moral support or funding for effective primary prevention of such alcohol problems. (Could this be because the alcohol industry is a great contributor to campaign funds?) And most health care professionals are preoccupied with treating clinical alcoholics (if they have prepaid medical coverage) but are doing very little to promote primary prevention of alcohol problems—for at present there is little money to be made or professional status to be gained through promoting prevention.

"The alcoholism movement" (as the combination of pioneering nonprofit advocacy groups and government program administrators is often called) has been a huge success in getting the general public to accept the concept of alcoholism as a disease. It has also helped to guarantee that the insurance coverage of the majority of Americans includes some type of prepaid medical treatment for alcoholism. However, although the leaders of the movement to treat alcoholism had the best of intentions in urging the kinds of remedial programs that seemed plausible in the late 1960s, things have not turned out nearly as well as they had hoped.

This book is not a prohibitionist jeremiad on the evils of alcohol. Instead, it deals with alcohol from the standpoint of agent/host/environment relationships, in the same way that the public health field deals with other substances that affect health. From this public health perspective, alcohol is the "agent" connected with a broad range of problems for which people are the "host" and social and economic influences constitute the "environment." The goal is to find effective ways to intervene among these three variables to reduce alcohol problems to a workable minimum.

Overview of the Contents

Chapter One summarizes the findings of several recent large-scale national surveys and presents a brief review of America's drinking history, which helps to explain why drinking problems in America are not really diminishing very rapidly in response to all the effort and money expended in the last couple of decades. The chapter emphasizes the costliness of alcohol misuse—in physical deterioration and in fiscal costs to society—and explains why we should not be so preoccupied with the primarily medically oriented concept of alcoholism as a disease that we neglect to deal with the variety of other serious drinking problems in our society.

Chapter Two provides a brief account of America's drinking history, demonstrating that our attitudes and behaviors relating to alcohol have changed over the last 350 years in response to dramatic changes in our way of life. From our history it is not hard to see why our inconsistency in dealing with alcohol problems is attributable to our contradictory objectives and values about alcohol, rather than to a lack of zeal and effort on the part of officials.

Chapters Three and Four discuss the efforts of federal, state, and local governments and private agencies to combat alcoholism and to control drunken driving and a few of the other conspicuous results of overconsumption. While these efforts have been generally praiseworthy, these severely underfunded agencies have had to fight an uphill battle against the alcohol industry's astute lobbying with Congress and the White House to prevent the adoption of more effective controls over alcohol in the interest of public health and social welfare.

Chapter Five discusses the marketing techniques of the alcohol industry, which has been very effective in dividing and co-opting the institutions set up to control alcohol problems. However, there are now signs that the industry is beginning to lose ground in its battles against increased controls on the sale and taxation of alcohol, despite its constant assertion that alcohol problems are caused by genetic heritage or personal mental health problems, rather than by excessive drinking.

Chapter Six describes the efforts of a new generation of public health and public policy specialists, who are helping to bring about better research-based programs of primary prevention. These specialists contend that effective treatment should not preclude effective prevention and that we must develop a broader perspective on how alcohol problems develop and are reinforced. To this end they are urging the adoption of new programs to improve public cooperation in testing various prevention strategies—for example, reducing alcohol-impaired driving and many other alcohol-related problems through selective taxation; reducing the present subsidies to the alcohol industry in the form of tax deductions for advertising; and exercising better control over the selling and serving of alcohol.

Chapter Seven describes the various modes of alcoholism treatment and their apparent effectiveness, and discusses some of the often heated controversies among professional practitioners over what alcoholism really is and how to treat it. There has been a great gulf between those of the Alcoholics Anonymous persuasion, who contend that alcoholics can never resume normal drinking, and the therapists who maintain that it is better to retrain the drinking habits of those not yet ready to accept abstention than to turn them away. As the chapter demonstrates, a newer generation of professionals is learning to reconcile these two points of view. Considerable evidence is presented that a larger number of excessive drinkers may be brought into rehabilitation programs if we deal with alcohol addiction in much the same way that we deal with tobacco addiction—as a tenacious habit which can be broken only through determined effort on the part of the sufferers, aided by sympathetic but firm moral support from those around them.

Chapter Eight shows how the last two decades of substantial federal budgets and the enormous growth of third-party payments from insurance and government sources for alcoholism treatment have contributed to the steep rise in the general cost of medical care without much demonstrable improvement in the treatment of alcoholics. Because of such increased coverage and mounting costs, and the government's understandable efforts toward cost containment, treatment for alcoholism is becoming dependent on insurance coverage and bureaucratic considerations rather than on the sufferer's actual needs.

The chapter also indicates that the overmedicalization of problems has led to ineffectual treatment of alcoholism and waste of public funds through overuse of expensive hospital resources. This primary concentration on clinically defined alcoholics has diverted too much attention away from the environmental and cultural influences that have contributed to the misuse of alcohol, especially among youth. As a consequence, our country until very recently has almost completely neglected the obvious need to prevent alcohol problems from developing in the first place, or at least to apply reasonable social controls to keep alcohol problems from getting any worse.

The last three chapters discuss ways in which the findings of the many surveys and staff studies commissioned by government agencies and private foundations can be put to profitable use by administrators and members of professional groups that are—or should be—concerned with alcohol problems. Chapter Nine considers the appropriate roles of various professionals in alcohol treatment and prevention and describes the current programs for training alcoholism counselors and the mechanisms for certifying them. Chapter Ten contains recommendations for research programs, and Chapter Eleven lists specific recommendations for action agencies.

Clearly, the present social pressures toward heavy alcohol consumption need to be reduced if we hope to do a better job of controlling alcohol problems. Neither traditional alcohol education nor the expensive treatment of clinical alcoholics is coping with the new crop of problems drinkers emerging every year. Effective primary prevention is likely to require reduction in alcohol-marketing pressures through such measures as constraints on alcohol advertising and increases in alcohol taxes. The present public acceptance of controls over smoking and other environmental hazards may well carry over into acceptance of similar controls over alcohol—if such controls are advocated in the interest of sound public health and are not made part of a moral crusade similar to the crusade that resulted in the excesses of prohibition.

Acknowledgments

The following specialists have provided helpful advice and insights on the alcohol scene through extended discussions or correspondence: Henrik Blum, professor of public health (emeritus), University of California, Berkeley; William Butynski, executive director of the National Association of State Alcohol and Drug Abuse Directors (NASADAD), Washington, D.C.; Robert Denniston, director of the Division of Prevention and Research Dissemination, National Institute on Alcohol Abuse and Alcoholism (NIAAA), Washington, D.C.; Susan Farrell, director, Office of Policy Analysis, NIAAA; George Hacker, director for alcohol policies, Center for Science in the Public Interest, Washington, D.C.; Jay Lewis, editor of *The Alcoholism Report*, Washington, D.C.; Stephen Long, chief, Planning and Financial Management Branch, NIAAA; Christine Lubinski, Washington representative of the National Council on Alcoholism; Larry Meredith, deputy director for operations, Department of Public Health, City and

County of San Francisco; Lorraine Midanik, assistant professor of social welfare, University of California, Berkeley; Robert Reynolds, alcohol program administrator, San Diego County; Robert Straus, chairman of the Department of Behavioral Science, College of Medicine, University of Kentucky; and Al Wright, director of the Office of Alcohol Programs for the County of Los Angeles.

My former colleagues at the two NIAAA-sponsored Alcohol Research Centers in Berkeley have provided much useful information, although, of course, the conclusions I have drawn are my own. I especially thank the following members of the Alcohol Research Group: Robin Room (director), Raul Caetano, Denise Herd, Mike Hilton, Ron Roizen, Richard Speiglman, and Connie Weisner. Jim Mosher of the Trauma Foundation and Larry Wallack of the Prevention Research Center have also been most helpful. A special note of appreciation is due Andrea Mitchell, information specialist at the Alcohol Research Group, who has always sensed what kinds of information were needed for this book and who, with the able assistance of Judith Lubina, has coped so well with the almost endless process of tracking it all down. And I am most especially indebted to my wife, Ellen Cahalan, for her helpful editing and encouragement.

I am also grateful for the helpful counsel provided by two colleagues who reviewed the completed manuscript in its entirety: Ron Stall, assistant professor of urban studies, Rutgers University, and William R. Miller, professor of psychology and psychiatry and director of clinical training, University of New Mexico.

Finally, I wish to dedicate this book to the memory of two colleagues who contributed a great deal to alcohol research and education. Ira H. Cisin, professor of sociology and director of the Social Research Group of George Washington University, was one of the principal founders of nationwide probability sample research on drinking practices and drug use. Herman Kregel, D.D. and colonel in the Chaplains Corps, U.S. Army (ret.), for years directed a federally funded training program at the Pacific School of Religion in Berkeley, California. His hardheaded yet compassionate perspectives on alcoholics and other problem drinkers were an inspiration to a whole generation of his students and colleagues in the California State Department of Public Health. Ira and Herman will be much missed by many, not only for their professional contributions, but also for their personal warmth and unique leadership qualities.

Berkeley, California   Don Cahalan
July 1987

The Author

Don Cahalan is professor of public health (emeritus) at the University of California, Berkeley. He received his B.A. (1937) and M.A. (1938) degrees from the University of Iowa in psychology, and his Ph.D. degree (1968) from George Washington University in social psychology. His career in conducting social surveys has spanned fifty years. During the last twenty years, he has directed national and regional studies of drinking behavior and problems, sponsored primarily by the National Institute on Alcohol Abuse and Alcoholism and its predecessors. Out of these studies he has published more than forty articles and three books, *American Drinking Practices* (1969, with Ira H. Cisin and Helen M. Crossley), *Problem Drinkers* (1970), and *Problem Drinking Among American Men* (1974, with Robin Room).

Earlier, Cahalan served as associate professor of psychology and social science at the University of Denver, as director of attitude research for the Army and Air Force in Europe, and as senior research analyst in the National Opinion Research Center in Chicago. After several years directing market research surveys in the New York area, he moved to George Washington University in 1962 to work with Ira Cisin in his Social Research Group, helping to direct the first national probability sampling survey of American drinking practices. In 1968 he moved to Berkeley, where he combined the research resources initially set up a decade earlier in the State Department of Public Health by Wendell Lipscomb, Ira Cisin, and Genevieve Knupfer. Until his retirement in 1979, he organized and directed the Alcohol Research Group in the School of Public Health and its ongoing federally funded alcohol research and training program.

He is a life member of the American Psychological Association and the American Association for Public Opinion Research. He is also a member of the Society for the Psychological Study of Social Issues and the American Public Health Association and serves on the advisory boards of several journals concerned with alcohol and other drugs.

Understanding
America's Drinking Problem

1

⩗⩗⩗⩗⩗⩗⩗⩗

How Much of a Drinking Problem Do We Have?

Alcoholic beverages have been used in almost all cultures since the dawn of civilization. Alcoholic drinks are legal in all but a few counties in the United States, and the vast majority of Americans now drink at least occasionally. Figures 1 and 2 show "apparent consumption" (as estimated from alcohol tax records) between 1850 and 1981. As these figures indicate, there were great changes during these years in the types of alcoholic beverages consumed; however, except for the prohibition period and a couple of years thereafter, the level of consumption never fell below two gallons of absolute alcohol—the equivalent of more than four gallons of whiskey per year—for every man, woman, and youth of fifteen or older. Total alcohol consumption rose rapidly in the 1860s and 1870s, dropped a bit in the 1880s, and rose again about 1910. A couple of years after repeal, consumption rose rapidly again through World War II, dropped slightly in 1950, and then rose steadily until 1981 (the end year of Figure 2). As Robert Niven, then director of the National Institute on Alcohol Abuse and Alcoholism (NIAAA), put it: "Since 1950, alcohol consumption has continued on a steady upward path, from somewhat more than 2 gallons of absolute alcohol per capita

1

Figure 1. Apparent Consumption of Absolute Alcohol from Each
Major Beverage Class, in U.S. Gallons Per Person in the
Drinking-Age Population, 1850–1970.

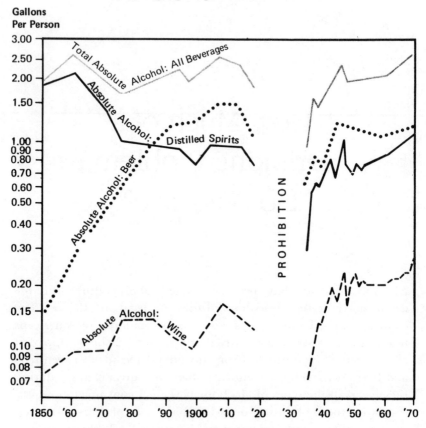

Source: National Institute on Alcohol Abuse and Alcoholism, 1971, p. 15.
Notes: "Apparent Consumption" was calculated according to tax-paid
withdrawals, as shown in alcohol tax records.
"Drinking-age population" = Age 15+.
For the period labeled "Prohibition," figures are unavailable.
This figure is drawn on a semilogarithmic scale.

to nearly 3 gallons in 1981. . . . That is about 591 12-oz. cans of beer
or 115 fifths of table wine or 35 fifths of 80-proof whiskey, gin, or
vodka" (Niven, 1984, p. 1913). However, consumption may
have hit a plateau recently: it fell off slightly in 1982 to 2.72

Figure 2. Apparent United States Consumption of Alcoholic Beverages in Gallons of Ethanol Per Capita 1950–1981.

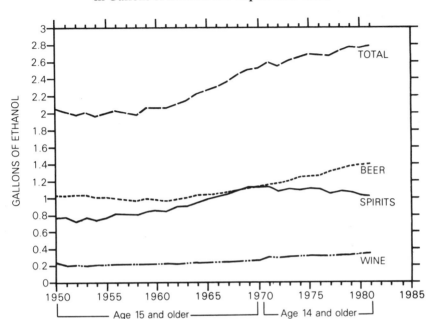

Source: National Institute on Alcohol Abuse and Alcoholism, 1983, p. 2.

gallons and then to 2.69 gallons per capita in 1983 (Lewis, *Alcoholism Report*, Jan. 17, 1986).

To summarize: (1) Drinking habits in America have been subject to large changes over long periods of time. (2) Although the aggregate consumption of alcohol has remained relatively constant, there have been considerable swings in the consumption of individual types of beverages. Chapter Two will consider the historical reasons for some of these trends, including the effects of successive waves of immigrants who brought their European drinking habits with them; and Chapter Five will show how alcohol marketing and the alcohol industry's lobbying efforts following World War II have paid off in increased consumption.

Although the United States was only thirteenth out of twenty-seven countries in per capita (age fifteen or older) consumption of alcohol in the mid-1970s, it was one of the leaders in consumption of hard liquor (Hyman and others, 1980). The only countries among the twenty-seven that exceeded the United States in per capita consumption of hard liquor were Poland and the Soviet Union (which have since been trying to crack down on vodka consumption). The only countries topping the United States in aggregate consumption were wine- or beer-drinking Portugal, France, Italy, Switzerland, Spain, West Germany, Austria, Belgium, Hungary, New Zealand, and Czechoslovakia. Lowest in consumption of the twenty-seven were Bahrein and Israel.

Figure 3 shows that within the United States the highest apparent consumption (again, estimated from tax figures) is in the more urbanized areas of the Northeast and Illinois, some of the Pacific states (including Alaska and Hawaii), and several of the Plains states. The lowest consumption is in the more rural areas of the Southeast and cross-country through Kansas, with highly Mormon Utah being the lowest of all. These 1981 findings—which are consistent with our 1964–1967 national survey (Cahalan, Cisin, and Crossley, 1969) and with differences in alcohol control laws from state to state (Mosher, 1984a)—imply that, if some of the stringent alcohol control practices discussed in Chapter Five are to be effective, due regard must be given to local differences in habits and attitudes, which often have deep historical roots.

Another survey of United States drinking behavior, a Gallup Poll, found that the proportion of adults twenty-one or older who drank at least occasionally rose from 65 percent of men and about 40 percent of women before World War II to nearly 80 percent of men and 60 percent of women by the end of the 1960s (National Institute on Alcohol Abuse and Alcoholism, 1971, pp. 17–18). Our national survey found that 68 percent of the adult population reported drinking at least once a year and only 22 percent said they had never drunk alcohol (Cahalan, Cisin, and Crossley, 1969, p. 22).

Costliness of Alcohol Problems

Obviously, such a large number of people would not be drinking unless they were getting real or fancied benefits from alcohol as a social lubricant, a picker-upper, the socially approved "thing to do," or as "medication" for anxiety or depression.

**Figure 3. Apparent Consumption of Ethanol from All Alcoholic Beverages
in U.S. Gallons Per Capita of the Population
Age Fourteen and Older, 1981.**

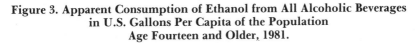

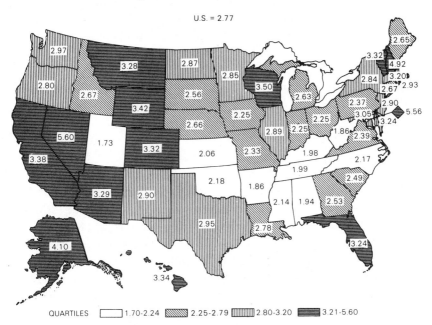

Source: National Institute on Alcohol Abuse and Alcoholism, 1983, p. 3.

However, most authorities who study the physical effects of alcohol would agree with Ernest Noble, former director of the NIAAA, in his description of alcohol as "the dirtiest drug of all" because of its adverse effects on so many physical and mental functions. Although evidently few think of alcohol as a drug, because "drug" is a dirty word reserved for illegal mind-altering substances, it would take many fat volumes to describe in detail all the damage alcohol can do to the liver, pancreas, digestive tract, vascular system, muscles, and the brain and the rest of the nervous system (Hoffman, 1983; Julien, 1978; Goodwin and Guze, 1984; Segal, 1987).

The NIAAA reports to Congress often have summarized such damage, a recent one saying that alcohol plays a role in 10 percent of all deaths in the United States and is the *principal* cause of deaths through accidents among those aged fifteen to twenty-four

(National Institute on Alcohol Abuse and Alcoholism, 1983, p. vi). A reinterview in 1966 of our 1964–65 national sample found that the heavier drinkers had suffered a significantly higher rate of accidents within the prior year (Brenner, Cisin, and Newcomb, 1966). Drinking data from our national and San Francisco surveys conducted 1962–1971 were checked against death certificates for interviewees who had died by the late 1970s, with the finding that high levels of drinking were associated with higher mortality rates (Room and Day, 1974; Day, 1979). And Waller (1976) estimated that about 8,000 alcohol-connected fatal accidents and 3.2 million nonfatal injuries occur in homes each year, plus 7,400 fatal and 2.8 million nonfatal injuries in nonhighway settings.

In addition, all available evidence indicates that, even though alcohol is a legal drug used by at least two-thirds of our adult citizenry, its side effects are very costly. The official estimate for 1980 of the fiscal costs to society is a whopping $89+ billion. When projected forward to 1983, the costs were guesstimated at the even more astronomical figure of $116.7 billion (Harwood and others, 1984). These are much larger sums than the tentatively suggested figures for drug abuse (about $47 billion) or mental illness (about $54 billion). More than half of those estimated losses attributed to alcohol are from diminished productivity, which may be difficult to estimate accurately. However, these estimates also include some rather large hard figures—such as the more than $10 billion estimated as spent for 1980 treatment of alcoholics, more than $2 billion in property losses because of alcohol-involved auto accidents, and more than $2 billion in the costs of alcohol-related crime and violence.

That estimating the costs of alcohol misuse is at best a perilous pursuit is seen when we look back at the NIAAA's *Annual Report to Congress* (1972), in which it said (p. 1) that "Alcohol abuse and alcoholism drain the United States economy of an estimated $15 billion a year." A Senator Proxmire might wisecrack that something must be wrong with the management of alcohol programs if the country has spent so many million dollars to combat alcohol abuse, and yet after fourteen years the problem has grown sixfold! Of course, how one estimates the costs of a national problem depends on how one defines the problem and on the assumptions made in the course of estimating its scope. But most will agree that even the most conservative estimate for the cost of damage associated with alcohol would be far higher than the estimated $12.5 billion in federal, state, and local taxes for spirits, beer, and wine collected in 1984 (Distilled Spirits Council of the United States, 1985, p. iii).

National Surveys of Drinking Problems

Aggregate dollar-sign statistics may be inflated, but even they cannot reflect all the indirect and intangible social costs of problems related to drinking. The most feasible—although expensive and admittedly imperfect—way to measure these costs is through scientifically conducted sample surveys, in which people are asked details about their own drinking problems; for my colleagues and I discovered that individuals are more accurate in reporting their own drinking-related problems than those of even their own spouses (Cahalan, Cisin, and Crossley, 1969, p. 80). So we use self-reports rather than the opinions of other informants as the main source for estimates of drinking problems.

Because correlation does not prove causality, the official federally sponsored projections of figures for the incidence of alcohol-related illness, accidents, crimes, or other social disruptions probably are somewhat higher than the disruptions actually "caused" by alcohol. To try to get around this difficulty, in our national surveys we measure the individual's *own* perception that drinking was the cause of his or her self-recognized problems. Since heavy drinkers tend to minimize their problems to some extent in talking to an interviewer, survey-based estimates of the proportions of persons with drinking problems will tend to err on the conservative side.

How have we defined "alcohol problems"? Here we have used Knupfer's (1967, p. 974) simple, commonsense definition: "A problem—any problem—connected fairly closely with drinking constitutes a drinking problem." As noted in *Problem Drinkers* (Cahalan, 1970, p. 12), this definition makes no assumptions about whether the drinking caused the problem or whether the problem may have caused the drinking.

In the 1967 survey of adults (aged twenty-one or older when initially interviewed in 1964–65) presented in *Problem Drinkers* (Chap. 3), we asked the respondents whether they had *ever* had any of eleven types of problems related to drinking, and whether any of those problems had occurred during the last three years. The problems included: getting intoxicated frequently, binge drinking, "symptomatic drinking" (a score on seven items, such as drinking to get rid of a hangover, or having alcohol-related lapses of memory, or sneaking drinks), "psychological dependence" (drinking to alleviate depression or nervousness or to escape from problems), problems with spouse or relatives or friends or neighbors, alcohol-related problems on the job, or alcohol-related accidents or problems with the police. These actual or potential problems were based primarily on the items used in the pioneering San Francisco survey reported by Knupfer (1967) and Clark (1966), which items in turn were drawn from the behaviors or experiences commonly described for various forms of alcoholism by such recognized authorities as Jellinek (1952, 1960).

In the 1967 survey, the most common problem for men during the prior three years was frequent intoxication (14 percent), followed by difficulty in stopping drinking, having blackouts, sneaking drinks, "psychological dependence," and problems with spouse or relatives (8 percent each). Women reported far fewer problems, the most frequent fairly severe problem being impaired health because of drinking (4 percent). Among the less serious problems, 15 percent of women reported that they had to some extent been dependent on alcohol to make them feel better, and 8 percent said that drinking had made them belligerent at some time within the preceding three years.

The highest correlates of having a high score on drinking ·problems consisted of a combination of demographic and attitudinal and environmental factors. For example, we were able to isolate one group with a 63 percent rate of high problem-drinking scores (Cahalan, 1970, p. 108). This group consisted of men with a favorable or tolerant attitude toward heavy drinking, who also had high scores on an "impulsivity" (doing things on the spur of the moment) attitude scale and on a scale of environmental supports for heavy drinking (friends and associates drank a lot, had relatives or friends with drinking problems, or those closest to him would think it all right for him to drink eight or more drinks on some occasions). Throughout this book we will see many other examples of how attitudes and social environments interact in determining whether people will get into trouble over drinking and how well they can work their way out of it.

Another national survey, conducted by the Berkeley Alcohol Research Group (ARG) in 1984, permits comparisons of drinking problems over a seventeen-year span (Clark and Hilton, 1986). More men (24.5 percent compared to 20.1 percent) in the 1984 survey said they had abstained from drinking during the prior twelve months than was the case seventeen years earlier. Men's increase in abstention was greatest among those under forty and those sixty or older. Women also showed an apparent slight increase in abstention, especially among those under thirty and in their forties.

Among men, despite the increase in abstainers, there were higher figures for most drinking problems in 1984 than in 1967, especially on loss of memory (blackouts), skipping meals while drinking, and damage to friendships or social life, marriage or home life, and work or employment opportunities. Among women there were relatively few differences in rates of problems over the seventeen-year span.

Consistent with recent increases in the aggregate national per capita consumption of wine and beer and the slight decrease in consumption of spirits (Distilled Spirits Council of the United States, 1985), the 1984 survey found that the proportion of drinkers who reported having five or six drinks of wine "at least once in a while" was 7 percent in 1967 and 15 percent in 1984; the comparable figures for beer were 21 and 31 percent; and for distilled beverages, 27 percent in 1967 as against a slightly lower 23 percent in 1984. The implications of these changes in beverage preferences are discussed in Chapter Five.

Our initial 1964–65 national survey found many large differences in drinking behavior between men and women and by age, income, and educational levels, regions of the country, and ethnic origins (Cahalan, Cisin, and Crossley, 1969). Particularly noteworthy were the differences by age. Among the men there was a significant increase from 1967 to 1984 in the proportions of abstainers among those in the youngest and the oldest groups; however, there was relatively little difference from one age group to another in change in heavier drinking. The highest proportions of heavier drinkers in both surveys were found among men in their twenties and thirties—which is consistent with findings of all known national surveys, and at odds with the considerably older levels among alcoholics in clinics (Malzberg, 1960, p. 6). The reasons for the disparity in ages in the clinical and nonclinical populations are discussed in Chapter Seven.

Women in the two surveys showed somewhat the same patterns as the men regarding relative rates of abstainers in the two surveys. There was no statistically significant difference in rates of heavier drinking. However, the rate more than doubled for women in their twenties, even though there was also a significant increase in the percentage of abstainers in this youngest group.

The social settings in which drinking occurs are worthy of more intensive study, in the light of findings from these two national surveys twenty years apart, which show important changes (Hilton, forthcoming). For example, in 1984 respondents were considerably *less* likely than in the initial 1964-65 survey to report that they got together in social occasions with people from work or with neighbors or people from the same church. This may well reflect a trend toward greater privatization in America or less cohesiveness of social ties in an age where there are fewer intact families and more commuting and probably more disruption of roots through successive moves. The average person now lives in thirty different places over a lifetime ("Harper's Index," 1986). However, in 1984, when survey respondents *did* get together with people from work or with close neighbors or friends, alcohol was reported as being served "nearly ever time" much more often than in 1964-65. This was especially true for getting together with people from work—for both men and women (particularly the women, of whom more are now in the work force), and for all age groups, for all educational levels, and among married and unmarried alike.

The Alcohol Research Group's 1984 national survey included a special supplementary representative sample of Blacks, so as to permit a more detailed examination of their drinking habits than in our previous surveys. Some of the conclusions emerging from an analysis by Herd (1987) of that special sample and of the findings from other surveys are as follows:

Medical problems associated with drinking among Blacks have increased dramatically since World War II. Rates of drinking problems for Blacks and Whites seem to be coming closer together. White and Black men have very similar drinking patterns. However, Black men exhibit a higher prevalence of all types of alcohol-related problems except drinking-driving. The difference between Black and White men is greatest for alcohol-related health problems. The higher the socioeconomic status of Black men, the lower the rate of drinking problems. However, southern Blacks, reputed in the past to have low rates of heavy drinking and drinking problems, now have relatively high rates. Black women differ from White women in having significantly higher rates of abstention and lower rates of frequent drinking.

The younger Blacks are not as heavy drinkers as the younger Whites are. Only after age twenty-nine do alcohol problems begin to rise among Blacks, while declining among Whites. However, except for young adults, substantial numbers of Blacks at all ages appear at risk for alcohol-related problems.

The 1984 survey also included another expanded sample (1,453) of those of Spanish-speaking origin. Some of the findings, as analyzed by Caetano (1987b), are as follows:

While, as with the Anglo (other White) population, the Hispanic men drink more than the women, and drinking is positively associated with income and education, the percentage of drinking problems does not decline with age in the same way as among the Anglos. Heavy drinking actually increases among Hispanics after age thirty. This finding is consistent with Hispanic attitudes in this survey, which accord men thirty and forty years of age more freedom to drink than younger men.

Within the Hispanic population (drawn from many Spanish-speaking subcultures from the southwestern United States and Latin America and the Caribbean), men of Mexican ancestry were found to drink more than the other Hispanic men and also to be more prone to drinking problems. However, as compared to other women of Spanish-speaking origin, women of Mexican origin showed a relatively higher level of abstention and almost no heavy drinking.

Even when national surveys are conducted by different organizations with somewhat different questions, the general findings tend to be quite similar. Clark, Knupfer, and Midanik (1981), in reporting the results of another ARG survey conducted in 1979, compared their findings with those from seven other national surveys of the United States adult population conducted by the ARG and other groups from 1971 through 1979. Although the questions and criteria for grouping differed somewhat from survey to survey, they found little difference in rates of abstaining (about one-third in most surveys) and of heavy drinking (about 10 percent in each survey were listed in the heavier-drinking class).

Still another very recent national survey, conducted by the National Center for Health Statistics (NCHS), is of special interest because it included drinking questions as part of the 1985 National Health Interview Survey, and thus will permit an analysis of the relationship between alcohol use and respondents' health and lifestyles. The survey was conducted with very high standards: interviews were completed with persons eighteen or older in 96 percent of the households assigned, resulting in about 16,780 completed questionnaires. A preliminary summary report (Thornberry, Wilson, and Golden, 1986) found the same patterns of heavier drinking by men and younger people as in the recent Alcohol Research Group surveys, and also summarized the public's alcohol knowledge levels as follows (p. 2):

> With the exception of cirrhosis of the liver, the adult population appears less knowledgeable about the effects of alcohol on health than the effects of smoking. Whereas 95 percent felt that heavy alcohol consumption increased the chances of getting cirrhosis of the liver, only about one-third recognized the association between heavy alcohol use and cancers of the throat (39 percent) and mouth (31 percent). Eight percent of adults were classified as heavier drinkers (two or more drinks per day), 21 percent as moderate drinkers, and 24 percent as lighter drinkers (3 drinks

or less per week). Twelve percent of adults admitted to driving at least once in the last year when they perhaps had had too much to drink and almost a quarter of young adults admitted to doing so.

Still another, and much larger, national survey (22,418 personal interviews) was conducted two years earlier by the National Center for Health Statistics in cooperation with the NIAAA. This Alcohol/Health Practices Supplement of the 1983 National Health Interview Survey included questions on drinking and health practices, health conditions, and problems associated with drinking. The study was preceded by a large-scale methodological survey to establish the statistical reliability of the methods used (Williams, Aitken, and Malin, 1985). A preliminary report (Malin, Wilson, and Williams, 1985) yielded findings consistent with those reported above for other surveys, including indications that the proportion of abstainers appears to have increased in recent years (especially among women)—which the authors note is also consistent with the drop in per capita consumption estimated from sales data.

This NCHS survey also found that moderate drinkers had fewer health problems than either abstainers or heavy drinkers. This finding—which held true even when age, sex, and former-drinker status of abstainers were controlled for—has cropped up in a number of other studies reviewed at an American Heart Association meeting (Cahalan, 1981). However, caution is needed in interpreting such findings, since the better health of moderate drinkers may be attributable to a generally even-keel lifestyle rather than to moderate drinking as such.

In any case, the very large sample size for that NCHS 1983 survey, and its inclusion of general health habits and conditions along with drinking behavior and problems, should generate great interest on the part of alcohol researchers in more detailed analysis of this rich body of data. It is hoped that the NCHS and the NIAAA will fund outcome studies of subsamples of this large sample in order to trace changes in drinking behavior and health status, and ultimately of mortality rates for respondents varying in their drinking and health habits.

Brentwood School Library
155 S. Layton Drive
Los Angeles, CA 90049
(213) 476-9633

Definitions of Alcoholism

There are many definitions of alcoholism, some of which are
summarized in the first chapter of *Problem Drinkers* (Cahalan,
1970). The chapter also discusses a number of other questions about
alcoholism. One is whether it is a unitary disease process, with
symptoms of graded severity, which cumulate until they constitute
a full-blown disease. This notion has been largely disproved by
national and regional studies of the general population, which
show that symptoms do not cumulate in a regular order and that
many people move rapidly into and out of the problem-drinking
class (Clark and Cahalan, 1976; Roizen, Cahalan, and Shanks,
1978). Knupfer (1972) found that about 25 percent of those in a
representative sample in a West Coast city who had marked
drinking problems no longer had those problems a couple of years
later, *without* any treatment at all. That finding suggests that
probably a large proportion of those who appear to improve after
alcoholism treatment would have gotten better without any
treatment. Indeed, Fingarette (1985) contends that there is no solid
evidence that "treatment" in any form has made any material
difference in recovery from alcoholism; instead, he believes, recovery
is entirely dependent on the person's resolve and ability to change
his or her way of life. However, as he says, the rub is that, despite
our culture-bound emphasis on "free will," we are all very much
the prisoners of our own lifestyles and environment—and hence the
proper treatment of heavy drinkers is to show them, step by step,
how to change their habits.

Another question that must be resolved before we can assess
the effectiveness of alcoholism treatment is: What kind, or kinds, of
alcoholism are we talking about? Mandell (1983) notes that there are
four current definitions of alcoholism:

One is the World Health Organization's definition: "Alcoholics are those excessive drinkers whose dependence upon alcohol
has attained such a degree that it shows a noticeable mental
disturbance or an interference with their bodily and mental health,
their interpersonal relations, and their smooth social and economic
functioning; or [those] who show the prodromal signs of such
developments" (Mandell, 1983, p. 415). This definition is so broad,

using weasel words like "noticeable" and "smooth social and economic functioning" and "prodromal," that it can be of little guidance in clinical diagnosis.

Another well-known concept is that alcoholism is a unitary disease, "identifiable by its history, symptoms, and signs, which form a recognizable pattern" (p. 416). This, Mandell infers, is the traditional position of the National Council on Alcoholism (NCA), although the NCA's position may be subject to change. As mentioned, our longitudinal studies have established that few problem drinkers really do fit into such a classical pattern.

A third definition is offered by Pattison, Sobell, and Sobell (1977): that there is no single entity which can be defined as alcoholism; rather, a collection of symptoms and behaviors with psychological or sociocultural or genetic origins lead to the inappropriate use of alcohol.

A fourth position was taken by Jellinek (1952, 1960), one of the founders of the Center of Alcohol Studies at Yale University in the 1940s and long the guru of those who assert that alcoholism is a disease. Jellinek identified several alleged species of alcoholism and specified that the disease element attaches only to alcohol addicts—that is, those who display a "loss of control" over drinking (so-called gamma alcoholism)—and not to nonaddictive alcoholics—that is, "habitual symptomatic excessive drinkers" (1952, p. 674).

Mandell likens Jellinek's position to the definition of "alcohol dependence syndrome" that appears in the 1977 statement of the Committee on Alcohol-Related Disabilities of the World Health Organization (WHO) (Edwards and others, 1977). "Alcohol dependence syndrome" covers the following elements: (1) a narrowing (regularity) in drinking repertoire, (2) salience (dominance) of drink-seeking behavior, (3) increased physiological tolerance of alcohol, (4) repeated withdrawal symptoms, (5) repeated relief or avoidance of withdrawal by further drinking, (6) subjective awareness of a compulsion to drink, and (7) reinstatement of the syndrome after abstinence.

In his writings Jellinek set forth elaborate and sometimes equivocal definitions of alcoholism. In his 1960 version (pp. 36–39), he distinguished the following types: alpha alcoholism, a purely psychological dependence; beta alcoholism, involving physical complications such as alcohol-caused gastritis or cirrhosis without dependence on alcohol; and gamma alcoholism, entailing acquired tissue tolerance for alcohol, withdrawal symptoms and physical dependence, and loss of control over drinking. It is the gamma form of alcoholism, involving physical dependence and loss of control, that is most commonly referred to in discussions of clinical treatment; for it is the form of alcohol involvement that is the most likely to present some risk of withdrawal symptoms and attendant complications. Jellinek adds that "Gamma alcoholism is apparently (but not with certainty) the *predominating* species of alcoholism in the United States and Canada, as well as in other Anglo-Saxon countries. It is what members of Alcoholics Anonymous recognize as alcoholism to the exclusion of all other species" (p. 38).

Jellinek described an elaborate series of steps of degradation through which the gamma alcoholic passes on the path from mere overdependence on alcohol to development of serious health problems and loss of social supports. In fact, he based most of his theories about gamma alcoholism (including the concept of a "drunkard's progress" through specific stages) on the beliefs of AA members as expressed in an informal AA poll of only ninety-eight members (Jellinek, 1946)—hardly a conclusive way of developing scientific theory.

Mark Keller, a colleague of Jellinek's at Yale and founding editor of the *Journal of Studies on Alcohol*, did not think it necessary to require any specific series of steps on the road to becoming an alcoholic. In a letter to Robin Room (dated Oct. 20, 1969), Keller said, "I think [alcoholism] is a disease because the alcoholic can't consistently choose whether or not he shall engage in self-injurious behavior—that is, any of the alcoholism drinking patterns. I think of it as a psychological disablement."

Problem Drinkers Versus Alcoholics

What is the connection between the heavier drinkers and problem drinkers, as measured in surveys of the general public, and the "alcoholics" who presumably are in need of medical or related treatment? If one uses Keller's "psychological disablement" as a criterion of alcoholism, perhaps the closest fit to this criterion among the items in our national surveys is the "high" score on our ad hoc "psychological dependence" scale. This scale includes five items: (1) helpfulness of a drink when depressed, (2) drinking because of nervousness, (3) drinking to forget everything, (4) drinking to help forget one's worries, (5) drinking to cheer one up when in a bad mood. When a respondent rated at least one of these items as very helpful or important, and two more of the five items as fairly helpful or important, during the prior three years, that respondent obtained a high score. In our 1967 survey, 8 percent of the men and 3 percent of the women had such a score (Cahalan, 1970, p. 37). This finding, as well as the 9 percent of the total having an arbitrarily chosen score of seven or more out of fifty-eight items measuring problems within the last three years, was seized on by spokesmen for the NIAAA in 1970 (when congressional votes on budgets might have been at stake) as warranting an estimate of 9 million alcoholics for the United States (Gross, 1983, pp. 119-121). This was a more impressive statistic than Keller's (1962) estimate of about 4.5 million alcoholics. However, when the *First Special Report to the U.S. Congress on Alcohol and Health* (National Institute on Alcohol Abuse and Alcoholism, 1971, p. vi) was released, this 9 million figure was tempered by the statement, "An estimated 5 percent of the adult population manifest the behaviors of alcohol abuse and alcoholism. Among the more than 95 million drinkers in the nation, about 9 million men and women are alcohol abusers and alcoholic individuals."

The following disclaimer in *Problem Drinkers* was adopted in a vain effort to forestall some interest groups' eagerness to include estimates of "problem drinkers" with estimates of "alcoholics":

> The proportion of "problem drinkers" according to one rather arbitrary (but statistically useful) definition later in this book was found to be about 9 percent (although plausible alternative definitions yielded a range of from about 3 percent to 30 percent). Thus the prevalence of alcoholism and problem

drinking can be interpreted as being rather closely congruent or as being in wide disagreement, depending upon the necessarily arbitrary definitions one prefers to use. However, comparing estimates of alcoholics and problem drinkers is a rather futile exercise, because the concepts of alcoholism and problem drinking are not very similar, do not necessarily apply to the same sufferers, and may have quite different implications for etiology and preventive public health measures and treatment [Cahalan, 1970, pp. 2-3].

Alcohol researchers have learned to be very wary about estimating the total number of "alcoholics" or "problem drinkers" in the country, because such figures are almost always taken out of context by lobbyists who are trying to maximize or minimize the problem. Many researchers prefer, instead, to draw from the considerable store of recent survey data and publicly available aggregate statistics to provide detailed estimates in answer to specific issues, for agencies pledged not to misuse such estimates.

Lack of congruence between the concept of "problem drinking" and "alcoholism" is especially evident when we look at the findings of surveys of drinking behavior in the armed forces (Cahalan and others, 1972; Cahalan and Cisin, 1975; Burt and Biegel, 1980; Polich and Orvis, 1979). These surveys found that while there was a lot of heavy drinking going on within the military (which might be expected in a population consisting largely of young men who are mostly single or away from their families and ordinary civilian social environments), and many were drinking so much as to be at risk of developing medical problems in the long run, the drinking problems these men had were primarily disciplinary ones—absenteeism, getting into brawls, accidents, and so forth—rather than medical problems.

Thus, in their large survey of all the armed forces, Burt and Biegel found that more than 80 percent of all ranks and grades had drunk alcoholic beverages at least once during the prior thirty days (p. 25). Among these, 21 percent were rated as "heavy drinkers" of beer (eight or more cans in a single day at least once a week during the past twelve months), 5 percent as "heavy drinkers" of wine, and 11 percent as "heavy drinkers" of hard liquor (p. 27). While 22 percent said that their work performance was impaired because of alcohol use (p. 33), relatively few *as yet* had developed obvious medical problems or the high level of physiological tolerance that goes with alcohol addiction. However, the drinking habits of many in the military (most of them in their twenties or thirties) would, if continued, put them at high risk of medical complications in their forties—the age of the average clinical alcoholic. These findings among military personnel help demonstrate that, within our culture at least, life cycle and environment need to be taken into account in assessing the implications of drinking behavior that might put a person in jeopardy of becoming a clinically defined alcoholic.

Again, literal reliance on Jellinek's elaborate criteria on the progressive nature of alcoholism is put into question by two longitudinal surveys we conducted in San Francisco and nationally, in which the same people were interviewed twice over a span of several years about their drinking habits and problems. These studies conclusively established that, in the nonclinical population, having a specific problem is a poor predictor of having the *same* problem several years later.

There was also a great deal of apparent remission or temporary suspension of problems, even though the sample was drawn from a population in which the overall level of drinking problems was either stable or increasing. Such results are consistent with the commonsense observation that most people tend to settle down as they grow older, as reflected in our first survey's finding that, even among men, the proportion of heavier drinkers drops off from 30 percent at ages forty-five to forty-nine to only 7 percent among those sixty-five or older (Cahalan, Cisin, and Crossley, 1969, p. 22).

While these findings are not in themselves proof that alcoholism is not a disease, they provide grounds for skepticism regarding the practicality of using any one sequence of development of symptoms as characterizing clinical alcoholism.

Teenage Drinking

These national surveys of adults do not—by definition—include information on the drinking habits and problems of youth. Other surveys have established that much heavy drinking goes on even down to the age of fourteen or younger. The Research Triangle Institute's national survey, cited in the NIAAA report to Congress for the fiscal year 1977, showed that about one-fifth of youth aged fourteen to seventeen were getting drunk six or more times a year or were having specific self-admitted problems with alcohol (National Institute on Alcohol Abuse and Alcoholism, 1977b). A report on high school students' use of drugs (including alcohol) from 1975 to 1984 indicates that teenagers' use of alcohol, although diminishing slightly, is still high (Johnston, O'Malley, and Bachman, 1985):

The percentage of high school seniors who reported that they had used alcohol within the last thirty days dropped slightly, from 72 percent in 1975 to 67 percent in 1984. The percentage of seniors reporting that they drank every day or almost every day dropped from 7 percent to 5 percent; and the percentage of those who said that they had had five or more drinks in a row during the prior two weeks fell off very slightly, from 41 percent to 39 percent. The sex difference narrowed from 1975 to 1984. Drinking during the last thirty days in 1975 was down slightly for males (75 percent as against 71.4 percent) but up slightly for females (62.2 percent as against 62.8 percent). Similarly, the percentage of those who drank five or more drinks in a row within the prior two weeks fell from 49 percent to 47.5 percent for males and rose from 26.4 percent to 29.6 percent for females (p. 48).

Few of these students could have begun drinking in their senior year. Every year from 1975 through 1984, about 10 percent of the seniors reported that they had begun drinking by the sixth grade, about 30 percent by the eighth grade, more than 50 percent by the ninth grade, and about three-fourths by the tenth grade (p. 88).

Thus, while drinking among high school seniors appears to be falling off a little, it is hardly cause for rejoicing that the percentage of those who have five or more drinks in a row within a two-week period decreased in 1984 to 39 percent from the 41 percent registered for the prior year. Almost all these seniors are below legal drinking age; and seniors figure prominently in the statistics for alcohol-related auto accident deaths. The vulnerability of youth to accidents after drinking is reflected in the recent finding that United States death rates are declining except for youths aged fifteen to twenty-four, who are dying at increasing rates ("U.S. Death Rates Decline," 1983). The development of insightful and realistic preventive activities for this group will be especially crucial. Some such preventive programs are discussed in Chapter Five.

Those who make forecasts of the prevalence of alcohol problems (and of alcohol-related delinquency) will do well to focus on the possible effects of rapid changes in the *age* makeup of the population. One estimate is that the number of eighteen-year-olds will have dropped by 25 percent between 1979 and 1994 ("The Best Students Money Can Buy," 1986). Since the heaviest drinking occurs among men aged eighteen to twenty-nine, this demographic change in itself might result in a lowered rate of alcohol problems— particularly drunken driving—for the population as a whole within the next few years, all other things being equal. Other projected demographic changes—such as increases in the Hispanic population through immigration or higher-than-average birthrates, and increases in Asian populations, primarily on the West Coast—will no doubt have at least some localized effects in what people drink, how much they drink, and whether they get into problems because of their drinking.

Cross-National Comparisons

Studies of the effectiveness of different countries' techniques for controlling alcohol-related problems have been helpful in demonstrating which methods work best under what circumstances (Cahalan, 1987, p. 370). International exchanges of methods and findings have helped American researchers improve their techniques and gain better insight into the drinking heritage of immigrant groups. Particularly helpful have been the interchanges with the Addiction Research Foundation of Canada and with

English and Scandinavian researchers, especially those in the Finnish Foundation for Alcohol Studies. The comparative studies sponsored by the NIAAA and the World Health Organization (WHO) have also been helpful. One of the studies with especially interesting results is the WHO project on Community Response to Alcohol-Related Problems, conducted in communities in Mexico, Zambia, Scotland, and the United States (California). Communities in these countries were chosen for study because their cultural traditions concerning alcohol are so different. For example, Zambian drinking is usually a group occasion; Mexican drinking is more sporadic than in the United States and is accompanied by more negative feelings about alcohol on the part of women; and people's attitudes about the appropriateness of drinking under varying circumstances differ considerably from country to country (Roizen, 1981; Rootman and Moser, 1984, chap. 6). Similarly, in their study of new-immigrant groups in the United States, Bennett and Ames (1985) found, for example, that the drinking practices of Spanish-speaking immigrants differ greatly depending on the country and subculture of origin.

Most of the major anthropological studies of the last generation are spelled out in detail in Dwight Heath's excellent review (1976). It reveals the enormous differences in drinking practices and values, not only between different cultures and subgroups but over time. The changes in drinking behavior throughout the relatively short history of the United States, for example, were influenced by the country's growth, industrialization, and influx of immigrants. These changes will be discussed in the next chapter, on our heritage of drinking habits and problems.

2

Ups and Downs in Our Drinking History

America's historic love-hate relationship with alcohol is typified in this speech by a Mississippi state senator (Gross, 1983, pp. 23-24):

> You have asked me how I feel about whiskey. All right, here is just how I stand on this question:
>
> If, when you say whiskey, you mean the devil's brew, the poison scourge, the bloody monster that defiles innocents, yea, literally takes the bread from the mouths of little children; if you mean the evil drink that topples the Christian man and woman from the pinnacles of righteous, gracious living into the bottomless pit of degradation and despair, shame and helplessness and hopelessness, then certainly I am against it with all of my power.
>
> But if, when you say whiskey, you mean the oil of conversation, the philosophic wine, the stuff that is consumed when good fellows get together, that puts a song in their hearts and laughter on their lips and the warm glow of contentment in their eyes; if you mean Christmas cheer; if you mean the stimulating drink that puts the spring in the old gentleman's step

on a frosty morning; if you mean the drink that
enables a man to magnify his joy, and his happiness,
and to forget, if only for a little while, life's great
tragedies and heartbreaks and sorrows, if you mean
that drink, the sale of which pours into our treasuries
untold millions of dollars, which are used to provide
tender care for our little children, our blind, our deaf,
our dumb, our pitiful aged and infirm, to build
highways, hospitals, and schools, then certainly I am
in favor of it.

This is my stand. I will not retreat from it; I
will not compromise.

Ever since the Pilgrims landed at Plymouth Rock, our
politicians and the rest of us have see-sawed up and down on
whether and how to control alcohol problems. In trying to
understand why our country has put up with wild swings in its
people's drinking behavior and problems, we should keep in mind
Santayana's old saw: that those who will not study history will be
doomed to repeat it.

Rum and True Religion

Although we think of the Puritan forefathers as stern and
righteous people, they did like their drink. They often spoke of
whiskey as "the good creature of God" (Levine, 1983b) because of
its comforting and presumed medicinal efficacy for a variety of
ailments. As soon as they landed, they set about making beer and
hard cider and wine from native fruits and berries; and while they
occasionally would put the town drunkard into the stocks for not
being a productive worker, they did not regard excessive drinking
as much of a problem—even though they came from an England
soon to suffer from an epidemic of alcoholism in which a part of
London became known as "Beer Street, Gin Lane" (Coffey, 1966).

Indeed, alcohol in colonial days was considered a universal
medicament at a time when few other palliatives were available. It
was prescribed for colds, fever, snakebites, frosted toes, and broken
legs, and as a pain reliever and relaxant (Rorabaugh, 1976; cited by

Levine, 1983b, p. 115). A historian of the early temperance movement summed up colonial dependence on alcohol thus (Krout, 1925; cited by Levine, 1983b, p. 115):

> Parents gave it to children for many of the minor ills of childhood, and its wholesomeness for those in health, it appeared, was only surpassed by its healing properties in case of disease. No other element seemed capable of satisfying so many human needs. It contributed to the success of any festive occasion and inspirited those in sorrow and distress. It gave courage to the soldier, endurance to the traveller, foresight to the statesman, and inspiration to the preacher. It sustained the sailor and plowman, the trader and trapper. By it were lighted the fires of revelry and of devotion. Few doubted that it was a great boon to mankind.

Relatively few worried about alcohol problems during the 150 years between the first European settlements in America and the Revolution. In fact, tavern keepers were among the most respected of community leaders (Levine, 1978). Rations of whiskey or beer or rum were considered a normal part of a workingman's pay, and the earliest alcohol tax statistics reflect a remarkable consumption of high-proof whiskey or rum. The heaviness of much colonial drinking is illustrated by Levine (1978) in two church-related events: At the funeral of a Boston minister's wife in 1678, the mourners consumed 51 1/2 gallons of wine (Dorchester, 1888). And at the ordination of a minister in Woburn, Massachusetts, the guests drank 6 1/2 barrels of cider, 25 gallons of wine, 2 gallons of brandy, and 4 gallons of rum (Kobler, 1973).

By 1700 rum was being distilled in Boston, and whiskey was being made throughout the colonies; the number of taverns was increasing rapidly, and so was public drunkenness (Austin, 1978). Bacon (1967; cited by Austin, 1978, p. 104) reminds us that during the 1700s wine and beer were largely supplanted by imported or domestic distilled spirits, which were four or five times as powerful; and that the increase of immigration and the spreading out of the population from the eastern seaboard "led to a loosening of all manner of social controls." In reaction, throughout the 1700s there was much preaching against drunkenness, and by 1773 Methodist John Wesley was advocating the prohibition of all distilling. Even so, the American Revolution of 1776 was ushered in by continuing increases in consumption of whiskey and rum, and much public drunkenness.

During colonial days the only group to which alcohol was denied by law was the Indians, whose traditional violence while drunk may well have been learned from their watching how White frontiersmen drank (MacAndrew and Edgerton, 1969). But as time went on, the settlers evolved from closely knit small communities of farmers and fishermen with very similar Protestant cultural backgrounds, to become much more varied in religious and cultural origins. And as cities grew and the colonies experienced the ups and downs of prosperous and hard times, differences widened between the more well-to-do and the poor, between the hard-working and those without skill or ambition, and between the rough frontiersmen and the community leaders concerned with moral and economic uplift. The growing stratification of America into socioeconomic and ethnic groupings with conflicting values led to increased perception of the poor and feckless as the primary source of alcohol problems; and to status conflicts, with the employer and churchgoing classes trying to impose sanctions to control drunkenness among the working class (Gusfield, 1962).

Growth of the Temperance Movement

Gradually, increasing concern over public drunkenness led to licensing of taverns and saloons in the Massachusetts Bay Territory as early as 1633, excise taxes on wines in Massachusetts, and on beer, wine, and brandy in New York in 1644 and similar restrictions in Connecticut in 1650. By 1694 popular feelings about the need for more temperance had increased enough to encourage Cotton Mather to petition the General Court of Massachusetts for stricter regulation of taverns, and to launch a campaign against the "flood of excessive drinking" that he felt was drowning out religiosity in the colonies (Austin, 1978).

The medical profession in postrevolutionary days became increasingly concerned about the effects of alcohol on public health as well as morals. In 1795 the physician Benjamin Rush published his *Inquiry into the Effects of Ardent Spirits upon Body and Mind,* in which he called the intemperate use of distilled liquor a "disease"; and a few years later, he organized physicians' appeals to Congress to impose heavy duties on all distilled spirits. Levine (1978) credits Rush with being not only a forefather of the temperance movement in America but also the author of the first systematic public health model of alcoholism. Rush identified distilled liquor as the causal agent, diagnosed the drunkard's condition as a disease, and prescribed total abstinence as the only realistic cure. (This is much the same model of alcoholism advocated by Alcoholics Anonymous today, except that AA adherents go beyond Rush to say that beer and wine can be as dangerous to alcoholics as hard liquor.) As reported by Levine (1978, p. 152), Rush spoke of habitual drunkenness as a "disease of the will" (the same as today's alcohologists' concepts of "inability to refrain" and "loss of control"). He gave this example: "When [a habitual drunkard was] strongly urged to stop drinking, he said 'Were a keg of rum in one corner of a room, and were a cannon constantly discharging balls between me and it, I could not refrain from passing before that cannon, in order to get at the rum.'"

In 1833 the American Temperance Society summarized a growing medical and moral concern (Levine, 1981b, p. 13) thus: "Ardent spirit, as a drink, is not needful, or useful. It is a poison, which injures the body and the soul. It deranges healthy action, and disturbs the functions of life. It blinds the understanding, sears the conscience, pollutes the affections and hardens the heart. It leads men into temptation."

Even so, as Austin says (1978, p. 107), "Between 1790 and 1830, Americans seem[ed] to go on an alcoholic binge." In the Whiskey Rebellion of 1794, western Pennsylvania farmers rose up against the imposition of a federal excise tax on liquor, which threatened their marketing of their backwoods grain in transportable liquid form. During the presidential terms of Thomas Jefferson and Andrew Jackson (1800–1808 and 1829–1837), personal freedom was emphasized and rough frontier manners were idealized. Saloons were everywhere, and heavy drinking was commonplace.

In reaction, temperance and prohibitionist sentiments grew; and in 1825 the preacher Lyman Beecher began leading a movement urging total abstinence. As Levine says (1983b, p. 126), the half-century from 1776 to 1826 saw a transition in American thinking about alcohol. At the beginning of this period, alcohol was considered "the good creature of God" by almost everyone; at the end, a growing minority had concluded that distilled spirits was a "demon" and a "destroyer." Twenty years later several million had signed a pledge to give up the use of alcohol entirely. The growth of temperance organizations between 1830 and 1850 was correlated with a decrease in alcohol consumption, from about 2.5 gallons of absolute alcohol per capita in 1790 to a low of 1 gallon by the 1850s (Austin, 1978, p. 109). A wave of prohibition laws started in Oregon Territory in 1843, and by 1855 there were thirteen states with such laws; but because they were found to be unenforceable, they were all repealed or modified by the beginning of the Civil War in 1861.

"Temperance" Turns into Prohibition

The growing industrialization and settling down of America after the primitive frontier days before the Civil War were accompanied by a fairly steady increase in the power of temperance and prohibitionist movements beginning about 1850, particularly when women such as Susan B. Anthony combined campaigns for women's rights with ringing pleas for reducing the evils of drunkenness and attendant violence and poverty. A latent but pervasive motivation back of prohibitionist drives was the conflict in values and styles between the established farmers and business leaders (joined by their upwardly mobile wives), who were concerned with moral standards and efficiency; and the laboring classes and migratory traders, trappers, and frontiersmen, who sought solace and temporary relief from hardship through indulgence in booze (Gusfield, 1962). There was also a close connection between the nativist antiforeigner and anti-Catholic feelings vented by adherents of evangelical Protestant sects against the drinking of Irish and German immigrants, who came to constitute a large part of the labor supply after the potato famine of 1845–1850 in Ireland and the European depression and wars of the late nineteenth century.

The prohibitionist movement really shifted into high gear under the leadership of Frances Willard, who was elected leader of the Women's Christian Temperance Union (WCTU) in 1879. She coupled temperance with the liberal reform movement by saying, "We believe in a living wage; in an eight-hour day; in courts of conciliation and arbitration, in justice as opposed to greed in gain" (Austin, 1978, p. 117). In the 1880s and 1890s, a second wave of state prohibition laws was passed; but most of these were also repealed by 1904. However, the WCTU by 1900 had pushed through laws in all states to require temperance education in the public schools; and many of these laws remain in effect today.

In the 1890s the Anti-Saloon League began a relentless campaign for national prohibition, operating from state to state with blunt admonitions to politicians either to get aboard their bandwagon or face the league's well-organized opposition in the next election. These tactics paid off ultimately in the passage of laws prohibiting alcoholic beverage sales in twenty-six states by the time America entered World War I in 1917. The Anti-Saloon League traded on war hysteria by calling the liquor traffic un-American, pro-German, crime-producing, food-wasting, youth-corrupting, home-wrecking, and treasonable (Austin, 1978, p. 120). And thus, by January 1919, the Eighteenth Amendment was ratified by the necessary thirty-six states, to become effective one year later.

In October 1919—one month before the end of the war—Congress passed the Volstead National Prohibition Act (over President Wilson's veto) to implement the Eighteenth Amendment. The Act provided for bootlegging penalties of up to five years in jail and $10,000 fines; and only physicians could write legal prescriptions for spiritous drinks. However, the ambivalence of Congress regarding the Volstead Act is seen in its making no provision for penalties for *drinking* or keeping liquor, but only for selling it; and gearing up for enforcement did not really begin until the late 1920s. Since enforcement varied because it was largely left up to the states, people in many sections of the country (especially in urban and coastal areas) still consumed a lot of liquor, although the use of spirits dropped off sharply about 1921–22, with a corresponding drop in cirrhosis rates.

Repeal and Its Aftermath

Soon after passage of the Volstead Act, antiprohibition leaders began to muster their forces. By 1928 the DuPont industrial family of Delaware quit supporting the dry cause; in 1932 John D. Rockefeller and S. S. Kresge, the dime store king, joined with John J. Raskob of General Motors in the antiprohibitionist Association Against the Prohibition Amendment movement (Levine, 1985). One strong motivation for their objection to prohibition was the effect of the new income tax: they reasoned that both personal and corporate income taxes could be abolished if liquor taxes could be restored. President Hoover, though in favor of continuing prohibition ("the noble experiment"), established the Wickersham Commission (National Commission on Enforcement of the Prohibition Laws), made up of prominent industrialists, educators, and other professionals, to review the effects of prohibition. The commission deliberated for two years and finally came forth with a tepid opposition to repeal, but accompanied by strong statements on how much damage was being done to public respect for law and order. Thus, the commission's report really set the stage for the renewed drive for repeal that was mounted during the 1932 presidential campaign.

Much of the intellectual groundwork for the form that repeal finally took had been established many years before by the "Committee of Fifty," a group of distinguished educators, industrialists, and professional men who were active from 1893 to 1903 in a special privately financed task force that published many volumes of facts and arguments about alcohol in American society (Levine, 1983a). While they were opposed to prohibition as ineffectual and voiced the prophetic prediction that it would be likely to lead to the breakdown of respect for law, they had many specific recommendations for control of the liquor trade, which ultimately were put into effect after prohibition had come and gone thirty years later. These included provisions against selling alcohol to minors or inebriates, closing of liquor outlets on established holidays, strict control over hours, and many other conditions of sale and the licensing of outlets.

In 1932 both the Democrats and the Republicans came out against national prohibition, the Republicans preferring resubmission of the Eighteenth Amendment to the states and the Democrats demanding outright repeal. Upon Franklin D. Roosevelt's election, he took immediate steps to declare light beer to be nonalcoholic and thus legal; and the Eighteenth Amendment was repealed the following year by passage of the Twenty-First Amendment. Factors that weighed heavily in the demise of prohibition after only thirteen years included, as mentioned, wealthy industrialists' hopes for income tax relief through the return of alcohol taxes, as well as their fear—in a time of economic depression and growing unrest in poverty-stricken areas all across the country—that growing disrespect for law could become contagious enough to threaten property rights unless something was done to alleviate popular unrest. So most of the nation's leading tycoons, whose pronouncements were still highly respected, came out for legalization of beer and then for outright repeal. Their arguments were bolstered by claims that resumption of legal alcohol sales would help reduce unemployment at a time when there were long breadlines in midwestern and eastern cities—a point on which organized labor then generally agreed.

Thus, we see that a concerted lobbying campaign and the intensive propaganda efforts by the Anti-Saloon League and the WCTU brought about prohibition, and that much the same types of tactics (through appeals by some of the very same individuals, such as the DuPonts and Rockefellers) in turn brought about repeal. This was indeed a massive turnabout within less than a generation, and well worthy of study by anyone interested in understanding how public opinion and legislative action can be influenced. However, the climate was ripe for repeal: while prohibition had reduced cirrhosis rates materially, evidently many of the American people never really were strongly in favor of prohibition. And, as we will see in later chapters, after repeal had turned the problems of control over alcohol back to the states, many people uneasily continued to drink wet while they voted dry.

After repeal the federal government kept part of the responsibility for controlling alcohol, but primarily for the purpose of regulating the orderly production and marketing of alcoholic beverages rather than to restrain consumption. Since 1972 such controls have been lodged in the Treasury Department's Bureau of Alcohol, Tobacco, and Firearms (BATF). The BATF's stewardship is discussed in the next chapter. It should be sufficient for the moment to note that the agency plays virtually no role in attempting to reduce any adverse effects of legally acquired alcohol on American public health and welfare, other than to stipulate some rather arm's-length and underfunded rules on the stewardship of taverns and other places of sale concerning serving underaged and intoxicated persons. The BATF also established certain rules in the interest of preserving orderly markets for alcohol, such as prohibiting "tied-houses" (retail establishments controlled by alcohol producers), and regulations regarding purity. As also discussed in Chapter Three, the individual states' alcoholic beverage control (ABC) agencies also have operated more in the interest of orderly marketing than in attempting to reduce excessive alcoholic consumption (Mosher, 1979).

After repeal seven states continued with prohibition, though beer was legal in five of these; twelve states permitted liquor for home consumption only; and twenty-nine allowed liquor by the glass. Eighteen states eventually adopted systems of state-monopoly stores; and these and the other states where alcohol was sold through state licensing of package liquor stores or taverns or eating estblishments were heavily dependent on alcohol taxes to help restore their depression-depleted revenues so that they could provide needed public services (Aaron and Musto, 1981). Thus, the climate was permissive for a gradual relaxation of alcohol controls—particularly since the American public wanted to forget all about the dark days of prohibition and the depression. Thanks also to astute lobbying and shrewd marketing and advertising by the alcohol industry (see Chapter Five), all fifty states had abandoned prohibition by 1966, although a scattering of counties (chiefly in the South and Midwest) are still officially dry. The steadily increasing efficiency of alcohol advertising and marketing through the media and in taverns, bars, grocery stores, and even gasoline filling stations has been associated with a high level of alcohol sales, although (as discussed in Chapter Five) the sale of distilled beverages recently has leveled off in response to shifts in popular tastes toward lighter drinks.

Hindsight Is a Dear School, But . . .

What can we learn about controlling America's alcohol problems through a reassessment of our history? We have seen many fitful attempts at better control: moral suasion, then prohibition, then repeal with fairly strict control over sales, then the recent laissez-faire situation of mounting consumption and problems, and the current linking of the good-health-and-exercise movement with a hope for better primary prevention measures. Perhaps we will see the picture better if we look at ourselves through the eyes of outsiders.

One early observer of America was Alexis de Tocqueville, a French aristocrat and amateur historian of the early nineteenth century who visited America and wrote his reflections in *Democracy in America,* published in 1835. As described in *Habits of the Heart* (Bellah and others, 1985), de Tocqueville believed that Americans were destined for future greatness because of their form of government and the liberal traditions on which the country was founded; but he also recognized the inherent conflicts between their desire for individual freedom and their desire for public order through the rule of laws that impinge on those individual freedoms. Such contradictions in our national character are still manifested in our ambivalence over whether (and how) to control alcohol problems.

The thoughts of another Frenchman, Emile Durkheim, concerning "anomie" (the state of normlessness) may be helpful in understanding American drinking habits. In his book on suicide, published in 1897, Durkheim described anomie as a condition that leads to alienation from one's fellow beings, accompanied by a pervasive sense of hopelessness and lack of confidence in the efficacy of social institutions. Although he was writing about the role of anomie in suicide rather than necessarily about alcoholism, his thoughts are relevant to alcohol problems because high suicide rates and alcoholism generally go together. Many sociologists see anomie as an almost endemic condition of life for many Americans; for many of us do not have comfortably deep roots in any culture, social class, or philosophical belief, or even a specific geographical spot of earth that we can call a home.

Americans have been always on the move, eager to improve their condition by changing their residences or their jobs or their lifestyles. Some of this restlessness comes from our emphasis on individualism; some of it, from events in our history—such as the opening up of free lands in the Midwest and West, the California gold rush, and oil booms. Because of this feverish mobility, many Americans have not developed a close network of supportive family and friends and hence have often resorted to alcohol to stave off loneliness. All our national surveys have shown a high correlation between alcohol problems and a lack of family or friends. Our emphasis on individualism makes us reluctant to obey rules and regulations intended to serve the common good; we evade them whenever they cramp our style.

Our individualism and our made-in-Hollywood folk legends about rough pioneers and cowboys make us sympathetic to macho heroes who can drink anyone under the table and can still outshoot all the foreign hordes that try to overpower them. These legends have been exploited most cleverly by those who are advertising products that dare us to use them dangerously: sports cars screaming around mountain curves, cigarettes puffed energetically by sun-burned cowboys, or alcoholic beverages guzzled by outdoor sports figures.

Our diverse ethnic and cultural backgrounds make it hard for us to accept each other's ways of drinking or nondrinking. Therefore, it is more difficult for us to arrive at a workable consensus on standards for appropriate conduct than is true in countries with much longer continuity of cultures, such as Sweden or Japan.

Still, we do have the capacity to resolve problems if we are given sufficient challenge. We often get irritated at how our government works; but ours is the only republic in the world that has survived with the same form of government and the same basic Constitution for the last 200 years. We have managed to heal the wounds from a devastating Civil War and to survive two world wars and a severe economic depression that might have led to a revolution had it occurred in a country without our balance-wheel constitutional safeguards. We may be slowly—very, very slowly—learning from our mistakes in Korea and Vietnam and Latin America. Thus, perhaps it is not too much to hope that we can do a better job than we have with such internal problems as overuse of alcohol and drugs. Some options on how we might begin to solve our national drinking problem are discussed in the chapters that follow.

Using the lessons of history in predicting future trends in alcohol problems and their control is certainly a risky endeavor. Central to the prediction of future trends in drinking behavior is a good understanding of the attitudes and values of the main subcultures in our population; but analysts will differ in the weight they give to different variables. Some will emphasize the role of individual leaders (such as Benjamin Rush, Andrew Jackson, Frances Willard, Franklin D. Roosevelt, or Senator Harold Hughes, whose vigorous campaign brought about the birth of the NIAAA). Others will give greatest weight to the effects of national watershed events (such as the westward migration, the Civil War, and the 1930s depression). Others will emphasize the efforts of organized groups (such as the Anti-Saloon League, the repeal coalition, and the National Council on Alcoholism.).

The following chapters discuss the role of other factors that can materially affect the amount and consequences of drinking: new avenues of communication (such as radio and television), leading to changes in American habits and values and to greater alcohol-marketing pressure; innovations in alcohol production and economics; changing diet and health habits; changing values that affect drinking and alcoholism treatment indirectly (such as rising expectations that we will be protected by insurance or government action or the miracles of modern medicine against most health risks, coupled with related readiness to sue somebody if something does not turn out as well as expected); and changes in government activities (such as changes in taxes and tax deductibles affecting alcohol prices, and changes in controls over alcohol advertising and marketing).

Of course, major trends are always influenced by several variables. Particularly because alcoholic beverages have played such a strong role in our lives, and because the alcohol industry is so strong politically, alcohol problems in America are unlikely to be materially reduced unless national, state, and community leaders and organizations make an extended and systematic effort to reshape the general public's attitude toward heavy drinking. As discussed in subsequent chapters, this is not likely to happen until those who wish to bring about more effective control of alcohol problems develop more political clout than the alcohol industry and its many powerful friends.

3

Undernourished Government Alcohol Programs

Experience since repeal has proved that the health and efficiency of the congressionally mandated and supported federal agencies involved with alcohol are crucial to the maintenance of reasonable standards of control and the funding of alcohol prevention and treatment programs on the state level. This chapter presents a brief history of recent developments in federal alcohol control programs, as background for understanding why very limited progress has been made and why the future course of remedial measures is uncertain.

In Chapter One we saw that, as of 1980, alcohol-related deaths, disability, violence and lost productivity were costing our nation a total variously estimated at $89 billion to more than $116 billion per year—a much larger sum than even for drug abuse or mental illness. But, as shown by the following figures (correspondence submitted to me by S. Long, chief of the NIAAA's Planning and Financial Branch, July 31, 1986), the national alcohol research effort is very thinly funded in comparison with money spent on other health-related federal research:

The NIAAA research appropriation of $57 million for fiscal year (FY) 1986 comprised only 1.1 per cent of the total National Institutes of Health

37

(NIH) and Alcohol, Drug and Mental Health Administration (ADAMHA) appropriation for research.

In 1981, economic costs of alcoholism were
estimated at $75 billion per year, for cancer at $33
billion, for heart and vascular disease at $80 billion,
and for respiratory diseases at $33 billion. However,
for every $1,000 of the estimated costs of these
problems, the Federal Government spent only 30 cents
for alcoholism research while spending $23 for cancer
research, $4 on heart and vascular disease, and $2 on
respiratory ailments.

In 1981, the prevalence of alcoholism and
alcohol abuse was estimated at 13 million persons
affected; there were 3 million with a history of cancer;
48 million with heart and vascular disease; and 66
million with respiratory diseases. However, per
chronic case, research funding was $2 for alcohol, $257
for cancer, $7 for heart and vascular disease, and $1 for
respiratory disease.

Although alcohol abuse and alcoholism made
up ten per cent of the chronic cases, alcohol research
dollars were only three per cent of the total spent on
research for those four ailments in 1981.

The picture is even grimmer for funding of alcohol programs
from the private sector. As noted by Joseph Califano, former
secretary of health, education and welfare, in his book *America's
Health Care Revolution* (1986, p. 208), "Despite the widespread
diseases alcoholism and alcohol abuse cause, they are near the
bottom of the list in private research support: alcoholism gets 30
cents per victim, while cancer gets $66, cystic fibrosis $131, and
muscular distrophy $173."

Why do alcohol problems rate so low on the national totem
pole? The answers are easy to guess: It is harder to work up a
sympathy for alcoholics, whose problems are popularly seen as
largely self-inflicted. Also, as shown in Chapter Two, our country
has tried to get rid of alcohol problems through legislation, but has
failed; thus, many legislators are loath to vote more money to deal

with such a controversial problem. Then too, alcohol is a legal beverage, and most legislators drink; so it is politically safer to make speeches denouncing the illegal *demon drug traffic* and to vote more money to combat it than to try to drum up support for combating alcohol problems in the face of possible opposition from the powerful alcohol industry lobby. As we will see further on in this chapter, the constituency for dealing with alcohol problems has been materially weakened in recent years by the virtual elimination of the NIAAA's role in supporting alcoholism treatment facilities, by the Reagan administration's emphasis on decentralization of treatment through removing money from the NIAAA's budgets and putting it into block grants to the states.

Federal Alcohol Control Agencies

This chapter deals primarily with the achievements and trials of the NIAAA, because it is the federal agency that is primarily responsible for research on alcohol and for monitoring the treatment of alcoholism in a general way, although it no longer has funds to dispense on direct treatment activities. The NIAAA never has been assigned significant regulatory responsibilities. However, a number of federal agencies have at least a tangential responsibility for alcohol regulation, as well as for treatment or rehabilitation programs for their employees. Mosher and Mottl (1981) have distinguished four types of jurisdiction: land-based, transportation-based, safety-based, and economic-based agencies:

The principal *land-based* federal agencies with authority to regulate the availability of alcohol within their jurisdictions include the Department of Defense, the National Forest Service, the National Park Service, the Bureau of Land Management, the Army Corps of Engineers, and the Bureau of Indian Affairs. Taken together, these agencies have more alcohol under their jurisdictions than any of our largest states. The Department of Defense is of special interest because military personnel consist mostly of males in the heaviest-drinking age range, eighteen to thirty-nine. Mosher and Mottl (1981, p. 399) cite several surveys that confirm the high rates of drinking problems among military personnel. When one considers the sensitive nature of military operations and the ever-increasing requirement for finely tuned skills and a clear head, these findings—as Mosher and Mottl point out—are occasion for concern. Mosher and Mottl provide many details about the high volume of alcohol sold through the approximately 500 service-run package stores (plus the numerous on-post clubs) run by the Army, Navy, and Air Force, which racked up $356.1 million in alcohol sales in fiscal 1977. The authors give credit to the Department of Defense for its recent attempts to deglamorize alcohol and constrain consumption through prohibition of such practices as "happy hours" (periods of reduced drink prices), increasing vigilance and training for those serving alcohol in the clubs, cutting back on number of alcohol outlets and hours of service, and tightening up disciplinary actions for drunkenness and alcohol-related absenteeism or inefficiency.

Federal *safety-based* jurisdiction over alcohol (report Mosher and Mottl) involves such agencies as the Occupational Safety and Health Administration, the Consumer Product Safety Commission, the Federal Drug Administration, the Environmental Protection Agency, the National Highway Transportation Safety Administration, the Nuclear Regulatory Commission, the National Transportation Safety Board, the Coast Guard, and the Bureau of Mines. Space does not permit repeating here all the alcohol-concerned activities of these agencies, which the authors describe as crucial to health and safety. Their article contains many suggestions for better prevention of accidents and for protection of consumers through better labeling and marketing practices.

Federal *transportation-based* jurisdiction over alcohol is necessary, as Mosher and Mottl point out, because most forms of travel involve crossing state lines. Federal jurisdiction covers employee practices in the transportation industry, equipment specifications and maintenance, and passenger and operator practices. Transportation agencies include the National Transportation Safety Board (which investigates air, land, and sea accidents), the Department of Transportation, the Federal Aviation Administration (which has established stringent rules against serving drinks to intoxicated passengers and against crew members' drinking during flights or for eight hours prior to flights), the Federal Railroad Administration (which recently has been trying to push enforcement of its strict rules against intoxication or use of alcohol by workers while on duty or on call), and the United States Coast Guard (which has jurisdiction over sales and consumption on board vessels and in Coast Guard establishments). The Small Business Administration is involved in the alcohol traffic through loans to bars and liquor stores. The Mosher and Mottl article provides many details on these agencies' efforts to reduce alcohol-related transportation accidents and on how their effectiveness could be improved through more stringent enforcement of long-existing rules.

The Internal Revenue Service has a very real effect on alcohol consumption, note Mosher and Mottl (p. 446), because of tax deductions currently permitted for gifts of alcohol and purchases of drinks for "business purposes" and deductions of well over $200 million per year for alcohol advertising. (Some of these deductions may be reduced and more closely scrutinized under the new tax reform bill.)

The federal agency primarily responsible for the *economic* aspects of alcohol is the Bureau of Alcohol, Tobacco, and Firearms (BATF). Its primary duty is to see that excise and import taxes are collected. It is the oldest of the federal agencies directly concerned with alcohol. Local governments in America imposed alcohol taxes well before the Revolutionary War; the first internal revenue statute passed by Congress, the Revenue Act of 1791, called for taxes on distilled spirits and tobacco, thus establishing the forerunners of the BATF. Soon thereafter came the Whiskey Rebellion in Pennsylvania, where embattled farmers' armed struggle to preserve local "rights" to sell untaxed whiskey was quelled after President Washington called out the militia (National Association of State Alcohol and Drug Abuse Directors, 1980).

Jefferson repealed excises in 1802, referring to the "infernal" excise system, "hostile to the genius of a free people." Federal taxes on alcohol and tobacco were not invoked again until 1862, when the Office of the Commissioner of Internal Revenue was established and another forerunner for today's BATF was set up. The Commissioner of Internal Revenue was charged with primary responsibility for enforcement of the Volstead Act under prohibition in the 1920s; and repeal in 1934 saw the formation of an Alcohol Tax Unit within the Bureau of Internal Revenue to enforce liquor tax laws.

In 1940 the Alcohol Tax Unit was integrated with the Federal Alcohol Administration to combine both tax collection and alcohol regulatory functions. In 1972 these activities were combined with gun control and tobacco tax collection under the present BATF in the Treasury Department.

As noted in the 1980 National Association of State Alcohol and Drug Abuse Directors (NASADAD) report (p. 45), the BATF collects about $8 billion in excise taxes on alcohol and tobacco, in 1980 the third largest source of federal revenue. Much of the BATF's authority rests upon the 1935 Federal Alcohol Administration Act, which issues permits to engage in interstate or foreign commerce in alcohol beverages, prohibits anticompetitive practices (such as "tied-houses" linking alcohol producers and retail outlets), and provides for regulation of alcohol labeling and advertising.

Recently there have been many attempts by consumer groups to get the BATF to put warning labels on bottles or cans containing alcohol. Covered under the BATF's labeling and advertising jurisdiction are the approval of labels for all alcoholic beverage containers in interstate trade, standardization of sizes of containers, and setting standards for alcohol strength or proof.

At the present time, the media impose a few voluntary controls over alcohol advertising (for example, distilled spirits are not advertised on television, and current sports figures are not supposed to appear in alcohol commercials). The BATF has resisted the imposition of further controls, such as banning alcohol advertising altogether or clamping down on suggestions that alcohol improves one's status in society or with the opposite sex. BATF hearings on alcohol advertising have been dragging along for years with little significant resolution, partly because the BATF sees its authority to control advertising as very limited, and partly because the alcohol industry has been lobbying effectively against further constraints on advertising. The NASADAD report concludes (p. 10):

> But as concern builds over the potential health hazards of alcoholic beverages serious questions remain: are BATF health actions to date merely token steps taken to placate critics? Is BATF too close to the

alcohol industry? Can BATF be effective in influenc-
ing industry voluntary efforts? Will BATF require
warning labels if evidence indicates the need and the
voluntary effort is not successful? Will Treasury
continue to call for action on health protection? The
findings and recommendations of the forthcoming
health hazards report may provide some insight into
these questions. The answers must await future agency actions.

However, the "health hazards report" (U.S. Departments of
Treasury and Health and Human Services, 1980) did not turn out
to be any blockbuster. While this thin report enumerated most of
the types of health hazards (for example, cirrhosis and pancreatitis)
in which alcohol may be a factor, it put its primary emphasis on
the relatively rare fetal alcohol syndrome (which affects some
infants' facial and other bodily characteristics) and nowhere
provided any statistics on the estimated incidence of specific
alcohol-related health disorders, fatal crashes, and other accidents.

Regarding the use of health warning labels, the report
hedged (p. 41): "After concluding the consultation process, reading
communications literature and reviewing the aforementioned
government experience with health warning labels, the Departments agreed that it would be premature to recommend health
warning labels for alcoholic beverages at this time." This decision
was based primarily on the dubious grounds that "it has not been
established that moderate alcohol consumption is hazardous for
most alcohol consumers" and that "the public is becoming jaded
over government warnings." And whom did Treasury and HHS
consult at a special meeting of the National Advisory Council on
Alcohol Abuse and Alcoholism? Of the fifty-five names listed,
fifteen were from the ranks of the beer, wine, and liquor interests—
understandable since the BATF was running the show, and the
BATF is closely allied with the alcohol industry, whose taxes
support its budget. Thus, it is not surprising that—after years of
agitation on the part of public health authorities for more control
over alcohol advertising or at least to have warnings of alcohol's
dangers placed on the bottles (as is done for less dangerous

tobacco)—at this writing the BATF has done nothing to implement any tightening up on alcohol advertising or labeling.

The alcoholic beverage control (ABC) agencies in each of the fifty states have functions very similar to those of the federal BATF. As noted by Room and Mosher (1979/80) in their paper on state alcohol agencies, the intent back of the control codes enacted in each state after repeal was the promotion of temperance; but an NIAAA-funded study by Medicine in the Public Interest (1979) found that those in charge of these state control systems saw their main functions as providing an orderly market for alcoholic beverages, reducing the role of criminal elements in the alcohol trade, and generating tax revenues. It is widely believed that both the BATF and the state ABC agencies are unduly influenced by the alcohol industry because of incessant industry lobbying and frequent transfers of personnel between control agencies and the industry. There have been many complaints that they do not do a good job of operating in the public interest: that they should apply more stringent measures to control violations of laws against sales to minors and intoxicated persons and should impose tighter controls over issuance of alcohol licenses and over alcohol advertising. While most states also have statewide or local alcoholism authorities, whose primary purpose is to deal with alcoholism and alcohol problems, Room and Mosher (1979/80, p. 13) note that "These offices usually have little or no input into ABC policy decisons. Likewise, they generally have shown little or no interest in using ABC enforcement as a tool for prevention."

National Institute on Alcohol Abuse and Alcoholism

The NIAAA is the primary federal agency charged with a broad range of responsibilities for programs of public action and education to help minimize drinking problems. The rest of this chapter will be devoted to summarizing its accomplishments and problems since its founding in 1970.

As noted in the NASADAD alcohol and drug report for 1984 (Butynski, 1984, p. 2), prior to 1967 "alcoholism and alcohol abuse had been generally ignored by all levels of government. The major source of assistance for those with alcohol abuse problems was the private voluntary sector and a small number of private treatment clinics. [But] by 1967, alcoholism had been recognized as a disease by the World Health Organization, the American Medical Association, the American Hospital Association, and the American Psychiatric Association. In addition, several federal court cases had held that alcoholism is an illness or disease. During the late 1960s the alarmingly high incidence of the disease of alcoholism had also begun to be recognized by health officials."

This NASADAD account of the neglect of alcoholism treatment problems "by all levels of government" is somewhat misleading, for even as early as 1951 there were thirty-five states with alcohol agencies. However, the founding of the NIAAA did draw attention to the *national* scope of alcohol problems and provided many mechanisms and incentives for improvement of standards in research and treatment programs.

The steps that led to the founding of the NIAAA were described to me by Robert Straus in a recent interview (June 6, 1986). He was chairman of the Cooperative Commission on the Study of Alcoholism, an ad hoc group that came into being in 1959 through a grant from the National Institute of Mental Health (NIMH) to the North American Association of Alcoholism Programs. The commission's members included representatives of mental health and social welfare agencies in the United States and Canada who were interested in alcohol problems, and representatives of constituency groups such as the National Council on Alcoholism and the Alcohol Research Foundation of Ontario (later renamed the Addiction Research Foundation). Funds were raised from the National Institute of Mental Health for a five-year grant to establish a research unit at Stanford University to help in the planning of the objectives and scope of future alcohol research and treatment programs. Nevitt Sanford headed the unit, but the major output from it was provided by his deputy, Thomas F. Plaut, in his book *Alcohol Problems: A Report to the Nation by the Cooperative Commission on the Study of Alcoholism* (1967).

Straus recalls President Lyndon Johnson as being the first President of the United States to express much concern about alcohol problems. As an outgrowth of the Cooperative Commission's interim reports, Johnson directed NIMH to create a subcenter concerned with alcohol, and he ordered the secretary of health, education and welfare to appoint a consultative National Advisory Committee on Alcoholism. This committee (of which Straus was the first chairman) ultimately became the Advisory Council when the NIAAA was formed.

Building on the work of the Cooperative Commission, the National Advisory Committee (which included many members of the Cooperative Commission, with Straus again as chairman), issued a formal report (1968) to Johnson's top assistant for domestic affairs, Joseph Califano. The report recommended most of the primary program objectives soon adopted under the temporary stewardship of NIMH and then under the new NIAAA: emphasis on dealing with alcoholism as an illness, continuing advocacy of insurance and prepayment coverage for alcoholism, the decriminalization of public intoxication, and the expansion of alcoholism research coupled with research training.

The full history of the origins and achievements and disappointments in the NIAAA's career has yet to be written. In the most extensive account thus far, Jay Lewis, in a chapter in *Alcohol, Science and Society Revisited* (1982a, pp. 385-386), noted that a number of public policy and health issues concerning alcohol were coming to a head in the late 1960s:

> The foundation of the federal alcoholism effort was laid down during the late 60s with a series of studies, court decisions, legislation and bureaucratic moves, all aided and abetted by constituency groups. . . . Landmark court decisions in *Easter* v. *District of Columbia*, *Driver* v. *Hinnant* and *Powell* v. *Texas* affirmed the status of alcoholism as a disease. In Congress, leading up to the Comprehensive Alcohol Abuse and Alcoholism Prevention, Treatment and Rehabilitation Act of 1970 (the "Hughes Act") were a number of prior bills, including the Highway Safety Act of 1966, which required a report on alcohol and traffic safety; the Economic Opportunity Amendments of 1967 and 1969, which created the first federally funded alcoholism treatment programs, under the

Office of Economic Opportunity; and the Alcoholic Rehabilitation Act of 1968, which declared that alcoholism was a "major health and social problem" and led to the Community Mental Health Centers Amendments of 1970, which authorized direct grants for special alcoholism treatment projects.

As described by Stephen Nieberding of the NIAAA (1983), the agency ultimately grew out of activities in NIMH's Division of Special Mental Health Programs. In 1969 the division established a National Center for the Prevention and Control of Alcoholism, which funded sixty-eight research and twelve training grants and fellowships totaling $6.4 million in that initial fiscal year. In 1970, to give added visibility to the program, this center was redesignated the Division on Alcohol Abuse and Alcoholism, still within NIMH.

Jack Mendelson, a Harvard psychiatrist, came on board then to administer the program with one hand while running an experimental alcohol behavior research laboratory in the District of Columbia's mental hospital with the other. President Johnson, his assistant Joseph Califano (later secretary of health, education and welfare under President Carter), and Senator Harold Hughes of Iowa (former governor and a recovering alcoholic with a charismatic personality) were all strong advocates for federally funded alcoholism treatment programs. Their interest was stimulated by the lobbying of the National Council on Alcoholism (NCA) and other constituent groups, all pushing hard for increasing the scope and funding of this budding alcohol agency.

Their efforts finally led to the signing by President Nixon of Public Law 91-616, which established the NIAAA in 1971 and authorized alcohol treatment project grant and formula grant programs. Morris Chafetz, another Harvard psychiatrist, then headed the agency and immediately launched a great variety of programs, funded by a budget that soon jumped to $87.5 million per year. In 1974 Congress established an umbrella agency, the Alcohol, Drug, and Mental Health Administration (ADAMHA), which still superintends the operations of the NIAAA, the National Institute on Drug Abuse (NIDA), and NIMH.

The NIAAA inherited the alcohol research and training activities that had existed under NIMH, and Chafetz rapidly expanded congressionally mandated programs. Divisions within the NIAAA included Special Treatment and Rehabilitation, State and Community Assistance, and a skimpily funded one for Prevention. The NIAAA also expanded public service and media activities by setting up a National Clearinghouse for Alcohol Information.

In line with pressure from the NIAAA's advisory committee (largely drawn from the top ranks of the treatment-oriented National Council on Alcoholism), the Division of Special Treatment and Rehabilitation got the bulk of the funding (some $90 million in fiscal year 1974) for more than 700 programs focusing on community-based treatment of alcoholism, early intervention programs, programs to help corporations institute or strengthen alcohol treatment insurance programs for their employees, and many others. The Division of State and Community Assistance involved the NIAAA directly in state-based alcohol activities through formula grants that dispensed funds in every state for programs meeting NIAAA approval. These formula grants also provided the funding for an alcohol authority in each state, useful in promoting communications between the NIAAA and the states and among the states themselves.

An NIAAA summary sheet dated August 1975 enumerated its increase in budgets from $17 million in 1971 to $218 million in 1974, and its principal accomplishments within the first five years, as follows: passage of a Uniform Alcoholism and Intoxication Treatment Act (then accepted in twenty-seven states and since accepted in a majority of states) (Finn, 1985), which identified public drunkenness as a medical and not a criminal issue; increase in the acceptability of third-party payments from insurance organizations; a tenfold increase in outreach programs by businesses, to assist employees with alcohol problems; an increase in the effectiveness of treatment resources, which was claimed as more than offsetting federal expenditures on treatment programs; establishment of a National Center for Alcohol Education to develop manpower for prevention and treatment programs; the instituting of special programs focusing on Blacks, Hispanics, and

American Indians; cooperation with the Department of Transportation's Alcohol Safety Action Program for rehabilitation of drinking drivers; and development of standards for certification of treatment counselors. During that same period, substantial resources were also devoted to grants and contracts to support basic and applied alcohol-related research in the biomedical and behavioral sciences.

As described by Lewis (1982a), in the NIAAA's early days, severe federal constraints on staff size (less than 100) and refusals to expand grant-review mechanisms, coupled with sudden releases of some $80 million that had been withheld for a couple of years under President Nixon's impoundment practices, provided pressure toward spending considerable sums in outside contracts:

> The classic example of NIAAA unorthodoxy was a series of grants made to national organizations in 1974-1975 under the directorship of Chafetz. Some $23 million in awards to organizations, including both alcoholism field groups and associations representing broader constituencies, were dispensed in a fashion which was later criticized as highly irregular and for purposes seen as constituency-building in nature. The 16 grants were awarded to 14 organizations for a wide range of projects. Recipients included major alcoholism organizations, such as the National Council on Alcoholism (which had three large grants), the Association of Labor-Management Administrators and Consultants on Alcoholism, Council of State and Territorial Alcoholism Authorities, and the Association of Halfway House Alcoholism Programs.
>
> Other national associations included the National Congress of Parents and Teachers, United States Jaycees, League of Cities-Conference of Mayors, Boys Clubs of America, Legis 50 (formerly the Citizens Conference for State Legislatures), Education Commission of the States, National Association of Counties, Airline Pilots Association, Group Health

Association of America and the National Council on
Aging [Lewis, 1982a, p. 389].

These grants to constituencies generated a great deal of
enthusiasm in the benefactor organizations for a time. However,
pressure from Congress resulted in sudden cutbacks in most of these
grants. The cutbacks produced much bitterness and alienation in
some of the NIAAA's major constituencies, particularly the
National Council on Alcoholism, the nonprofit treatment-oriented
association discussed in the next chapter. This bitterness carried
over to affect relationships with the NIAAA after Chafetz left.

By 1976 the NIAAA had achieved significant credibility with
Congress, state alcohol treatment agencies, and the general public
as regards the seriousness of alcohol problems nationally. Ernest
Noble, Chafetz's successor, held credentials in biological research as
well as psychiatry; and thus his appointment was congruent with
Congress's putting a greater relative emphasis on alcohol research
than on treatment. After Chafetz departed, there was increased
emphasis on the commissioning of many studies of social and other
environmental aspects of alcoholism and other alcohol problems
and the stepping up of research on genetic, biological, and
metabolic factors in alcoholism.

In 1979 the NIAAA published its first comprehensive account
of its cooperation with other federal agencies on solving alcohol
problems, including two large studies to evaluate the effectiveness
of drinking-driving programs. Many projects were undertaken in
conjunction with such agencies as the Veterans Administration, the
Department of Justice, the Office of Education, various National
Institutes (National Institute of Arthritis, Metabolism, and
Digestive Diseases; Heart, Lung, and Blood Institute; National
Institute on Drug Abuse; National Cancer Institute; National
Institute of Child Health and Human Development; National
Institute on Aging; National Institute on Neurological and
Communicable Disease and Stroke; and National Institute of
General Medical Science), the Health Services Administration, and
the Department of Labor.

Also, there was vigorous continuance of attempts to
destigmatize alcoholism, assistance to health insurers in their

development and marketing of insurance coverage for alcoholism treatment, subsidization of training for medical students and physicians about alcohol, and studies of alcohol advertising and the presumed influence of alcohol taxes on consumption. Noble's later espousal of increases in alcohol taxes as a means of reducing consumption (and thereby ostensibly reducing alcohol problems) earned him the opposition from the alcohol industry. This opposition, coupled with his forthright public speeches about the importance of preserving a separate identity for the NIAAA, resulted in his ouster.

As related by Nieberding (1983), a new Title V authority established a separate funding for intramural grants and contracts totaling $20, $24, and $28 million annually for fiscal years 1977-1979, and a new national Alcohol Research Centers (ARC) program with $6 million annually for a three-year period. These ARCs were instituted in order to provide continuity of funding for a number of long-range research programs deemed important to the NIAAA's overall goals. At this writing the Alcohol Research Centers include the Berkeley Alcohol Research Group (ARG) of the Medical Research Institute, studying the social epidemiology of alcohol problems through national and community surveys; the Prevention Research Center of the Pacific Institute for Research and Evaluation, which assesses environmental factors and laws and regulations affecting alcohol problems; and ARCs at Washington University School of Medicine in St. Louis (neurobiological, genetic, and epidemiological factors in alcoholism), the University of Colorado (pharmacogenetic aspects of alcohol), the University of Connecticut (multidisciplinary models to predict treatment outcomes), Mount Sinai School of Medicine of the City University of New York (pathological effects of alcohol), the Scripps Clinic and Research Foundation in La Jolla (studies of the neurological basis for tolerance and dependence in animals and humans), Jefferson College of Medicine in Philadelphia (biochemical and biophysical aspects of cellular activity relevant to alcohol effects), and the University of Florida (alcohol problems among the elderly) ("The National Alcohol Research Centers," 1985).

The research potential of the NIAAA was enhanced by the expansion in 1985 of its Initial Review Group from fifteen to twenty-three members and the inclusion of two new subpanels, one on treatment and clinical research and one on epidemiological and prevention research ("NIAAA Announces Change in Grant Review Process," 1985). This move put a stronger priority on prevention research, an area in which the NIAAA traditionally has been weak. Some of the newer approaches intended to prevent or minimize alcohol problems are discussed in Chapter Six.

Under Noble, and then under John DeLuca and Robert Niven, the NIAAA shifted to a greater emphasis on research. Niven, in an interview for the *ADAMHA News* ("Dr. Robert Niven: Alcohol Research," 1985), said: "My primary interest is that the institute support good science—in whatever area of research it happens to be, permitting science itself to determine what the future directions are. This, of course, does not mean that we will support the esoteric pursuit of pure knowledge, but research that has the potential to reduce the present toll of alcohol abuse and alcoholism." He stressed the need for interdisciplinary approaches in tackling complex mechanisms of alcohol dependency. While he did not promise any imminent breakthroughs, he hoped that recent research advances would lead to a reduction in alcohol-related cirrhosis and brain damage within the next decade. He also pointed out that, since alcohol-related damage interacts with many other health problems, the NIAAA's research in the long run should have a cumulative impact in helping to treat health conditions not commonly thought of as related to alcoholism.

In 1978 and 1979, the NIAAA began shifting a number of its community-based treatment projects to administration by the states. Delegation of more activity to the states was accelerated when the Reagan administration took over in 1981. Its emphasis on the defederalizing of government programs led directly to the elimination of NIAAA funding authority for treatment and prevention demonstration purposes; the money was turned over to the states under block grants, and its distribution was no longer supervised by the NIAAA but by its umbrella agency, ADAMHA. NIAAA budgets are now allocated almost exclusively to research into alcoholism, other alcohol-related medical problems, alcohol-related deaths and injuries, prevention activities, and epidemiology;

limited funds also are available for public information activities and for training grants.

By eliminating NIAAA-administered formula grants and supplanting them with direct block grants to the states, the Reagan administration in effect weakened the NIAAA's influence on the states' alcohol programs and also weakened the ties to constituency groups who were no longer receiving direct or indirect funding through the NIAAA. As Jay Lewis recently has commented (in an interview with me on Aug. 25, 1986), David Stockman, director of the Office of Management and Budget under Reagan, made it clear in a much-publicized *Atlantic* article (Grieder, 1981) that he planned to weaken the pressure from constituencies by destroying such earmarked categorical grants.

Scope of Activities on the State Level

Treatment efforts in the individual states still continued on a substantial scale after the shift to state-administered block grants. The National Association of State Alcohol and Drug Abuse Directors (NASADAD), an information-coordinating agency established through funding by the NIAAA, has published a series of reports on drug and alcohol activities nationwide, the latest of which (Butynski, Record, and Yates, 1986) mentions these activities (and many more) for fiscal year 1985:

Total alcohol client treatment admissions reported by forty-eight states, the District of Columbia, Guam, Puerto Rico, and the Virgin Islands were more than 1.1 million: more than 76 percent were in nonhospital treatment units; 76 percent were male; 30.9 percent were between the ages of twenty-five and thirty-four; 71.3 percent were Whites, 16.1 percent Blacks, and 5.5 percent Hispanics. Alcohol treatment admissions increased by 6 percent from fiscal year (FY) 1984 to FY 1985.

Most states described unmet needs for treatment and prevention services, and also needs for increased services to youth, women, ethnic minorities, indigent persons, those in the criminal justice system, and chronic alcoholics and public inebriates. In addition, many states stressed a need to expand detoxification services, increase staffs, and raise salaries.

Many of the states indicated that the three top priorities should go to prevention and education, services for children and adolescents, and solving public and private health insurance issues.

Expenditures for *combined* alcohol and drug abuse treatment and prevention services totaled more than $1.3 billion. Of the total expenditures, states provided 52.7 percent; federal sources, 19.3 percent; county or local sources, 6.5 percent; and other sources (private health insurance, court fines, client fees, or assessments for treatment imposed on drunk drivers), 21.6 percent. Approximately 78.2 percent of the expenditures were for treatment services; 11.8 percent, for prevention services; and 9.9 percent, for other activities, such as training, research, and administration.

This report also contains much other information about the individual states' alcohol and drug programs and felt needs.

A separate NIAAA report (Reed and Sanchez, 1986) for FY 1984, based on 9,041 alcoholism service units (almost 90 percent of all then-known units in the United States), provides data on clients for one specified date. The findings were that 73 percent of the treatment units had provided services to both alcoholism and drug abuse clients. There were 6,963 alcoholism service units reporting treatment for that specified date, an increase of 64 percent over 1982 findings. Of the more than one-half million people in treatment for alcoholism on the date of the survey, 447,649 were active outpatients, 40,786 in an inpatient setting, and 51,976 in a residential (for example, halfway house) setting. Almost half of the alcoholism treatment units were free standing; 21 percent were in community health centers, and 19 percent were housed in hospitals.

Three-fourths of the alcoholism treatment units were proprietary in nature; the remaining 24 percent were publicly owned. The proprietary units run on a profit-making basis comprised 12 percent of the total, nearly double the number in a comparable survey two years earlier. Prevention services (kind not specified in this summary report) were offered by 49 percent of the units, and three-fourths of these units also offered treatment.

An earlier NASADAD report, for FY 1984 (Butynski, Record, and Yates, 1985), gathered data on prevention, intoxicated driver, and employee assistance programs (EAPs) in state agencies. Nearly 6.7 million persons were covered in prevention efforts; about 2,600 of these programs were school-based, and 3,600 were provided for nonschool populations. More than 850,000 intoxicated drivers were enrolled in treatment or rehabilitative programs. More than half of the state agencies reported that all state employees had access to an employee assistance program. For those having access to EAPs, from 1 to 3 percent of eligible employees received client services.

Downsizing of NIAAA

The implications of the shift in emphasis in NIAAA funding from treatment to research were indeed profound. Jay Lewis, author of the authoritative subscription newsletter *The Alcoholism Report,* noted (1982b) that

> the consequence has been a widespread notion in the field that NIAAA is an agency solely concerned with research, perceived in terms of biological studies carried out by bench scientists working with patients and monkeys. This misconception has served to weaken constituency support for the general effort by groups and individuals who feel that NIAAA, as a research agency—and a small one at that—is remote from their interests. Moreover, there is some feeling that NIAAA and the altered federal effort is no longer particularly relevant to the cause of the alcoholism field.
>
> . . . Two conclusions can be drawn from the recital of developments which amount to a sinking of the federal presence as it existed during the 1970s. One is that the federal effort has played itself out and, with research the only activity left, there is no longer any point in pushing for a return to the old days of budgets soaring near the $200 million mark and new initiatives being launched by the score with every reauthorization and budget cycle.
>
> The second is that NIAAA is now in need of heroic measures to keep it and the remnants of a federal presence alive in the coming years. The

recognition currently is taking shape that a federal
presence in the form of NIAAA may be vital to the
continuation of the field of alcoholism at large, from
the public sector programs to the growing and
flourishing proprietary sector, from the embryonic
prevention field to the occupational alcoholism or
employee assistance programs. An argument can be
made that the weakening of the federal identity in
alcoholism and diffusion of focus can have untoward
repercussions down the line into every segment of the
field. One of the major rationales for the creation of
the federal effort in the late 1960s was that the
alcoholism field needed an institute of its own in the
federal health establishment to achieve a modicum of
parity with other diseases and disorders. The question
can be legitimately raised as to whether the ground
gained during the 1970s can be retained in the absence
of a single national agency serving as a focal point for
the field.

Despite all the achievements of the NIAAA in its dozen hectic
first years, it has suffered from many bureaucratic and political
disadvantages that have hampered its ability to carry out its chief
missions. Again, one inherent difficulty in the NIAAA's striving for
status within the federal establishment is that sufferers from
alcoholism do not evoke the same sympathies from Congress as do
those afflicted with other serious ailments (such as cancer, heart
disease, or stroke) that are not so obviously self-inflicted. Another
is that the beer, wine, and liquor industry maintains very powerful
lobbies in Washington, which have the ear of influential members
of Congress and the administration; and whenever the NIAAA
threatens to recommend moves that might reduce alcohol consumption or hamper the advertising or marketing process, the industry
is quick to voice complaints. Thus, it is widely rumored that two
directors of the NIAAA (who serve at the pleasure of the President),
Ernest Noble and John DeLuca, were forced out of their positions
because of industry pressure. Also, the umbrella agency for the
NIAAA, the Alcohol, Drug, and Mental Health Administration

(ADAMHA), is not only somewhat of a redundancy that interferes with the NIAAA's freedom of action in relating to other federal agencies and power structures but has been markedly uncertain in its leadership, having had a succession of nine administrators from 1970 to 1983 (Alcohol, Drug, and Mental Health Administration, 1983). This instability in ADAMHA is reflected in rapid turnover in the NIAAA itself: it has had five directors in a dozen years.

While all the directors of the NIAAA except one have been M.D.s and most of them have been psychiatrists, they have differed considerably in operating philosophies and styles. Some of these differences are seen in an account of the 1982 New England Conference on Alcohol Issues, in which Chafetz, Noble, and John DeLuca appeared in a panel discussion (Room, 1984b).

Chafetz emphasized his public relations achievements in rallying the support of the Boys Clubs, the Chamber of Commerce, and similar public organizations to support NIMH's programs. "In his view, the period 1971-1975 was the only time everyone in the field was united—'and we made a difference' " (p. 38). The annual alcoholism conferences hosted by the NIAAA in those years grew from 300 to 4,500 participants, with "people like Mel Laird, David Brinkley, and Dick Van Dyke joining with us." As a side comment on the alcoholic beverage industry, Chafetz noted that in his view "the field can get more by cooperation than by confrontation" (p. 38). (Noble and DeLuca had clashed with the industry over their attempts to constrain consumption, thus hastening their departure.)

At the same meeting, Noble voiced his opposition to the concept of "responsible drinking" popularized by Chafetz during his administration of the NIAAA, saying that it was too ambiguous. (Noble often has said that this slogan puts a premium on the value of drinking and thus plays into the hands of the alcohol industry's marketers.)

DeLuca, Noble's successor, who came to the NIAAA at the behest of Joseph Califano (then secretary of HEW) and who shared his concern about integrating alcohol treatment into the general health system (Califano, 1986), said he was glad that he had been able to make some advances in restructuring the financing for alcoholism coverage through third-party health insurance payments; and he emphasized that the acceptance of alcoholism treatment by the health care system is important if provision of alcoholism treatment programs are to survive. He lamented that "Reagan has a strong philosophical commitment on government and its role—NIAAA was an extraordinary victim of it" (referring to the allocation of block grants to the states, with a cut in the NIAAA's budget from $220 million to $30 million) (p. 40). "Such radical change," he added, "is infrequent in Washington." In his brief three-year tenure, he noted, the agency had gone through two Presidents, three secretaries of HEW, and one reorganization. With such changes, "You lose the capability of holding onto your political support." DeLuca concluded (p. 40):

> When I left Washington, I left discouraged— the rules of the game had changed, and I don't understand the rules of the new game. The institute is different from what it was 18 months ago: it has the capacity to do basic research and that's it. If it stays that way (keeping to its more narrow issue of alcoholism; that's enough for it), it should find a new home in NIH—the prestige and maturity of that agency is a safer harbor for NIAAA. It's a desperate entity with a tiny budget in danger of disappearing or absorption—the excitement of growth is not there. It's almost like starting over.

Even the NIAAA's reduced role continues to be threatened by prospective budget cuts under the Gramm-Rudman-Hollings bill (Butynski, Record, and Yates, 1986). Reagan's proposed budget for fiscal year 1987 would have funded NIAAA research at $68.8 million, in contrast to $82.9 million for the National Institute on Drug Abuse (NIDA). Under Office of Management and Budget constraints, the number of new and competing NIAAA grants would have been reduced from 100 to 74. These reductions, if approved by Congress, would have resulted in substantial cuts in the NIAAA's activities, particularly in prevention and technical assistance and dissemination, which would have been reduced about 20 percent. Christine Lubinski, head of public policy for the NCA, protested at a congressional subcommittee hearing that there was urgent need for expansion rather than cuts in such activities, and that the NIAAA clinical training grants and pilot treatment demonstration programs should be restored. Earlier, only $1.327 million was to have been made available for research training, with only sixty-six trainees to be supported; and the funding for the nine national Alcohol Research Centers was to have been reduced by 4.3 percent and the National Clearinghouse for Alcohol Information (responsible for maintaining a data base for reports on scientific research findings vital to those engaged in alcohol research or treatment) reduced by 23 percent (Lewis, *Alcoholism Report,* Jan. 31, 1986).

The NIAAA was temporarily bailed out of this dilemma by funding from the new drug abuse initiative hastily passed by Congress in the fall of 1986. That additional funding restored some of the proposed cuts and provided increased funding for research training. However, this temporary funding does not change the basically precarious hand-to-mouth situation of the NIAAA. The Reagan administration's position still stands: to let lapse the current specific authority for the three institutes under the Alcohol, Drug, and Mental Health Administration (ADAMHA) umbrella administrative structure (the NIAAA, NIDA, and NIMH), which would mean transferring all of them to the general Public Health Service research authority.

Donald Macdonald, Reagan's appointee as director of ADAMHA, testified before House and Senate Appropriations Subcommittees in March 1986, presenting the view that under the current administration's plan the institutes would be in less jeopardy because they would no longer have to go before Congress every year or two to justify their existence. His stance was consistent with the Reagan administration's determined policy to reduce the number and scope of governmental units.

Some supporters of the NIAAA with primarily a research orientation would be relieved to see it become solely a research institute, with continuity of funding no longer jeopardized by involvement in controversial issues of alcohol control (such as increasing alcohol taxes and requiring warning labels) or being mired down in refereeing among factions competing for funding for alcoholism treatment and prevention programs. But a number of treatment and prevention constituency groups see that downsizing as a disaster and thus are continuing to plead the cause of preserving the NIAAA's roles in treatment monitoring and prevention advocacy rather than making it solely a research institute.

At present the NIAAA is conducting a holding operation, hoping to be able to stave off absorption by some larger federal agency (and thereby presumably reducing its visibility and influence) until there is a change in the administrative climate. A task force currently is studying what the NIAAA's future role should be. This task force's recommendations for an improved role for the NIAAA will be summarized in Chapter Eleven. However, the long-term outlook for an NIAAA that can continue to make a significant contribution to the control of alcohol problems is not going to improve materially unless and until a new administration and Congress make up their minds that they really *want* to see more effective controls established.

4

Movements to Institute Better Treatment and Control

Creating organizations is an all-American occupation, and over the years America has launched a large number of them to deal with alcohol problems. They have waxed and waned over time, but the same few basic organizing principles and operating philosophies have cropped up from generation to generation. This chapter will attempt to describe the origins of some of these alcohol-concerned organizations, as well as their achievements and shortcomings.

Varying Perspectives of Organizations

For the last two centuries, what we have defined as alcoholism—and how we should treat it—has varied in broad cycles that are more dependent on moral attitudes and political and economic considerations than on the state of medical, psychological, and sociological knowledge. At various times through our history, alcoholism has been seen primarily as the outcome of bad habits; at other times, primarily as a disease. But, throughout this period, a substantial number of people have regarded alcoholism as *both* self-

61

imposed *and* a disease (Cahalan, 1970, p. 6). As discussed in Chapter Two, in early colonial times alcohol was considered to be "the good creature of God," a comforter and a medicine; then, in Washington's day, Benjamin Rush finally convinced many that there was such a thing as "alcoholism" and that it was a disease. Baumohl and Room (1987) have shown that fashions on whether and how alcoholics should be punished or treated (or both) varied throughout the 1800s. In the mid-1900s, a popular consensus developed that alcoholism is indeed a disease, and that it should be treated and not punished. None of these shifts in public attitudes was accidental. All of them required concerted campaigns of education and propaganda and political lobbying: no mass campaign can be won without effectively organizing many true believers to work hard to put over their common goal.

Four main operating philosophies on what to do about drinking problems have contended for domination from the American Revolution to the present day. The relative success of each of them has varied in accordance with social and economic conditions, the strengths of leaders, and the efficiencies of campaigns. They can be described as (1) the punitive approach, (2) the humanistic approach, (3) the prohibitionist approach, and (4) the preventive approach. They do not operate in isolation, of course: some preventive activities can be called humanistic, and much prohibitionism has been punitive in application. Space does not permit detailed documentation of each occasion in history where each of these approaches was dominant; further illustrations appear in Baumohl and Room (1987), Baumohl (1986), and Morgan (1983).

The *punitive approach* has been favored by those who view drunkenness and alcoholism as perverse, immoral, evil, or wicked. (This is the principal approach applied by our government against dealers and users of illegal drugs today.) While, as described in Chapter Two, the Pilgrim fathers viewed alcohol as "the good creature of God" and a medicine or comforter for all occasions, Calvinism taught that man is responsible for his own behavior. The Pilgrim philosophy was also more than a little tinged with the Manichean view that man cannot be trusted and must be kept in stern control and that the elders are entitled to mind their neighbors' business. This philosophy, brought over by the Pilgrims, was strengthened by the harsh conditions they found in this country—the primitive housing, severe weather, and increasingly hostile Indians. Just as John Smith declared in Virginia, "Those who do not work shall not eat," the Pilgrims expected all the colonists to carry their own load and not make trouble for their overworked neighbors.

As the colonies grew in size and there was an influx of people who did not share the fervor and self-sacrifice of the original colonists, the punishment of drunkards became increasingly harsh: jail with little food or comfort, the stocks, and whippings for repeated offenses. The punitive approach also tended to be applied to alcoholics during economic crises, when numbers of homeless men wandered about and were considered threats to peace and good order. While the stocks and whippings are no longer resorted to as a means of dissuading public drunkenness, many of our major cities still throw skid row drunks into dirty, crowded drunk tanks and make things very uncomfortable for them in the hope that they will move on to a different area. While many jurisdictions have decriminalized drunkenness, many drunks are still kept in jail for actionable offenses or under the guise of "protective custody" or are given negatively reinforcing "treatment," such as a choice of Antabuse or jail.

The punitive approach is also seen in the insane asylums of the nineteenth and twentieth centuries, where people were warehoused in locked wards, to protect them from each other and especially to protect the general public from crazies who could do harm if they wandered around loose. Warehousing may not be intended to be punitive, but it is common in situations where the society does not put a sufficiently high value on the lives of derelicts or insane people to warrant spending the money and other resources to provide decent treatment.

The *humanistic approach* assumes that man's essential goodness can be strengthened through kind treatment and many social supports. This approach, congruent with the philosophies of Jean-Jacques Rousseau and John Locke, was evident in the "moral treatment" of mental hospital patients by Philippe Pinel of France and his followers (Baumohl, 1986). One early example of this approach was the "Washingtonian" movement of the early 1840s (Baumohl and Room, 1987). This movement featured the use of "experience lecturers," former drunkards who helped to keep themselves sober by meeting with problem drinkers interested in staying on the wagon. Many of the Washingtonians' features were the same as in the Alcoholics Anonymous movement of today, including a plea that every convert to the cause should go out and bring in additional converts, an emphasis on frequent meetings to discuss each other's problems and to provide other moral supports, and encouragement of the organization of lodging houses for temporary rehabilitation. The impact of the Washingtonian movement on the rehabilitation of alcoholics is summarized in this passage from Baumohl and Room (1987, p. 139):

> Although short-lived, the Washingtonian move-ment inspired other, similar efforts. The Boston lodg-ing house was reorganized as a formal inebriate home in 1857; in San Francisco, a self-help temperance group known as the Dashaway Association founded a Home for the Care of the Inebriate in 1859; and the Washingtonian Home of Chicago was organized in 1863. In a historical survey of institutions for the treat-ment of inebriates conducted in the 1920s, Cherring-ton and his associates [1926] found that the first such endeavors in many countries were inebriate homes founded under temperance or religious auspices.
>
> By the late 1860s, the Washingtonians largely had passed from the American scene, to be succeeded by a variety of new, secret temperance fraternities: the Sons of Temperance (founded 1842), the Independent Order of Rechabites (England, 1835; U.S., 1842), the United Brothers of Temperance (1844), the Order of Good Samaritans (1847), the Temple of Honor (1849), and the Independent Order of Good Templars (1851). In addition, there were Irish-American societies, both parochial and ecumenical, which can be traced back to 1835. However, like the societies inspired by Father

Theobald Mathew in Ireland, beginning in 1838, it is not clear that these groups were interested primarily in the reclamation of habitual drunkards.

Like the Washingtonians, the secret, fraternal societies were at arm's length from organized religion and represented an unchurched Christianity. Good Templary was described by one of its officials as "a mild kind of freemasonry tempered by Methodism." While individual clerics participated in these groups, they received little formal support from Protestant sects and the Catholic Church was positively hostile. The large-scale involvement of religious groups in assistance for the drunkard came only with the evolution of the nondenominational Skid Row gospel mission in the 1870s and the founding of the Salvation Army in the 1880s, both offshoots of the Protestant city mission movement, which had strong temperance ties.

Here the term "temperance" means voluntary abstention from alcohol rather than compulsory prohibition. The temperance pledge approach, coupled with social supports against backsliding, was a central feature of Father Mathew–inspired campaigns in both Ireland and America (Bretherton, 1987). His approach was more popular among Irish or German Catholics than campaigns against drunkenness initiated by upper-status Protestants, which were often seen as inspired by a desire to dominate or suppress the newer immigrants (Gusfield, 1962). The Mathew pledge approach, like the Catholic confessional, did not reject the sinner for occasional lapses.

The *prohibitionist approach* is really a special case of the punitive approach, entailing as it does the attempt to apply the force of law in imposing abstention on everyone, with legal penalties for those who disobey. This approach, along with the principal organizations that backed prohibition in sporadic campaigns at intervals from the early 1800s through repeal in the 1930s, was discussed in Chapter Two (see Austin, 1978, for more details). It traditionally has been avoided by those espousing a humanistic approach, partially out of tender-mindedness and partially out of practicality (prohibition has not seemed to work in America).

The *preventive approach* is based on the conviction that treatment and humane control of drunkards, although necessary after the fact, are tantamount to locking the barn door after the horse is stolen; instead, appropriate measures should be taken to minimize the likelihood that drunkenness will occur. The preventive approach, which is very popular these days in public health circles, is a combination of the humanistic approach (with its efforts toward public reeducation and provision of alcohol alternatives for recreational and stress-reduction purposes) and the punitive approach (with its efforts to control drunken driving or alcohol-related violence through applying more certain and timely constraints). The prevention movement and its strategies and tactics are discussed in detail in Chapter Six.

NASADAD Inventory of Alcohol Organizations

Since the founding of the NIAAA in 1970, many nonprofit organizations have sprung up in response to the opportunities either to cooperate with the government in building action programs to combat alcohol problems or (in the case of alcoholic beverage companies) to try to redirect governmental actions away from increased taxes or other activities likely to lessen alcohol profits. A *Resource Directory* published by the National Association of State Alcohol and Drug Abuse Directors (NASADAD) (Butynski, 1985) provides an overview of ninety-three national organizations whose primary purpose relates to the use or abuse of alcohol. Thirty-five of the listed organizations are nonprofit citizen groups concerned primarily with the treatment of alcoholics. These include some founded well before the NIAAA, including Alcoholics Anonymous (1935) and its affiliates Al-Anon and Al-Ateen (1951), the National Council on Alcoholism (1953), and the Alcohol and Drug Problems Association (1949). Also included are volunteer organizations representing special populations, such as Hispanics, American Indians, and Blacks; and also a wide range of professionals (physicians, attorneys, clergy, nurses, psychologists, and alcoholism and drug abuse counselors).

Listed also in this NASADAD *Resource Directory* are a number of special service organizations founded to effect liaison between the NIAAA and state and local agencies or associations, including NASADAD itself, the Association of Labor-Management Administrators and Consultants on Alcoholism (ALMACA), the National Association of Alcoholism Treatment Programs (NAATP), and the National Association of Alcoholism and Drug Abuse Counselors (NAADAC). There are also quite a number of lobbies to maintain stricter controls over alcohol-impaired drivers (Mothers Against Drunk Driving, Students Against Driving Drunk, National Federation of Parents for Drug-Free Youth, National Center for Drunk Driving Control, and National Commission Against Drunk Driving). Sprinkled among the listings are also a number of associations formed to advance the interests of the alcoholic beverage manufacturers and wholesalers (see Chapter Five).

The oldest organization listed is the Women's Christian Temperance Union, founded in 1874. In its heyday the WCTU was one of the leaders in the struggle to bring about prohibition. It still has a staff of about eighteen and provides temperance pamphlets, books, filmstrips, teachers' manuals, and other educational materials for elementary and secondary schools. The WCTU also holds an annual convention.

This NASADAD *Resource Directory* provides much useful information on the functions of each organization, names and addresses of contact persons, and services and publications available. (It may be obtained through its sponsors, the NIAAA or the National Institute on Drug Abuse.) Space does not permit a detailed discussion of the work of all these agencies; but some of them are discussed in Chapter Eleven, which suggests what action agencies and professional organizations of the future should be doing to mitigate alcohol problems.

For a historical perspective on public attitudes about alcoholism forty years ago, before the advent of most of the organizations listed in the NASADAD inventory, let us look at the reminiscences of an early member of the staff of the Yale Center of Alcohol Studies, Robert Straus (1986, pp. 1–2):

In the mid 1940s in the United States, alcoholism was rarely mentioned in polite society, alcoholics were stigmatized and this stigma was often extended to or derived by persons who were associated with alcoholics including scientists who did research on drinking problems. It was often assumed by their peers that such investigators must have something wrong with them or they would be giving their attention to important mainstream questions. No research on alcohol problems was receiving Federal funding and most major foundations had unwritten but firm policies against supporting research on alcohol related questions. Today, in contrast, many mainstream scientists are engaged in alcohol research and they are respected for it. Stigma and derived stigma have been greatly reduced and both the Federal government and several foundations are supporting alcohol research. These changes have clearly been interactive. The reduction in stigma removed barriers from research funding and activity and research findings in turn helped clear away misconceptions and stereotypes that supported stigma.

Following are a few of the assumptions that prevailed in this field when I first became involved.

Alcoholism was assumed to be primarily a problem of homeless derelicts, disturbed persons, or the jail population of repeatedly arrested inebriates. These were the conspicuous and captive problem drinkers and the only ones whose characteristics had been studied and reported. This assumption reinforced the stigmatization of alcoholics and because of the stigma, alcoholics who did not fit the stereotype were often hidden by their friends or coworkers and supported in their denial of alcoholism.

Alcoholism was considered primarily a problem of middle-aged men.

The health problems of heavy drinkers were

attributed to malnutrition, not to the toxic effects of alcohol.

Suggestions that genetic factors might be significant in the etiology of alcoholism were dismissed as improbable.

Alcoholics were assumed to experience a common progression until they "hit bottom," and the metabolism of alcohol within the body was assumed to follow a standardized course and rate varying only with body weight.

It was assumed that blood alcohol levels were correlated with predictable and describable behavioral responses.

Generally unrecognized in the 1940's were the significance of fetal damage from alcohol; many of the common alcohol-related diseases; the variety of metabolic rates and pathways, blood factors, and isoenzymes; and the variances in response to alcohol sometimes associated with circadian, menstrual, seasonal and life cycles.

Much of the rest of this chapter will be devoted to a discussion of the recent history of two large alcohol-related organizations, which date back more than forty years—well before the NIAAA—and which played a material role in founding and establishing the character of such governmental alcohol programs. The two—Alcoholics Anonymous and its action arm, the National Council on Alcoholism—basically relate to the humanistic model. Both of these organizations are classic illustrations of Carolyn Wiener's statement (1981) that one can draw attention to the social problem of alcoholism by knowing how to animate, legitimize, and demonstrate the magnitude of social problems.

Alcoholics Anonymous

AA claims to be not really an "organization," for it has no dues and keeps no membership lists. It is widely regarded as the most effective avenue for treatment of alcoholism, although there has been little actual research to bear this out (National Institute on Alcohol Abuse and Alcoholism, 1983), and folklore has it that only about 10 percent of those with the most severe drinking problems ever avail themselves of AA. It was founded in the mid-1930s by William G. Wilson and Robert L. Smith, a stockbroker and a physician; and the Twelve Steps of AA were inscribed in the organization's "Big Book" (*Alcoholics Anonymous*, 1976) as follows:

1. We admitted we were powerless over alcohol—that our lives had become unmanageable.
2. Came to believe that a Power greater than ourselves could restore us to sanity.
3. Made a decision to turn our will and our lives over to the care of God as we understood him.
4. Made a searching and fearless moral inventory of ourselves.
5. Admitted to God, to ourselves, and another human being, the exact nature of our wrongs.
6. Were entirely ready to have God remove all these defects of character.
7. Humbly asked Him to remove our shortcomings.
8. Made a list of all persons we had harmed, and became willing to make amends to them all.
9. Made direct amends to such people whenever possible, except when to do so would injure them or others.
10. Continued to take personal inventory and when we were wrong promptly admitted it.
11. Sought through prayer and meditation to improve our conscious contact with God as we understood Him, praying only for knowledge of His will for us and the power to carry that out.
12. Having had a spiritual awakening as the result of these steps, we tried to carry this message to alcoholics, and to practice these principles in all our affairs.

AA also has Twelve Traditions, which include precepts that the only requirement for membership is a desire to stop drinking; that AA never endorses outside enterprises or accepts outside contributions; and that members are to remain anonymous, so as to place principles before personalities.

Maxwell (1982), who has been observing AA for many years, emphasizes that AA actually uses very low-pressure methods in getting the alcoholic to accept the principle that alcoholism is a disease of the will: that he can "arrest" his problem but will always remain one drink away from getting hooked again and that, through the support of the fellowship of AA (and the support he can give to others like himself), he can find a new way of life—a life so much better that he will not yield to the temptations of his old life.

Mary Catherine Taylor, who conducted her dissertation fieldwork by observing many AA meetings, describes the usual AA experience as going through a number of stages: a "simplification" stage, in which the member is aided by the group in focusing all his or her efforts on the single goal of staying sober; a sometimes lengthy conversion experience, in which the new member internalizes the AA ideology; a "honeymoon" phase of self-satisfaction, usually followed by self-doubts (and perhaps a return to drinking); and (if the person stays with AA long enough) a final recovery phase, in which AA is made the basis of a reformulated lifestyle (Taylor, 1977).

David Doroff (1977, p. 237) offers additional insight into the dynamics of AA. One key element is the friendly confrontation of the new recruit to face up to his or her processes of denial that abstention is necessary if one is to be a recovering alcoholic. Another is the provision of continual positive reinforcements: the alcoholic is immediately made welcome into a group, treated as worthy of respect and friendship regardless of past transgressions, and reassured that other members will immediately be available if called upon to get or keep the recoverer out of further trouble with alcohol. "The alcoholic is both allowed and encouraged to experience himself as the infant who is the apple of his mother's eye. He can call up anyone at any time. He need not long experience the frustration and stress of having to curb his desires. If he calls instead of drinking, he will almost certainly be rewarded for doing so. In short, the alcoholic seeking sobriety is offered therapeutic regression as an alternative to intoxication. Further, he is allowed to control the degree of involvement with any single individual by spreading his attachment to the group, or to others in it" (p. 239).

The timing of AA's "Big Book" was perfect for attracting nationwide attention to AA, because in the early 1940s, only a few years after repeal, the country seemed to be sliding into much heavy drinking again. The *Saturday Evening Post*, seeing merit in the AA movement, publicized it in a lengthy article in March 1941, and a number of middle-class alcoholics joined up and passed the word on the worth of this new movement. The AA movement spread like wildfire: Maxwell (1982) reports that by 1980 there were about 26,000 AA groups and about 800,000 members in the United States and Canada, and at least an additional 14,000 groups in ninety other countries.

AA may be limiting its clientele because five of the Twelve Steps invoke God; and much of the AA literature has a religious tone that might make agnostics wary of preachments. Bissell and Haberman (1984) asked a convenience "sample" of 407 AA members, primarily around the New York area, who had been dry for a year or more, how AA's religious emphasis had affected them; 22 percent said that they had expected it to "turn them off," and 12 percent actually did find it to be a problem. However, AA is still the primary resource that physicians and other professionals draw on in treating alcoholics once they have gone through the detoxification stage; and no doubt individual AA chapters will become even more effective as they learn to tailor the religious emphasis to their particular clientele. Certainly, chapters do differ a great deal in their membership, some of them being composed primarily of middle-class professional or business people, others having primarily blue-collar members, and some catering to a younger or to an elderly clientele. Since the membership of AA is so large, in most areas those who are really interested in joining AA can find a group composed of people much like themselves.

National Council on Alcoholism

The NCA started as an offshoot of the National Committee for Education on Alcoholism (NCEA), which was founded in 1944 at the Yale Center of Alcohol Studies (Earle, 1982; Room, 1982).

Marty Mann, a successful public relations counselor in New York, was executive director until 1949. Fired with the zeal of a recovering alcoholic, she was assisted in setting up the organization by four interested professors at Yale—Selden D. Bacon, Howard W. Haggard, E. M. Jellinek, and Edward G. Baird—and by Edgar Lockwood, vice-president of Guaranty Trust in New York. Haggard was director of Yale's Laboratory of Applied Physiology, Bacon was assistant professor of sociology, Jellinek was director of the Yale Summer School of Alcohol Studies, and Baird worked in the Research Division of the Yale Plan, under which clinics had been set up in New Haven and Hartford to treat alcoholics. The NCEA's linkage with Yale (which sponsored the *Quarterly Journal of Studies on Alcohol,* the Yale Summer School of Alcohol Studies, and the Yale Plan Clinics) "greatly increased the credibility of NCEA's message to the nation" (Earle, 1982, p. 685).

Drawing on the success of AA and the research findings and plans of the fledgling Laboratory of Applied Physiology at Yale, the NCEA began operating enthusiastically with the optimistic premise that if the known scientific information about alcoholism was imparted to the general public, heavy drinkers previously ignorant of the facts would somehow curtail their intake because it would be the only logical thing to do. The NCEA's primary tenets were that alcoholism is a disease, that alcoholics are treatable, that they are worth treating, and that alcoholism is a public health problem and therefore a public responsibility. Marty Mann and her associates launched a whirlwind campaign to bring this message to many groups across the country: women's groups, AA groups, newspapers, radio stations, social service agencies, libraries, schools, hospitals, churches, civic groups, medical associations, probation and parole departments, labor unions, state liquor commissions, and other prominent community organizations and individuals.

Until recently the NCA's almost exclusive theme has been that alcoholism is a disease and that the NCA's primary mission is to bring alcoholics into treatment. To further this mission, the NCA provides resources for dissemination of information about alcoholism; serves as a referral agency for alcoholics, to get them in touch with AA and clinics in which AA members served as counselors; and lobbies for governmental resources for alcoholism treatment.

Founded just when America was recovering from its disillusioning episode with prohibition, the NCA fought shy of getting involved with any activity that might smack of "prohibitionism," such as constraints that might reduce the consumption of alcohol. This stance helped the NCA get the cooperation of the alcohol industry in its campaigns. As I noted in a 1979 article, the NCA wound up making common cause with the industry in contending that the problem of alcoholism came from the man, not the bottle.

The NCA—which always has needed to raise substantial amounts of money to support the work of a fairly large national staff and to hold meetings and to maintain contacts with its affiliates throughout the country—accepted grants from the alcohol industry for years. A number of NCA affiliates across the country have been at least partially supported through industry contributions. This is not to say that the alcohol industry was bribing the NCA to dissociate itself from policies directed at reducing the sale of alcohol; but certainly for many years there existed a close community of interest.

For a long time, the alcohol industry had three members on the NCA's National Board, out of a total of eight; and as recently as January 1978, its National Board approved the hedging position that "more research is needed" to determine whether alcohol beverage control laws, health warning labels, alcohol taxes earmarked for alcoholism treatment, and other control measures would be relevant to combating alcoholism (Lewis, 1982a, p. 394). In fact, when Ernest Noble, former director of the NIAAA, accepted the job of executive vice-president of the NCA and immediately moved to get the alcohol industry representatives off the National Board and to come out with a manifesto calling for constraints on alcohol consumption, a number of the NCA affiliate agencies across the country passed resolutions censuring his stand. Some said in their local board meetings that his recommendations would mean the drying up of support funds from the industry.

The NCA Executive Committee's approval of Noble's manifesto in June 1982 was accompanied by a statement (reported by Lewis in *The Alcoholism Report* for June 30, 1982) to board members and affiliates, noting that the NCA had "worked for more than forty years to erase the stigma associated with alcoholism, and

to educate the public about this treatable—and beatable—disease"
(p. 3). Citing "tremendous success in these efforts," the statement
added:

> This is the past, and it is an important part of
> our future. But an equally important part of our future
> is to respond to growing public awareness about
> alcohol-related problems which has occurred as a nat-
> ural evolution of our work on the disease of alcoholism.
>   . . . Today's environment is permeated by more
> than a billion dollars of advertising which either
> directly or indirectly encourages the consumption of
> alcoholic beverages and has promoted positive mes-
> sages about alcohol use in the arts, the media and
> society as a whole. Drinking is associated with "the
> good life," with health, with success, and with
> sexuality.
>   In addition, this has been matched by a general
> trend of relaxation of controls on availability and
> price of alcoholic beverages which has, in turn, been
> followed by steady and frightening increases in
> alcohol-related problems, epecially among young
> people and in the workplace throughout the country.
>   These problems are broadly based, and cannot
> be effectively approached except through broad,
> general measures of prevention policies. Problems of
> this magnitude affect not just particular groups of
> Americans, but affect nearly every American.
>   The National Council on Alcoholism can be a
> vital public force in the coming decade by providing
> information to counter the growing public perception
> that drinking alcohol is a healthy and even safe thing
> to do. To do this, NCA must add to its existing prior-
> ities for research, public policy and education, bold
> new stances to the prevention of alcohol problems.

The Noble-inspired Executive Committee manifesto calling
for a substantial redirection of the organization's efforts toward

advocating primary prevention programs to limit alcohol consumption resulted in considerable disaffection within the ranks of
the organization for a time. But there are signs that the ranks are
being closed again and are now falling in line behind Noble's
recommendations for a much stronger emphasis on primary
prevention.

In the past the NCA traditionally concentrated exclusively on
getting the alcoholic more effective treatment and tried to dissociate
itself from movements that might be labeled neo-prohibitionist.
However, Noble's 1982 leadership in getting the alcohol industry's
representatives off the NCA's National Board, and in the issuing of
the 1982 manifesto calling attention to the dangers inherent in
heavy alcohol advertising budgets and relaxation of controls on
availability of alcohol, has been followed up by a strong emphasis
on primary prevention on the part of the NCA's national directors.
The NCA has now established an active office in Washington, D.C.,
which devotes much of its attention to lobbying before congressional committees and with individual legislators for increased
controls over alcohol advertising, for putting health warning labels
on the containers, and for increasing taxes on alcohol. The NCA
has also played a central role in lobbying successfully to induce
states to raise the drinking age to twenty-one. In these prevention-
oriented campaigns, it is joining with more than a score of
organizations in an association called "Project SMART" (for "Stop
Marketing Alcohol on Radio and Television"), spearheaded by the
consumer-oriented Center for Science in the Public Interest (CSPI),
whose activities are described in more detail below.

It remains to be seen whether the enthusiasm of NCA staffs
for more constraints on alcohol marketing can be translated into the
same type of evangelical fervor that has characterized the NCA's
grass-roots adherents in the past. Probably most of the members of
the NCA's approximately 200 affiliate branches and state associations came into the fold because they are recovering alcoholics
whose main interest is in getting better treatment of alcoholism.
Whether such members can be mobilized in the cause of promoting
state and national constraints on the availability of alcohol as a
means of reducing alcohol problems remains to be seen, particularly since some local affiliates still have members who are unhappy

because the NCA national headquarters issued the 1982 prevention manifesto without consulting the local chapters or taking into account that the manifesto might result in the cutting off of some financial support from the alcohol industry. The NCA needs also to implement more effective incentives if it wishes to attract younger, prevention-oriented members with the enthusiasm for volunteer lobbying on the state and local levels for increased controls on alcohol marketing.

As Wiener says (1981, p. 34), "NCA has a much harder time raising money than comparable health associations. To quote one respondent, 'The Heart Association does very well with memorials, but people don't want to say Joe died of alcoholism.'" The NCA had suffered from the severe budget cuts necessitated by the sudden withdrawal of the NIAAA grants when they were challenged by Congress back in the 1970s (see preceding chapter); and again from the alienation of some of its traditional funding sources because of its decision to lay some of the blame for alcoholism on the bottle as well as the person. However, the NCA is still the leading organization in the field of alcoholism. Because of its alliance and much common membership with the dedicated ranks of AA, and because it still has about 200 local affiliates across the country, if it stays receptive to changing times—such as the new emphasis on prevention through constraints on consumption—it should remain an influence to be reckoned with into the twenty-first century.

Center for Science in the Public Interest

The CSPI is a nonprofit organization founded in 1971 by three scientists who had worked in a consulting capacity with Ralph Nader on consumer-rights issues. It is currently headed by Michael Jacobson, with George Hacker serving as director for alcohol policies. Its primary mission is serving as a watchdog and advocate for better controls on consumer products, especially food and drink. Most of its funding comes from 80,000 subscribers to its nutrition and health newsletters and from sales of other publications. About 15 percent of its program budget is supported by foundations; the CSPI does not accept funding from any government or corporate organizations (Hacker, personal interview, Aug.

26, 1986). One of its primary current missions includes leadership of Project SMART and other lobbying efforts to curb alcohol advertising and raise alcohol taxes in the interest of reducing alcoholism and other alcohol problems.

Project SMART is aimed at paralleling the success in the alcohol field of John Banzhaf III's campaign of the late 1960s, which invoked the Fairness doctrine in forcing television and radio stations to carry antismoking appeals to match paid cigarette advertising. The Project SMART campaign, working through more than a score of citizen groups, has gathered over a million signatures calling either for an end to wine and beer advertising on broadcast media (as has happened voluntarily with advertising for liquors) or for equal time devoted to warnings on the dangers of alcohol. The campaign has focused on Congress and other elected officials, in the hope of bringing about a Federal Communications Commission requirement of equal time. This battle is still being waged at this writing. If it succeeds in the face of intensive counterlobbying by both the alcohol and the broadcast industries, it might result in a drop in alcohol sales (as happened with cigarettes) sufficient to occasion the alcohol industry's dropping broadcast advertising altogether in order to get rid of the negative warning messages.

The apparent effectiveness of the CSPI's alcohol control lobbying may be traced to two principal forces. One is that the emphasis is on *public health* arguments rather than on moralistic prohibitionist appeals. Another is that Jacobson and Hacker have a journalistic flair for publicizing attention-getting horrible examples of objectionable alcoholic beverage advertising, such as the ones cited in Chapter Five. Their press releases and public appearances have drawn much favorable media attention—even in the broadcasting publications—because of their timeliness and acid humor.

Mothers Against Drunk Driving

MADD is an organization that deserves notice for its mushroom growth and its impact on legislation to curb alcohol-impaired driving (Reinarman, 1985). It was founded in 1980 by Candy Lightner of California, whose daughter was struck and killed by a drunken hit-and-run driver who was out on probation for previous driving-under-the-influence (DUI) convictions and also out on bail for another hit-and-run DUI offense a few days before. Because of Lightner's charismatic leadership and television appeal, MADD's campaign to get drunk drivers off the road achieved immediate national media and legislative attention. By January 1985 MADD had some 600,000 members and donors and more than 320 chapters across the country. The organization now has a national headquarters with a full-time staff of more than twenty and an annual budget (national and local) of about $3 million. MADD has lobbied for anti-drunk-driving legislation through testimony before legislative bodies and through television and newspaper appeals for concerned citizens to write or call their representatives to take action. The organization can take major credit for the appointment of a Presidential Commission on Drunk Driving; legislation to raise the minimum drinking age to twenty-one (passed by most states); the passage of more than 230 individual laws on drinking-driving issues between 1981 and 1984, including higher fines and license suspensions; the banning of "happy hours"; and the passage of dram shop laws, which hold the servers of alcohol liable for damages from alcohol-related accidents.

Not all has been sweetness and light within MADD, however. Some local chapter members resented Lightner's $75,000 salary (plus a car and all expenses) and the allegedly high-handed way she ran the organization. She was ultimately deposed as president of MADD but is still playing a prominent role as consultant and media and legislative liaison activist. Also, there was some dissension within the organization over the acceptance of substantial grants from the alcohol industry and the failure to advocate increased taxes or other efforts to limit aggregate alcohol consumption.

MADD's mushroom growth may well taper off if it does not emulate the March of Dimes by broadening its objectives. However, the organization's immediate success in attracting attention to its anti-drunk-driving campaigns and its effective legislative lobbying could well serve as a tactical model to other, more broadly based, alcohol-concerned organizations, such as the National Council on Alcoholism.

Cooperation Among Advocacy Groups

It remains to be seen whether the old-line organizations (such as the NCA), which in the past have focused primarily on treatment of alcoholism, and the newer organizations (such as the CSPI), which are primarily interested in prevention, can sustain their present effective working relationships over the long haul, since their traditions and even their tactics are different. Fortunately, the national leaders of the NCA and the CSPI are cooperating with each other and with the NIAAA in working toward a greater emphasis on long-term primary prevention programs, within the limits set by their current underfunding and understaffing.

The NCA and the CSPI currently are the only alcohol-concerned organizations with any continuing Washington lobbying and watchdog activities. Both groups have only a few people who spend most of their time keeping track of alcohol-relevant legislation and legislative actions and marshaling the support of other groups in the furtherance of their prevention-oriented action programs. With intensified membership drives and appeals for foundation support to increase their staffs, they may one day be able to compete against the much more formidable lobbying resources of the alcoholic beverage industry.

5

5

〽〽〽〽〽〽〽〽

The Alcohol Merchants

The manufacturing and marketing of alcoholic beverages in America is big business indeed, with consumer purchases totaling $66.4 billion in 1984, an increase of 5.3 percent over 1983 sales of liquor, beer, and wine (Distilled Spirits Council of the United States, 1985). Of course, as we discussed in Chapter Two, booze has had its ups and downs here over the last three centuries, starting out in colonial times as "the good creature of God"; enduring growing calumny and abstention campaigns, culminating in national prohibition in 1920; but then making a quick turnabout to repeal in 1933 and a skyrocketing climb in sales in the 1960s. And now that the alcohol merchants are encountering some rough times again and are shoring up the barricades against assaults on alcohol labeling and advertising and threats of raising alcohol taxes to reduce consumption, eternal vigilance and expert lobbying are even more essential in the alcohol business.

Enjoying its status as a legal beverage for the last half-century, alcohol is important to the American economy. It claims to provide employment for at least 784,000 people, with payrolls of $18 billion. Alcohol provides federal, state, and local tax funds that totaled $12.5 billion in 1984 for spirits, beer, and wine combined, with distilled spirits alone accounting for $6.9 billion. (Of course, the alcohol industry's tax "contributions" are only an estimated one-tenth of the estimated economic and social cost of problems associated with alcohol.) The industry takes pride in its creation of many jobs in collateral commodities and services—grain and fruit and sugar, containers, transportation, advertising, printing, and public relations lobbying.

However, the alcohol business is beginning to feel the pinch of anxiety about the possibility of higher taxes in the near future. The industry is fighting back by contending that what is good for the alcohol business is good for America. Witness this impassioned statement from the president of the Distilled Spirits Council of the United States (DISCUS), the public relations arm of the distilled spirits interests (1985, p. iii):

> Additional taxes would disrupt the contributions of this important industry to employment, incomes, and government revenues. Before new tax increases are imposed on the industry, careful consideration should be given to the economic and revenue consequences of such increases, especially since expected revenues may not be realized as consumption declines and reduces the amount of spirits that can be taxed.
>
> Perpetually rising taxes have increased the burden carried by distilled spirits to the point of diminishing or no returns. Despite all indications that would advise against imposing new taxes on this industry, it continues to be a target for further increases.
>
> The distilled spirits industry is already shouldering more than its fair share of taxes and should not be subject to the discriminatory treatment that often characterizes the taxes levied on its products. The industry markets its products responsibly and performs functions that serve to meet the legitimate demands of American consumers. Tax discrimination against distilled spirits is not warranted.

This DISCUS *Annual Statistical Review* for 1984–85 goes on to lament that adult per capita consumption (called "apparent consumption" in the trade because it is measured indirectly, through tax revenues) of distilled spirits in 1984 was 14.6 percent below the peak level of 1974 and 2.4 percent lower than 1983, dropping to a still-sizable 2.46 gallons in 1984. DISCUS attributes the decline in drinking largely to changing lifestyles, adverse publicity about drinking-driving, legal liability under stiffening dram shop laws, and changes in the legal drinking age (p. 50). Between January 1, 1984, and July 31, 1985, fourteen states raised the legal drinking age to twenty-one; and, according to the DISCUS report, "Most other states . . . are expected to follow . . . as the result of federal legislation that links transfer of federal highway funds to states that have a minimum drinking age of twenty-one" (p. 50). "Efforts by the beverage alcohol industry and others to encourage moderation in the consumption of alcohol beverages also appear to be having an effect" (p. v).

Of the $66.4 billion in alcohol sales, beer accounted for more than half (53.6 percent); spirits, about one-third (33.9 percent); and wine, the rest (12.4 percent). Wine showed the most rapid growth since soon after World War II, dollar volume (not adjusted for inflation) rising in 1984 to 16.5 times its 1949 level, while beer was rising about sevenfold and spirits fivefold. Of the $66.4 billion sales in 1984, $53 billion was for private consumption; but an estimated $13 billion, or one-fifth of total retail expenditures, was spent for tax-deductible business consumption (Mosher, 1983). Consumption in eating places, bars, or other on-premise outlets was estimated at 37.8 percent of the total sales in 1983, and off-premise (largely for home use) sales accounted for about two-thirds (62.2 percent).

The alcohol industry never was completely out of business during the prohibition years. Distillers continued to make alcohol for industrial uses (some of which was illegally diverted to human rather than industrial consumption) and bottled a limited amount of whiskey to be sold for "medicinal purposes" in some states (I bought my first bottle of decent bonded bourbon on a trip through northern Texas in 1941, in an ostensibly "dry" state, through paying an obliging M.D. a dollar for the prescription). Breweries made a limited amount of legal near beer (which college kids used to spike with bootleg grain alcohol); and wineries survived by selling sacramental wines to the clergy and blocks of dehydrated grape concentrate, which somehow, miraculously, turned into wine in the cellars of the customers who flagrantly disregarded the "warnings" on the packages *not* to add water and yeast or it *might* turn into wine. Since making a fair amount of wine for one's own use was legal, some entrepreneurs even provided a service whereby grape concentrates were brought to the client's basement along with the bottles, corks, and yeast to produce wine and even bottle and label it (Bunce, 1979, p. 17).

As reflected in Figure 1, in Chapter One, although repeal had come to the rescue of the alcohol industry in 1933, alcohol sales never really got into high gear again until after World War II. In 1934, only twenty-eight states permitted sale of distilled spirits; and one state (Mississippi) was officially dry until 1965 (Distilled Spirits Council of the United States, 1985, Table 33). Even in states where liquor was legal, for years there were constraints on sales from rather strict provisions for state-run or state-licensed sales; some states even made liquor consumers use ration books, patterned after the *motbooks* in Scandinavia. Sale of liquor-by-the-drink was also prohibited in many states for years; and there was very little alcohol advertising and virtually no national distribution systems until the end of World War II. And, of course, during the war liquor was hard to get at any price because of the rationing of sugar and shortage of many other supplies and the diversion of manpower into the war effort.

Right after the end of prohibition, alcohol advertising was relatively modest in scope, primarily emphasizing brand quality and availability; but increasingly advertisers began to associate the product with glamor, prestige, and the sexual attractiveness or power of those drinking it. By 1975 the total advertising budget for distilled spirits was approaching the $200 million mark, while brewers were spending just under $140 million and vintners just under $60 million per year, for a total of just under $400 million. Ten years later the total yearly advertising budget for measured media (such as newspapers and television) alone had quadrupled to $1,293,700,000, with brewers now spending the most, at $777.7 million; distillers spending $303 million; and wine advertising budgets increasing fourfold to $213 million per year (August 1986 report from *Impact*, the alcohol trade publication). If the money spent on unmeasured media—such as many major sports events and special promotions—were counted, aggregate alcohol marketing expenditures easily could amount to more than $2 billion per year.

Alcohol sales really took off in the early 1950s with the end of wartime shortages and the advent of television and more sophisticated marketing and distribution systems. At first the makers of distilled spirits gained in their relative share of income from the alcohol market, garnering 50 percent of it in 1965 and holding more than 50 percent through 1969, but dropping to 33.9 percent in 1984. Beer sales rose to more than 50 percent in 1979 through 1984; and wine sales reached 10 percent of the alcohol market in 1977 and stood at 12.4 percent in 1984 (Distilled Spirits Council of the United States, 1985 Table 45). Today—thanks to the great American thirst, helped along by massive infusions of advertising—alcoholic beverages (in the urban centers in the east and west especially) seem to be available almost everywhere—in grocery stores, fast-food outlets, and even some gasoline stations, which stock cases or six-packs or singles of beer cans in refrigerator cases, adequately chilled for immediate consumption on the road or wherever.

Growth of Alcohol-Marketing Conglomerates

Just after the end of prohibition, most breweries and wineries and some distilleries were locally owned and operated. However, with the growth of mass marketing and distribution in the 1950s, merging of distilleries and breweries into large multinational corporations progressed apace. Such corporations were able to effect economies of scale in purchasing, advertising, and distribution, which smaller companies could not match. By the late 1970s, the increase in marketing efficiencies was paralleled by an increase in consumption of alcohol that had become a source of considerable concern not only to the NIAAA and its alcoholism-aware major constituencies and public health authorities but also to the World Health Organization, which launched an international study reported in the book *Alcoholic Beverages: Dimensions of Corporate Power* (Cavanagh and Clairmonte, 1985).

As summarized in McBride and Mosher's 1985 article on the public health implications of the international alcohol industry, the WHO-sponsored report presents some challenging findings on alcohol production and trade and on how transnational corporations have affected the industry's structure and marketing practices. The study shows that, during the last twenty-five years, while both production and trade have been centered in Europe and North America, the greatest growth of consumption has been in Asia, Africa, and Latin America. The spread of European-style alcoholic drinks has added to and changed older patterns of drinking instead of substituting for them; as a result, total consumption has increased. Another international study has found much the same tendency in Europe, Canada, and the U.S. (Mäkelä and others, 1981).

Alcohol-marketing conglomerates, often underwritten by large transnational banks, affect consumption and health in two ways: (1) a corporation can shift gains from one subsidiary to subsidize losses in another (for example, Philip Morris bought Miller Beer in 1969 and escalated it into the world's second largest beer brand by 1980); and (2) transnational corporations can buy into both alcohol and tobacco companies (which are sold in many of the same ways) and save much money by consolidating marketing and distribution resources. Thus, there emerged such marriages of convenience as between Philip Morris and Miller, R. J. Reynolds and Heublein, the Imperial Group and Courage, and the Rembrandt/Rothman's Group and its extensive wine interests (Cavanagh and Clairmonte, 1985).

The conglomerates have brought skills developed in cigarette marketing to alcohol sales, including expertise in market segmentation, brand differentiation, and sponsorship of sporting events. Two demographic groups especially targeted by both cigarette and alcohol marketing have been women and youth, who are deliberately catered to by the conglomerates in their drives to increase shares of markets. Thus, Jack Daniels became one of the first spirits brands to run advertisements in leading women's magazines; and very similar youth-centered commercials featuring dangerous or exciting pursuits are sponsored by the makers of sports cars as well as by beer and cigarette companies (as illustrated later in this chapter).

By 1980 there were twenty-seven global corporations in the alcohol trade, each of which generated alcohol sales of a billion dollars or more per year: nine based in the United Kingdom, five in the U.S., and four in Canada. Examples: Philip Morris, which owns Miller, also owns 22 percent of Rothman's International of Great Britain, which in turn owns 71 percent of Rothman's of Pall Mall of Canada, which in turn owns 50.1 percent of Carling O'Keefe of Canada. Thus, the second-largest U.S. brewer (Miller) is linked to the largest South African wine producer, which is linked to the third-largest Canadian brewer. Four of the twenty-seven global corporations rank among the world's twenty largest in food sales, and five are part of larger tobacco-based conglomerates.

Five corporations dominate the North American liquor market: Seagram, National Distillers, Heublein, Brown-Forman, and Hiram Walker, with combined 1980 sales of $10 billion. These five are also among the major marketers in Latin America, in wine as well as spirits. R. J. Reynolds' $1.4 billion takeover of Heublein made it one of the world's largest alcohol conglomerates; and it later merged with Del Monte to form a new beverage and food division.

Among beer producers, six of the top nine are based in the United States: Anheuser-Busch, Philip Morris (Miller), Pabst, Schlitz, Coors, and Heilemann. The growing consolidation of breweries is seen in these figures: there were 404 United States breweries in 1947, but only a tenth as many in 1979, although barrelage had more than doubled. By 1980 the top two brewery combines (Busch and Miller) had more than half of the United States market, and the top ten rang up all but 5 percent of beer sales. To give just one illustration of vertical integration, Busch has linkages backward into raw materials and forward into distribution. Its subsidiaries process barley into brewers' malt, produce bakers' yeast, make metal containers, and own vast rice handling and storage facilities, a trucking fleet, and a railroad. Also gathered into the Busch empire are entertainment enterprises, real estate, a major-league team, a soft-drink division, and a wide variety of snack foods. As August A. Busch III himself commented, "In 1977, we installed a programme which we called 'Total Marketing' which combines all of the key marketing elements into a single orchestrated thrust. Advertising was joined by sales promotion, merchandising, field sales, sales training, and sports programming, enabling us to market not only on a national plane, but also at the grass-roots level" (Cavanagh and Clairmonte, 1985, p. 125).

Regarding wine in the United States: four-fifths of it comes from California, where wine production topped $2 billion in 1980. In 1979, of the 724 bonded wineries in the United States, California alone had 450, of which 100 accounted for four-fifths of the United States wine output. Wine subsidiaries of five of the largest distilling corporations were selling almost half of the wine by the end of the 1970s: Heublein (18 percent), Seagrams (9 percent), National Distillers and Chemical Corporation (8 percent), Rapid American (7 percent), and Brown-Forman (5 percent). Heublein bought United Vintners in 1969 and also imports dozens of wine brands from Europe and Japan. Seagrams owns several wineries in New York and California through Paul Masson.

Coca-Cola entered wine markets in 1977 because it saw wine rising in sales and wanted to get maximum profits by combining wine marketing with its soft-drink distribution networks in 135 countries. It also benefited by hedging against price fluctuations in sugar. In just one year (1980), its fastest-growing division recouped its investments through sales outstripping $100 million. Although Coca-Cola later sold off most of its wine holdings, as did Seagrams, the entry of conglomerates into the wine business—consolidating merchandising, advertising, and distribution—has resulted in a growing liquidation of small, independent wineries.

Recently the beverage conglomerates have been promoting beer and wine as though they were refreshing soft drinks, appropriate for almost any occasion or time of day. Advertisements and commercials repeatedly refer to them as "light" drinks, even though they contain enough alcohol to be intoxicating if drunk in any quantity. In fact, the alcohol merchants see themselves as competing against the whole range of nonalcoholic beverages; for, as Cowan and Mosher point out (1985, p. 628), between 1972 and 1982, alcoholic beverages (as well as commercial soft drinks) materially increased their share of the total consumption of all beverages, particularly at the expense of milk and coffee. Not only is this relatively increased consumption of alcoholic beverages of questionable nutritional effect because of their "empty calories," but the implication that these drinks are as relatively harmless as commercial sodas can engineer the perception of alcoholic beverages as harmless, new, and entrancing varieties of soft drinks.

Drives to Increase Alcohol Taxes

In recent years public interest groups have stepped up the pressures on federal agencies and Congress to increase taxes on alcohol, for the primary purpose of reducing consumption as well as perhaps to set aside some tax moneys for the treatment of alcoholism. Many alcohol researchers have been contending for years that increasing alcohol taxes would lower the overall level of consumption and result in a sharper reduction of drinking by the heaviest drinkers, with an expected reduction in cirrhosis rates and other drinking problems (Bruun and others, 1975). While NIAAA officials in Chafetz's day did not see the raising of taxes as a solution, they later exhibited a cautiously receptive attitude toward tax increases, Noble saying at one point: "As far as taxes [are] concerned, we are not a regulatory agency. It is for us to provide information. If, in fact, increased consumption causes more problems, then I think that those in policy-making roles should then begin to make decisions based on fact. If taxation should be the best way of dealing with the issue, I think we should have enough data for the policy makers to make these decisions" (Wiener, 1981, p. 233, quoting *The Alcoholism Report*). A short time later, Noble came out for increased taxes, as have his successors. Thus, the president of DISCUS, the distilled spirits lobbying arm, said rather bitterly, in a speech at an international alcohol meeting in 1982, that the NIAAA has been a "strong supporter of the control concept," adding that it had been joined by the Addiction Research Foundation of Toronto and a National Academy of Sciences report. He added that one of DISCUS's "foremost priorities is intensifying its program to point out the fatal flaws in the control of consumption theory. . . . The control theory is inimical to the best long-range interests of the public and consumer; sound regulation; freedom of commercial speech; the majority of our customers who consume beverage alcohol in moderation and often with benefits to health; international trade;

as well as to the alcoholism treatment, research, and education communities" (quoted in Lewis, *Alcoholism Report,* June 15, 1982, p. 7).

He also noted that a "new major DISCUS priority" is the "health promotion concept," which is "grounded on research findings that establish the fact that moderate drinkers live longer than alcoholics or abstainers" (p. 7). These findings, however, may have stemmed from the generally even-keel lifestyles of regular but light drinkers, rather than from the salubrious effects of alcohol (Cahalan, 1981).

The president of DISCUS also estimated that, if alcohol tax increases resulted in a 10 percent reduction in consumption, the federal government would lose more than $600 million in revenues per year and the states would lose an additional $500 million. In his view the 10 percent reduction probably would come from less consumption by light and moderate drinkers, not alcoholics. "This would classify as one of the most expensive and least productive prevention programs in history" (quoted in Lewis, *Alcoholism Report,* June 15, 1982, p. 7).

The alcohol industry also has been assailed by those who question whether the cost of alcoholic beverages should be deductible from business taxes. At present the Internal Revenue Service allows more than $12 billion in deductions for business-related drinking, resulting in a government subsidy to the alcohol industry of $3 billion to $5 billion a year (Mosher, 1983). Mosher cites as an example the Oklahoma gas station owner who served more than $2,000 worth of tax-deductible free beer to his customers in two years in a promotional campaign of "All you can drink while I fill up your tank." The new tax laws probably will result in some cuts in such business deductions but will not eliminate them—because not only the alcohol industry but many businesses and also the restaurant and hotel industries are very much opposed to such a cut.

Alcohol Labeling and Advertising

Another proposed constraint on alcohol marketing is the advocacy of labeling of alcoholic beverage containers, at least with an inventory of substances that might cause allergies or other health dangers, and, more recently, advocacy of warning consumers of potential harm to fetuses as well as other injurious effects. One of the many organizations joining in this labeling campaign, the American Medical Association, has called for warning labels similar to those on cigarette packages. The AMA board's report recommended also that alcohol advertising not be aimed at youth; that TV programs not show irresponsible use of alcohol without showing its adverse consequences; and that alcohol labels carry accurate descriptions of contents, including listing percentages of alcohol rather than proofs, to avoid confusion ("AMA Wants Warnings on Liquor Bottles," 1986).

In 1980 the Bureau of Alcohol, Tobacco, and Firearms (BATF) of the Treasury Department actually had issued a regulation requiring that ingredients be listed on alcohol containers or that consumers be told how to obtain that information by mail; but in 1981, before the regulation was put into effect, the Reagan administration attempted to rescind it. A U.S. District Court judge in February 1983 ruled that the Treasury Department had acted illegally when it rescinded the rule. The department rescinded the regulation a second time in October 1983; and again the court ruled against the rescision (Lewis, *Alcoholism Report,* Nov. 18, 1985). At this writing the status of ingredient labeling is still uncertain.

The labeling campaign to put pressure on the BATF has been spearheaded by a number of public health officials and notably by the nonprofit citizens' lobby, the Center for Science in the Public Interest (CSPI), whose legal director has commented: "We hope that the government and the alcoholic beverage industry will stop the legal merry-go-round and start giving consumers the information they need to protect their health. Ingredients are listed on almost everything from dog food to shampoo—it's about time that the alcoholic beverage industry stopped hiding the ingredients of beer, wine, and liquor from the public" (quoted in Lewis, *Alcoholism Report,* Nov. 18, 1985, p. 5).

A separate campaign, designed to capitalize on the precedent of the warning labels on cigarette packages, calls for warnings on alcohol containers of the risks of cirrhosis, damage to unborn children, or auto accidents. Especially because many of the alcohol conglomerates have a financial stake also in cigarette sales and have suffered financial setbacks because of antismoking labeling, they are motivated to fight such alcohol warning labels to the last ditch. Although at this writing their lobbying has staved off all such labeling, in the long run they may be forced to give ground.

The alcohol industry also is under constant attack these days on the grounds of its advertising. Many studies show that alcohol advertising contains false or misleading claims and suggestions. One study (Breed and De Foe, 1979) of thirteen national magazines of high circulation entailed analysis of 454 alcohol ads. Most prominent were indirect appeals associating alcohol with desired outcomes or lifestyles. Wealth and prestige, social approval, relaxation and leisure, hedonistic pleasure, exotic associations, and sexiness were the major appeals. The ads contained very little description of the actual qualities of the beverages, and seldom was the need for caution in drinking mentioned at all. The article ends with this peroration (p. 521): "Alcohol ads present an unrealistic picture of alcohol and drinking. They show only the pleasant and relaxed face of alcohol while blacking out the ugly face, the one that mirrors the nation's alcohol problem. If the ads do not tell the truth, at least they should not imply falsehood. The burden of this advertising problem rests not upon researchers and alcohol educators like ourselves, but upon the alcohol industry, as well as the government agencies charged with regulating the industry."

The CSPI, the Washington-based nonprofit group described in Chapter Four, has been one of the liquor industry's principal gadflies for a number of years—advocating increased alcohol taxes, the use of warning labels, and reduction or elimination of alcohol advertising. Its paperback *The Booze Merchants* (Jacobson, Atkins, and Hacker, 1983) cites a great deal of research on alcohol-marketing practices in a way that must be vastly entertaining to advocates of more stringent controls, but not very entertaining to the merchants themselves. The book emphasizes how the alcohol industry appeals to heavier drinkers and to vulnerable youth through sponsoring sports events, using sports figures in alcohol advertisements, and associating alcohol with sex appeal, glamor, and hazardous adventure. Currently, both Anheuser-Busch and

Miller are running commercials of racing cars plastered with beer brand names, driven by leading contenders for the Indianapolis 500.

On the sports scene, the book notes that Anheuser-Busch alone sponsored 98 professional and 380 college sports events in a recent year; it also owns the St. Louis Cardinals and paid many millions to the Los Angeles Olympic Committee for the use of the Olympic seal in its beer packaging. Its Michelob Light also sponsors tennis tournaments, and Budweiser owns the world's leading speed boat and a "land rocket" that appears in Anheuser-Busch ads. Miller Beer was the chief sponsor of the 1984 Winter Olympics. The Anheuser-Busch group marketing manager, in an article in *Marketing Times,* explains that reaching the heavy drinkers through sports promotions is the key to Anheuser-Busch's preeminent position in beer sales: "We created a new media strategy to achieve a share of voice dominance within the industry and increased advertising expenditures fourfold with greater orientation towards sports programming to reach the heavy beer drinker" (quoted in Jacobson, Atkins, and Hacker, 1983, p. 32).

Despite industry claims to the contrary, *The Booze Merchants* presents much evidence that alcohol is constantly being advertised to people who in most states are not old enough to drink legally. The book is replete with illustrations of magazine and newspaper ads that associate beer drinking with manliness, risk-taking, and sexual attractiveness; some of the ads more than border on the raunchy ("Tony Roberts talks about his first time," "You never forget your first Girl," and the picture of the jailbait-looking, suggestively clad female standing over the caption "Two Fingers is all that it takes" (p. 119)).

The authors of *The Booze Merchants* suggest these steps for reforming alcoholic beverage marketing (pp. 139-141):

- The Federal Trade Commission or Bureau of Alcohol, Tobacco and Firearms should ban all advertising and marketing efforts aimed at heavy drinkers and young people. This would include activities on college campuses, ads on rock music stations and in youth magazines, commercials on sports broadcasts, and ads that suggest heavy consumption.

• Ads would either be (a) banned from radio and television, or (b) permitted without any limitation, but balanced by an equal number of professionally produced spots highlighting health problems related to alcohol and suggesting alternatives to alcohol.

• The Federal Communications Commission should encourage all broadcasters to run health-oriented and other alcohol-related public service announcements in prime-time, sports, and family-viewing time slots.

• Companies using print advertising [of alcohol products] should be required to either devote a significant space in each ad to health information or sponsor an equal number of equally well disseminated advertisements containing this information. The FTC or NIAAA could provide sample ads to insure that the public service advertisements are truly in the public interest and not so dull, redundant, or irrelevant that consumers would ignore them after the first few months.

• The content of alcohol advertisements should be limited to consumer information about the taste, price, and composition of products, with no puffery and no association with social, sexual, or financial success. Many retail liquor stores already run austere ads that just list product and price; these ads convey useful information without all the offensive Madison Avenue hype.

• The depiction of risky activities should not be permitted in alcohol advertising.

• Local governments should carefully regulate the time and place of sale of alcoholic beverages. The more outlets selling these beverages, the greater will be alcohol consumption and alcohol problems. Sale at supermarkets, gas stations, and other non-traditional outlets should be halted.

• Sports and other celebrities, active or retired, should not be permitted to appear in ads or otherwise help market alcoholic beverages.

As to industry demurrers that alcohol advertising only affects brand choices rather than increasing the sale of alcohol, *The Booze Merchants* quotes the sardonic remark of *Advertising Age,* the Bible of Madison Avenue: "A strange world it is, in which people spending millions on advertising must do their best to prove that advertising doesn't *do* very much" (p. 99).

College newspapers are especially laden with alcohol advertisements. De Foe and Breed (1979) reviewed the ads in a national sample of thirty-two college papers selected at random from the 400 campuses with the largest enrollment. While ten of the thirty-two papers carried no national alcohol ads at all, alcohol ads constituted over half of all national ads in the sample. (This finding is consistent with a 1977 *Wall Street Journal* estimate, cited by De Foe and Breed, that about two-thirds of all national advertising in campus newspapers was for alcoholic beverages.) The leading drink in the De Foe and Breed college newspaper study was found to be beer. Excerpts from beer ads, which the authors criticize as being really antieducation, included the following (pp. 196, 199):

Readers of these newspapers are getting a generous dose of Joe Cool humor and philosophy created to accomplish one purpose—sell youth more alcoholic beverages. Most of this advertising—particularly for beer—is especially designed to appeal to the young and new consumer immersed in the strivings, frustrations, and decision making that surrounds student life. It is important to note that these are lifestyle ads, created to make a wider statement about life and how to cope with it than ads that stress product quality only and urge the reader to drink one brand versus another.

Miller High Life offers an ad that is a takeoff on the familiar graduation picture. Five students in cap and gown, holding their diplomas rigidly in a

vertical position close to their hearts, fix the camera
with a most serious stare. But there is a sixth student,
in the middle of the front row, who wears a grin and
holds a bottle of Miller High Life, vertical position,
close to his heart. The caption reads "Now Comes
Miller Time."

Another ad shows three students coming out of
a bookstore. Walking one behind the other, the first
and last student are burdened with a stack of formidable looking tomes while the student in the middle
joyously carries three six-packs of beer. His smile is in
contrast to their concern. The caption reads "Now
Comes Miller Time."

Our hero, another Joe Cool–type, is not worry-
ing about term papers, reading assignments, and final
exams. He has a better way to cope. The hard work
involved in getting an education—a definite commitment and lifestyle—is compared with another lifestyle
which gives beer drinking a high priority. The beer
drinker emerges as a charming rascal, the serious
students as worried drones.

. . . An insight into the stakes involved [in
advertising alcoholic beverages in campus publica-
tions] comes from a marketing executive familiar with
the campus scene. He defended the large expenditures
for the specialized audience, speaking of college
students as being "ripe for picking." "Let's not
forget," he said, "that getting a freshman to choose a
certain brand of beer may mean that he will maintain
his brand loyalty for the next 20 years. If he turns out
to be a big drinker, the beer company has bought itself
an annuity."

Another recent study (Atkin, Neuendorf, and McDermott,
1983) of 1,200 respondents, mostly in the age range of twelve to
twenty-two, found that alcohol advertising "appears to contribute
to certain forms of problem drinking. . . . The evidence indicates
that advertising stimulates consumption levels, which in turn leads

to heavy drinking and to drinking in dangerous situations" (p. 313). While this Michigan study has been attacked on the grounds of being based on inadequate sampling and reporting people's inferences on the effects of advertising rather than its actual effects (Strickland, 1984), additional studies on the content and presumed effects of alcohol advertising will continue to draw public and congressional attention to the vulnerability of the industry to ultimate increases in control over its advertising.

The BATF has responsibility both for collecting alcohol taxes in the interest of the Treasury and for controlling alcohol marketing in the ostensible interest of the consumer—which occasions much conflict of interest in its protection of its golden goose (Mosher and Wallack, 1981). Currently, the BATF is catching flak from consumer advocates such as the CSPI and from public health officials for not improving on its regulations since the 1930s. Chapter Eleven will present further details on changes that have been proposed in the ways alcohol taxes are levied and in controls over advertising and marketing practices.

Again, the economic and political power of the alcohol industry is not easy to overestimate. A recent attempt by the CSPI and other consumer interest groups to get the BATF to require labels on alcoholic beverages describing the ingredients (such as flavorings and other additives) was summarily derailed by such industry-inspired protests as a letter signed by both senators and fourteen representatives from California, among whom only three had not been given 1980 campaign contributions by the alcohol industry. The industry was concerned lest a requirement for ingredient labeling might set a precedent for requiring warning labels about the potential harmful effects of alcohol drunk by expectant mothers or others susceptible to alcohol problems.

The marketers of wine, beer, and liquor will present a united front when they are equally threatened (such as by the labeling campaign), and many of them have a common interest because there is much overlapping ownership of manufacturing or marketing among the three types of beverages. But at present the distilled spirits interests are trying to regain some of their share of market lost to the lighter beverages during the last dozen years. One instance of competition between types of beverages was the 1985 campaign of the House of Seagram (Lewis, *Alcoholism Report,* Oct. 31, 1985, p. 6). Seagrams launched an advertising campaign on major cable television stations, charging the three major television networks with refusing to air its commercial about drinking and driving. The commercial, through which Seagram hoped to downplay the "lighter" appeals of wine and beer, emphasized that the most common servings of beer (12 ounces), wine (5 ounces), and liquor (1 1/4 ounces) are equal in alcohol content. (Subsequently, Seagrams withdrew from membership in the Wine Institute because of the institute's criticism of that competitive advertising campaign.)

Immediately, the Winegrowers of California publicly claimed that wine is the "beverage of moderation" and plays "an important and useful medical role." The representatives of major beer interests issued an "Open Letter on Alcohol Policy to Government Officials," accusing Seagrams of waging a "campaign which is as dangerous as it is devious," saying piously that "we strongly resent any attempt to 'capitalize' on the alcohol abuse issue or to use it to advance the sales and marketing objectives of individual companies." The wine and beer interests were not so competitive, however, as to mention the rather obvious point that while the size of a drink of wine or beer tends to be rather standard, the size of a personally administered dose of liquor can vary a good deal.

The Alcohol Industry on the Defensive

The press has been picking up recently on the mounting evidence that alcohol consumption is tapering off. In a *Business Week* article on February 25, 1985, Moskowitz and Pave cited a survey in which 45 percent of respondents said that they were drinking less than five years earlier, as compared to 31 percent on the same question in a 1971 survey. The authors attributed the apparent slackening in consumption to public forgetting of the tensions over prohibition of fifty years ago, the campaigns of Mothers Against Drunk Driving and other citizen groups, the physical fitness movement and increased knowledge about health hazards, and self-consciousness about the inconsistency of adults who drink heavily and yet condemn youths for using marijuana. Moskowitz and Pave conclude (p. 113): "Everywhere the evidence is

overwhelming that Americans are finding it increasingly acceptable—and sometimes desirable—to try to alter other people's
behavior. Ideologically, the change could be classified as a swing of
the pendulum from concern with personal rights to concern with
community rights. And all signs suggest that it will be a long time
before the pendulum swings back again."

In a *Business Week* article ("Sober Prospects for Distillers,"
1985), Vamos commented that the distilled spirits industry has not
yet found a way to counter the competition of wine and beer's
emphasis on "lightness." The magazine's annual scoreboard of
spirits retailing more than 500,000 cases found that, of the top sixty-
five brands, thirty-eight had lost ground between 1981 and 1983.

Today more of the newer generation of alcohol industry
leaders are emphasizing that they, too, want to cooperate in
promoting moderation in the use of their products and that they *are*
contributing to reduction of drinking problems through their
occasional sponsorship of ads promoting moderate drinking. In the
1960s, increasingly worried over their public image in the face of
growing public concern about drinking-driving among even
teenagers, alcohol-marketing companies began to sponsor magazine ads with a "know your limits" appeal for moderation. But a
cover story about alcoholism in *Time* ("Alcoholism: New Victims,
New Treatments," 1974) emphasized the "disease" aspects and said
nothing that could have offended the alcohol industry; the same
issue also carried thirteen ads (ten in full-page color) extolling
spirits or wine and beer and carrying no industry-sponsored pleas
for moderation.

Shortly thereafter, two writers for *Fortune,* while gathering
material for another prominently featured article—which turned
out to have the same "alcoholism is a disease" thrust—interviewed
me about our research on the increase in drinking problems; during
the interview they noted that the magazine would have to walk a
careful line because alcoholic beverages were among its largest
advertising accounts.

The question might well be raised: Why would a few
moderate-drinking ads make any difference anyway, if—as the
industry contends—all it is trying to do with its billions of dollars
in alcohol advertising is to change brand preferences, not necessar-

ily to increase the volume of alcohol consumed? Nowadays, more people are commenting that the industry can no longer have it both ways.

For many years the industry has subsidized numerous organizations and individuals working in the field of alcohol problems. In 1984 the president of the Distilled Spirits Council of the United States (DISCUS) wrote a letter to Nancy Reagan, outlining the liquor industry's history of research, education, and public service advertising to combat alcoholism or drunk driving. In the letter the following organizations are listed as currently being subsidized by DISCUS: the National Association of State Boards of Education, the Alcohol and Drug Problems Association, the National Education Association, the BACCHUS college anti-excessive-drinking program, Students Against Driving Drunk, the Rutgers Center of Alcohol Studies, the American Council on Alcoholism (not to be confused with the National Council on Alcoholism, which once was heavily subsidized but no longer is accepting industry money), the National Coalition for Adequate Alcohol Programs, the Health Education Foundation, the Salvation Army, the National Association of Alcoholism Treatment Programs, Boston University's School of Medicine, Pennsylvania State University, the Research Society on Alcoholism, Indiana University, and the Cottage Program of Utah (Lewis, *Alcoholism Report,* Jan. 17, 1984, p. 7).

George Hacker of the CSPI (in a personal interview, Aug. 26, 1986) has added to this list of industry-subsidized organizations the Association of Labor-Management Administrators and Consultants on Alcoholism, the Alliance for Traffic Safety, the National Association of Women Highway Safety Leaders, the Education Commission of the States, the General Federation of Women's Clubs, National Extension Homemakers Council, and Mothers Against Drunk Driving, as well as a long list of professors at universities.

It may well be said that the alcohol industry's partial support of these groups and individuals results in furtherance of campaigns against drunk driving, which are in the interest of improved public safety. However, George Hacker contends that these subsidies are highly correlated with the frequent refusal of subsidized organizations to join in on endorsements of legislation to increase alcohol taxes, put warnings on alcohol containers, or increase the controls on alcohol advertising. Certainly, when an organization accepts an industry subsidy, legitimate questions can be asked about what the industry gets out of these subsidies in return.

In light of growing public pressure to get. tougher with drunk drivers and to reduce drinking among those not yet of legal age, the alcohol industry soon may wind up going along with some controls over advertising and marketing to susceptible groups. Thus, the industry might decide, in the interest of good public relations, to drop its sponsorship of fraternity beer busts, its hiring of student beer brand representatives on campus, and its sponsorship of rock concerts that tend to get out of hand. The alternative may be to risk confiscatory taxes and more controls in the long run.

Possible Incentives for Industry Cooperation

One innovative way to secure more industry cooperation in controls over alcohol hazards would be to offer new tax incentives for the industry's actual promotion of moderation. This tax break could offset the revenue that the industry would lose through likely elimination of the present tax writeoffs for alcohol advertising.

However, some experts insist that alcohol problems will not be reduced until the production of alcoholic beverages is stabilized, so that the alcohol industry no longer will push the marketing of its product to increase sales at least 5 percent per year, which the industry appears to believe is necessary to insure sufficient profitability (National Institute on Alcohol Abuse and Alcoholism, 1977a). Perhaps the only effective way to lower the per capita consumption of alcohol will be to increase alcohol taxes and use part of the tax revenue to reimburse the industry for retiring some of the alcohol-producing resources, through such expedients as subsidies to growers to reduce the acreage devoted to wine grapes and the grains used in beer and spirits. We would thereby be buying off the politically powerful alcohol industry just as we protect other powerful interests—for instance, by paying farmers to reduce production. This might actually be a practical tactic, since the buying out of alcohol production resources could be financed from increased alcohol taxes rather than from the general fund. It might cost us a lot less in the long run if it resulted in a material lessening of our nation's present alcohol problems.

This rather cynical approach of "If you can't fight them, buy them out" may be the only practical means of prevailing against the political power of the alcohol merchants to stave off increased controls and taxes. Collectively, the wine, beer, and spirits manufacturers and wholesalers have staffs totaling more than 150 legislative liaison personnel, attorneys, research workers, and consultants on the alert to put out any fires threatening their freedom to maintain and expand their markets. They have the determination and the money to protect their interests against the skimpily funded and sporadic campaigns of the various citizen groups that mount campaigns for increased controls over alcohol. Unless the toll of drunken driving suddenly increases so dramatically as to warrant a rise in citizen alarm high enough to put much more pressure on Congress, our only hope for enacting controls over excessive alcohol consumption is to encourage brewers, vintners, and distillers to reduce their production of alcoholic beverages voluntarily. In any case, the pendulum appears to be swinging slowly toward acceptance of the public health perspective that more needs to be done to control the sale of alcohol if we are to have any hope of decreasing the nation's alcohol-related problems.

6

Primary Prevention and the Good-Health Movement

Here "primary prevention" refers to measures applied to the *general population* to keep alcohol problems from developing in the first place. Later chapters will deal with secondary and tertiary prevention, or attempts to help *individuals* get over the problems they already have.

The dictionary definition of "prevent" is variously "to deprive of power or hope of acting or succeeding," "to keep from happening or existing," or "to hold or keep back." After the sad experience of prohibition, American health and public policy authorities have had to settle for the last, least certain, definition of prevention of alcohol problems. This defensive stance is the result of popular reaction against the constraints of prohibition and the alcohol industry's emergence as a political and economic power dedicated to opening up new markets and increasing consumption everywhere it can. Thus, Robin Room's emphasis on "minimizing" rather than "preventing" alcohol problems (1974b) has been a realistic one in the political world of today.

Room borrowed his concept of "minimization" from one of the leading postprohibition alcohol researchers, the late Kettil Bruun of Finland (1973). It reflects the willingness of authorities to compromise with very real alcohol-related social and economic problems in order to keep the political ability to maintain any control over those problems at all. When the NIAAA was founded in 1970, this stance was reinforced by the preoccupation of the major constituency groups (notably the National Council on Alcoholism) with the clinical treatment of alcoholics. As a result, alcohol problems that were not primarily medical but were behavioral—such as drunken driving and alcohol-related violence and social disruptions of many kinds—were not effectively addressed. As Room points out, the primary prevention programs of the early 1970s fell into three relatively ineffectual categories: alcohol education for children and youth in the schools; public information campaigns to sell the concept of "responsible drinking"; and outreach or case-finding efforts to bring the "hidden alcoholic" into treatment.

Room (1974a) emphasizes the need for a redirection in our thinking about alcohol problems, distinguishing three somewhat conflicting images of alcohol: (1) as an irresistibly attractive but dangerous substance that merits restrictions on availability (a public health perspective); (2) as a substance associated with problems of disruptive behaviors ascribed to cultural conflicts (implying a need for general education campaigns); and (3) as a substance that leads to alcoholism only in those people who suffer from a specific disease of unknown but preexisting etiology (calling for case finding of "hidden alcoholics"). Room recommends prevention programs that encourage nondrinking behaviors, modify popular images of and reactions to drinking, and insulate drinking behavior from social damage.

Growth of the Prevention Movement

By the mid-1980s, research findings on the high incidence of nonmedical alcohol-related problems and the lobbying campaigns of such organizations as Mothers Against Drunk Driving had helped to bring about a changed emphasis in alcohol-problem prevention campaigns. Now in the forefront is a group of relatively young public health and social policy specialists. These prevention leaders are raising questions about how we might minimize alcohol problems through economic manipulation (such as increased alcohol taxes) and through constraints of many kinds: in the hours that bars can stay open, zoning regulations to control numbers and kinds of alcohol outlets, raising the legal age for purchasing alcoholic beverages, increasing controls over advertising and labeling, and passive restraints such as better highway lighting or airbags or improved seat belts. This chapter will cover such prevention efforts in some detail, after first discussing the conceptual issues that must be recognized in order to plan effective primary prevention programs.

Wallack (1984a) describes the general public health objective in primary prevention: to reduce the incidence or number of new cases of a particular problem, and thus in the long run to reduce the prevalence or number of cases of those who have the problem. To achieve this objective, one can—according to Wallack—reduce a person's exposure to the causal agent (in this case alcohol) or reduce the person's susceptibility. Three main strategies for reducing susceptibility are health promotion, disease prevention, and health protection. Health promotion advances skills and information conducive to healthy lifestyles; disease prevention provides specific services for those at high risk of particular problems, so as to keep problems from developing in full-blown form; and health protection entails taking steps to control the environment in ways that help to insulate people from potential problems.

Historically, Wallack says, the passive types of health protection (such as a clean water supply, pasteurization of milk, general sanitary practices, airbags or improved seat belts in automobiles, and improved highway design and lighting) have proved most effective because they do not require much cooperative effort once they are put into effect. However, they have been subject to the greatest resistance from vested interests—such as the determined defense of the alcohol industry against the reduction of consumption through increased alcohol taxes. As a result, according to Wallack, "For the past 50 years, the alcohol field has consistently relied on prevention

strategies that have the least potential for being successful" (p. 203)—
primarily alcohol education.

In Wallack's view, alcohol education is necessary—since
people should be informed about the dangers of drinking too
much—but it is not sufficient to prevent alcohol problems. It must
be coupled with "environmental strategies that seek to reduce the
risk for the individual by regulating the system in which the
individual exists" (p. 204). He notes the inconsistency between our
emphasis on alcohol education as a means of promoting individual
responsibility and, at the same time, our encouragement of alcohol
sales through increased marketing and tax-deductible advertising
efforts, greatly expanded numbers and kinds of alcohol outlets, and
significant reductions in alcohol prices in relation to other goods.

> This approach to understanding problems
> [that is, primary reliance on alcohol education] is
> popular because it provides a clear indication of what
> needs to be done in prevention. This [individual-
> centered] research process uncovers a need (an individ-
> ual deficiency) that is congruent with the existing
> skills of bureaucrats, planners, program developers,
> and researchers. Bureaucrats are satisfied, because
> these programs are usually politically safe and do
> little to alter existing arrangements. Educators and
> other kinds of program interventionists can develop
> programs to provide people with more self-esteem,
> better communication skills, or whatever the factor is
> they do not have. Some researchers can evaluate the
> outcome of these programs, while others can seek
> greater and greater precision regarding the relevant
> factors and perhaps find new factors internal to
> individuals that are more strongly correlated with the
> problem behavior. Finally, the alcoholic beverage
> industry is pleased, because the problem has been
> placed on the individual, and the product from which
> the industry derives their profits has been excluded
> from the problem definition. Alcohol and marketing
> and availability issues are seen as neutral forces that

do not infringe on the choices of individuals [Wallack, 1984a, p. 209].

Our policy makers, Wallack concludes, have been so preoccupied with the treatment of those who have drifted into clinically defined alcoholism that they have failed to invoke preventive measures which might stand a chance of being effective. In another publication (1984b, p. 79), he likens such policy makers to people who are busy rescuing drowning victims near the mouth of a dangerous river but are not doing enough upstream to keep more people from falling in.

In still another publication, Wallack concedes that "treatment of sick individuals is an important moral-ethical responsibility of our society. However, the moral-ethical responsibility to prevent problems from happening is surely as great if not greater. Ultimately, the treatment task will be made easier when prevention assumes a higher priority in the community. Those struggling to recover from alcoholism and other alcohol-related problems will be more likely to succeed if they return to a community with a social and physical environment that: supports, rather than questions, abstinence; is safe for those who elect to drink moderately; does not include policies at any level which directly or indirectly contribute to the pressure to drink; [and does not] increase the risk of injury when drinking does take place" (Wallack, 1984a, pp. 219–220).

George Albee, former president of the American Psychological Association, makes some of the same points in relation to American mental health in general, in his article "The Answer Is Prevention" (1985), in which he wryly observes (p. 62), "Conservatives strongly favor a constitutional-organic disease explanation, largely because no major social change is called for if the problems are all inside the skin."

A Systems Perspective on Social Problems

Problem Drinkers (Cahalan, 1970, p. 10), pointed out that the perception of alcoholism is strongly influenced by Western civilization's tendency to define things and people in absolutist terms. The youth who gets involved in some escapade is swiftly labeled a juvenile delinquent, and the man who continues to get into trouble because of his drinking is readily labeled an alcoholic. Such facile labeling helps to relieve the tensions and to reinforce the rectitude of the labeler, but it seldom contributes to efficiency in diagnosis or treatment of social ills. The great success of the medical "microbe hunters" during the last century in finding antidotes and inoculations against some very deadly diseases has lent further support to our looking for easy, magic-bullet solutions to long-term social problems such as alcoholism. The experimental method in modern science, in which only one thing is varied at a time, also has contributed to our thinking in "either/or" differential-diagnosis terms in relation to alcohol problems.

A systems approach to social problems is needed as an antidote for the "either/or" syndrome. As Holder and Wallack put it (1986, p. 336): "To approach the prevention of problems associated with alcoholic beverages as part of a system is consistent with our understanding of how things work in the world. As a natural consequence of a systems perspective, we would consider education and personal instruction in conjunction with alcoholic beverage control and regulation as well as the impact of economic and market forces. With this perspective, it becomes possible to identify those social, economic and psychological factors which we can realistically affect and to identify the factors outside our influence or control. In this way we increase the likelihood prevention will succeed."

The necessary complexities of any evaluation research or action program conducted within a systems perspective are well illustrated in Figure 4, which shows how various influences interact to cause drinking problems. One could add to the complexity of the model by adding more arrows to show additional pushing and pulling in real life—such as the pressure from the alcohol industry upon regulatory and control systems to keep the profitable alcohol market from being regulated enough to affect consumption.

Alcohol Education

Traditionally, since the mid 1800s, a great deal of information about the negative aspects of alcohol has been disseminated,

**Figure 4. A Conceptual Systems Model of Alcohol Use
and Alcohol-Related Problems.**

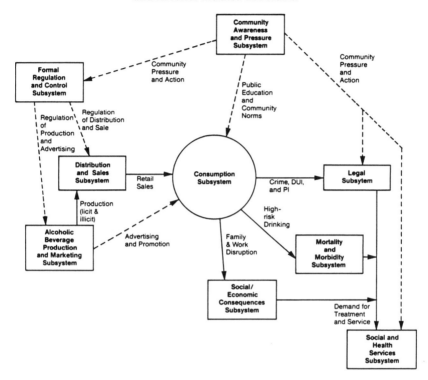

Legend:

──────▶ Flow of physical entities such as people, alcoholic beverages, money, etc.

─ ─ ─ ─▶ Flow of information such as advertising messages, regulations, public pressure, etc.

Source: Holder and Wallack, 1986, p. 331. Used by permission.

particularly for the captive audience of the young in school. This emphasis on alcohol education finds popular favor because Americans place high value on education in general and because we share the rationalist assumption that people will learn to behave well if they are informed of the bad consequences of doing things we don't want them to do. But because the vast majority of adults drink, we generally feel uncomfortable in warning other adults about the dangers of too much alcohol; so we prefer to emphasize alcohol education for the young, leaving it up to the teachers in the schools. Meanwhile, the young tend not to be too receptive to alcohol education when they see in their homes and many public places that adults do not practice what they preach. Thus, Howard Blane, a long-time specialist in alcohol education, in his definitive review of the status of education and the prevention of alcoholism, concedes that "The effect of public information and education programs on alteration of drinking patterns is indeterminate, although it is generally felt to be slight" (Blane, 1976, p. 537).

Alcohol education in the schools from the mid-1800s through World War II had a strong abstentionist and emotional emphasis; but, as Blane points out, by the late 1950s there was an increasing flow of scientifically objective information on alcohol's effects, and discussions of choices that young people can make regarding alcohol. Information on alcohol is included in the model curriculum guides for health education prepared by most state departments of education, though "the general impression is that alcohol education has never had much of an active place in the total education picture" (Blane, 1976, p. 553).

In reaction to knowledge that children in elementary school are heavily exposed to drinking behavior through the media and at home, and that many of them are drinking at a tender age, alcohol education is now being offered at the elementary school level. But although more alcohol information has been available in recent years, too often it is given out in canned lectures or pamphlets rather than through well-led discussions tha might lead students to make personal commitments to abstention or moderation in drinking.

Studies have shown that education on alcohol and other drugs may lead to changes in knowledge, but not to much favorable change in behavior over the long run. Part of the reason is that (as Blane says) the teachers in the schools are generally in the adversary position of trying to induce students to be more moderate in their drinking behavior than the adults they know, as well as more moderate than many of their peers and perhaps a few of their teachers.

A pioneering study by the Research Triangle Institute of North Carolina for the NIAAA (Bailey and Wakely, 1973) was candid in exploring the reasons why educational campaigns tend to be ineffectual. On the one hand, the health educator does not want to offend religious groups that advocate total abstinence. On the other hand, parents will resent it if their children are taught that adults who drink as much as their parents are harming themselves or their families. Thus, educational programs supported by the NIAAA in the 1970s tended merely to give information on alcohol's effects and on "the diversity of drinking patterns" but were "neutral on the desirability of these patterns" (p. 18).

There also was—and still is—quite an emphasis on "values clarification," which seeks through dialogues to get young people to make up their minds on what they want out of life. Nobody as yet has established that the values clarification approach has helped reduce teenage drinking. Many young people go in for excitement and immediate reinforcements, which overpower any values that call for postponement of gratification; and too often they have no adequate role models to follow among either their peers or adults to induce them to postpone the gratifications of alcohol in the interest of achieving longer-term goals.

The ethos of the leaders of the influential National Council on Alcoholism (which was founded soon after repeal and thus wanted to avoid the onus of being a dry organization) and the philosophy of the first director of the NIAAA, Morris Chafetz, led to a heavy emphasis in the early 1970s on a "responsible drinking" theme in the alcohol literature put out by the NCA and the NIAAA. Chafetz gained popularity in the alcohol industry by his advice for parents to introduce their children to small sips of alcoholic beverages at an early age, to get them started with moderate drinking habits, as is the case in many Jewish and Italian families. Yet the consumption of alcohol and the incidence of drinking problems and the prevalence of clinical alcoholism kept rising; and some critics said that Chafetz was confusing causes and effects—that introducing the children of hard-drinking parents to alcohol at home would merely lead to their drinking like their parents or their parents' friends. As noted in Chapter Three, Ernest Noble and his successors as director of the NIAAA ordered the deletion of the "responsible drinking" theme altogether from NIAAA-generated literature, although the theme is understandably still widely used in the institutional advertising put out by some of the companies within the alcohol industry.

The Moderate-Health-Habits Movement

The importance of health-related habits (including drinking behavior) in predicting death rates was underscored by the now-classic longitudinal study of the Human Population Laboratory of the California State Department of Health. A large probability sample of adult residents of Alameda County were interviewed regarding medical conditions and personal health practices, including weight control, moderation in smoking and drinking, participation in active sports or other exercise, eating regular meals, and getting enough sleep. Belloc's analysis (1973) showed that those who had the best scores on healthy lifestyles had a much lower mortality rate after some years than those with poorer scores: a good score on several lifestyle items was a better predictor of survival than any one item (such as drinking behavior) alone. The findings demonstrate that, because smoking and drinking and irregular health habits tend to go together, studies of mortality related to drinking should take into account other elements in the person's lifestyle. The findings also suggest that campaigns for moderation in drinking should also emphasize the importance of a generally healthy lifestyle with appropriate diet and exercise.

That the current media emphasis on healthy living may be having some effect is seen in a modest decrease in drinking among high school students within the last few years. Johnston, O'Malley, and Bachman (1985) reported that two-thirds of the high school seniors whom they interviewed in 1984 had drunk some alcoholic beverage within the last thirty days, a slight decline of 4.9 percentage points from the peak year of 1978. Also, the proportion who drank an alcoholic beverage on twenty or more occasions during the prior thirty days dropped from 6.9 to 4.8 percent, or a decline of about one-fifth. (At the same time, similarly frequent use of marijuana/hashish dropped more than 50 percent and similarly frequent cigarette smoking declined 37.5 percent.)

Wallack (1984b) emphasizes the importance of the media (especially *television*) in reaching both children and adults with messages on how to achieve good health and avoid trouble from drinking. He points out that the mass media are, de facto, health educators. Those who determine the content of television programming, create advertisements, and plan health promotion and prevention campaigns have an important responsibility to serve the public interest. His colleagues Breed and De Foe found in 1979 that television programs were unnecessarily showing a great many drinking scenes in a favorable light; but a few years later, television producers were willing to work with them in a constructive way to tone down the number of alcohol scenes and deglamorize drinking (Breed and De Foe, 1982).

In keeping with the documented importance of television in learning good or bad health habits, the NIAAA has launched a $1.135 million experimental two-year program directed at children from nine to thirteen years, and also toward those who influence children's attitudes and behavior (Lewis, *Alcoholism Report,* Oct. 31, 1985). The program is being planned by Macro Systems of Silver Spring, Maryland, and implemented by the Children's Television Workshop, the producers of *Sesame Street.* According to Robert Denniston, director of the NIAAA's Division of Prevention and Research Dissemination, the campaign's primary objectives are to delay the age of first drinking, to show children how to avoid pressures to use alcohol and other drugs, to inform parents and other role models on actions they can take to prevent children from developing alcohol problems, and to educate educational and other social agencies on how to help high-risk youth avoid alcohol and other drug problems.

Gradual Acceptance of Prevention Programs

According to the NIAAA's National Plan for 1986–1995 (National Institute on Alcohol Abuse and Alcoholism, 1986b), the principal NIAAA prevention goals for that period are to reduce alcohol abuse and alcoholism among adults by 20 percent, acute drinking problems among youth by 11 percent, motor vehicle accidental deaths involving drunk drivers (those with .10 percent blood alcohol levels) by 19 percent, alcohol-related traumatic injuries by 29 percent, liver cirrhosis deaths by 11 percent, and the incidence of fetal alcohol syndrome by 25 percent. Methods for achieving these goals include media campaigns, communication with other groups dedicated to these prevention goals, and prevention-oriented research.

In 1975, in the early NIAAA days, only about 6 percent of the NIAAA budget was allocated to prevention projects; and most of these amounted to secondary prevention—that is, to case-finding attempts to identify those in need of clinical alcoholism treatment. As Room (1984a) has illustrated, until the late 1970s, the climate was not ripe for serious discussions of practical ways and means of bringing about primary prevention of alcohol problems. In 1966, for instance, Milton Terris, former president of the American Public Health Association, presented a paper at a national conference in which he gave the evidence for a strong connection between alcohol consumption and mortality and argued in guarded terms that government measures might reduce mortality through reducing consumption; his paper was jocularly dismissed by other speakers, and it was actually omitted from the published account of the conference. Again, in the early 1970s, Terris presented his views at an NIAAA-sponsored strategy meeting attended by a small number of social scientists. He pointed out that—from the public health model of host, environment, and agent—alcohol unquestionably was the agent to be curbed. Despite his eminence as an epidemiologist, the general aversion of alcohologists to being tagged as "neoprohibitionists" was then so strong that I was not at all surprised when one of the founders of the NCA nudged me after Terris's presentation and whispered, "Where does this guy get off? What a crackpot! Does he want a return to prohibition?"

As Room (1984a) notes, Terris's views were uneasily regarded as illiberal by many members of his own public health profession. In the 1940s the founders of the Yale Plan clinics found it expedient to say that the alcoholism problem was in the person, not the bottle. At the time even Jellinek expressed skepticism about the link between drinking and cirrhosis and dismissed claims for a link between alcohol and cancer of the esophagus and birth defects.

However, as Room also notes, the stance of the public health profession toward alcohol has changed markedly within the last decade. An increasing number of public health leaders are taking a serious look at the possibility of reducing alcohol-related problems through constraints on consumption. Room attributes some of this change to the mounting evidence in international studies, which have shown reductions in cirrhosis and other alcohol problems in countries after they have adopted alcohol tax increases and related measures that reduce consumption of alcohol. For example, the relation between price and cirrhosis mortality "has turned out to be surprisingly strong: Cook (1982) estimates [on the basis of data on the apparent effects of state tax increases] that a doubling of the United States federal tax on spirits would result in a 20 percent decline in cirrhosis mortality. Findings such as these suggest that tax measures have at least as strong an effect on heavy drinkers as on the rest of the drinking population" (Room, 1984a, p. 308).

Often we can better understand American drinking problems when we look at international comparative studies, such as those reported by Mäkelä and his colleagues (1981) and by Bruun and his colleagues (1975). Mäkelä and his colleagues found a high negative correlation between the level of taxes on alcoholic beverages (especially higher-proof spirits) and cirrhosis rates. However, they point out certain pitfalls in alcohol control noticed in these international studies. For example, there is an essential conflict of interest in governments that both rely on alcohol taxes and are responsible for avoiding excessive consumption. Also, if governments make alcohol taxes too high, public resentment may rise sharply, and the bootlegger may become a romantic figure again.

Prevention Through Controls on Sales and Service

One specific constraint that might be imposed to reduce drinking problems is to put more emphasis on point-of-sale controls. These controls were most popular at the time of antisaloon campaigns before prohibition; they included (and in some states still include) a vast array of regulations on the number and kinds of off-premise and on-premise alcohol outlets to be permitted in a city or neighborhood, hours of service, minimum age of consumers, and even the lighting and seating arrangements in bars. Wittman (1982a) has written extensively about the alcohol-related problems that individual communities often have to face (pp. 8-9).

1. Problems of neighborhood tranquility: Rowdy outlets, litter and traffic congestion associated with convenience-type stores selling alcohol, late-night drinking and parties, teenage hanging out and drinking in parks and parking lots, conflicts over drinking styles among different population groups living in the same area.

2. Concerns about alcohol outlets: Sales to minors; neighbor concerns about establishing acceptable conditions of operation during the licensing process and obtaining adequate enforcement for same; concerns about "ratchet effect" licensing which makes it easier to put an outlet into a community than to remove it (this includes problems that people have with ABC regulations); concerns about the relationship of alcohol outlets to crime and vice, and unhealthy influences on young people; concerns about the exploitative effects that the presence of alcohol outlets has on the development of poverty/low income areas, and conversely, merchants concerned about the impact of too many outlets in booming "trendy" shopping areas.

3. Concerns about drinking and driving: These concerns appear mostly to be directed toward getting the drunk driver off the road, but also include protections for residential areas and denial of use permits to "mini-mart" type stores selling beer in gas stations.

4. Young peoples' and minors' use of alcohol: Parents' groups at the neighborhood and school district level have expressed concern about their children's purchase of alcoholic beverages and their use in community settings, including school yards.

Wittman also mentions the problem of coping with public inebriates. Several California cities, he notes, are currently trying to combine public and private resources to provide shelter and rehabilitative care. If such tertiary preventive measures are not pursued vigorously, the cost in dollars and human lives will be much higher; for (as he notes) under present conditions as many as half of the patients in county hospitals have serious alcohol problems. Fortunately, he reports some progress in dealing with public inebriates. One illustration is a unit in Albuquerque, which with one social worker and two paid aides managed to create a social-setting detoxification facility for inebriates, with space for counseling, some meals, listings of job opportunities, and a mail-drop. The program director scurried around among the major community organizations and within two years had made arrangements with the police, the county hospital, and the local mental health center to coordinate the handling of public drunks to avoid jailing, minimize hospitalization, and secure welfare benefits for those entitled. Arrangements were made with several old hotels to provide safe surroundings for vulnerable inebriates, and a job-retraining program was instituted. While few chronic alcoholics were thus completely rehabilitated, at least this temporary program "cleaned up" downtown Albuquerque for a time and reduced the need for police and hospital services.

Wittman warns that skill and patience are needed to cut through all the bureaucratic hurdles and inertia in getting city, county, state, and federal agencies to cooperate in effective community planning to cope with alcohol problems. In another article (1982b), in which he describes the intricacies of zoning, he notes that one has to cope with the alcohol lobby, the state alcoholic beverage control organization (which is usually more concerned about the orderly marketing of alcohol than about preventing alcohol-related problems), the state legislators (who are reluctant to offend the powerful liquor lobby or their local constituents who sell alcohol), the local city councils or supervisors (who are concerned about local alcohol retailers), and a myriad of local community groups.

But effective zoning can be accomplished; and a monograph by Wittman and Hilton (1984) (available from the California Department of Alcohol and Drug Programs, and also underwritten by the NIAAA) describes some of the ways to bring about better coordination among the public agencies concerned. Wallack (1984–85) has described one pilot program where some success has been achieved in getting community agencies in San Francisco to cooperate in bringing about better constraints on the number of alcohol outlets. Although success in controlling alcohol problems through this new project has been limited, at least it has resulted in the withdrawal of a major oil company's plans to alter a city ordinance to permit marketing beer and wine at its gasoline self-service stations. Another instance of effective community zoning was the action of the Los Angeles City Council in limiting the number of liquor outlets in a poverty area (J. Clayton, 1986). As a member of the South-Central Organizing Committee said in testimony before the council, "Some of these liquor stores are Club Meds for criminals. The loitering, the drinking, the drug activity that has been allowed to breed around liquor stores has got to be stopped and that's why we need the ordinance" (p. 1).

Better control over *drinking-driving* is dependent upon knowing more about *where* the drunken drivers are drinking, says Mary O'Donnell (1984), coordinator of the alcohol and drug abuse prevention program of the Student Health Service at the University of California, Berkeley. She notes that the heavier drinkers tend to drink in bars or lounges rather than in places (such as their own homes) where there is less occasion to drive after drinking; and she estimates that about half the drinking drivers on the road got their last drinks from licensed establishments, bars in particular. Knowing where the alcohol-impaired driver was last drinking is a practical means of pinpointing the establishments that are in need of more vigorous policing or reeducation of the bartenders.

Server intervention programs are growing in their coverage. Mosher, the attorney and social scientist who drafted the model law for dram shop liability (1985b), has written several position papers showing that public reaction against the laissez-faire mushrooming of alcohol outlets and the increases in drunken driving and other alcohol-related problems has led to a recent tightening up of control over outlets. Half or more of the states now impose civil "dram shop" liability laws on commercial servers (and some private hosts) if they serve drunks or minors who later cause harm to themselves or others. Increasingly, state alcoholic beverage control (ABC) authorities, which were set up originally to regulate the number of bars permissible in a locality and perhaps to establish price guidelines, now are prescribing how sellers can fulfill their responsibilities under dram shop laws (Mosher, 1984a).

As Mosher notes (1984b), the owners of bars and lounges can stave off potential liability lawsuits, as well as crackdowns from state and local regulatory agencies, if their bartenders and waitresses learn to avoid serving intoxicated patrons. Some insurance companies are offering as much as a 20 percent reduction in liability insurance rates to establishments whose servers have taken a course in how to avoid serving drunks. However, Mosher adds, to make such server intervention programs effective, the state ABC authority must have the backing of dram shop and liability insurance regulations and the trained personnel to carry out training programs and enforce the laws against serving alcohol to minors or drunks; all the licensees in an area must be stringent in their compliance with such laws, or else the cooperative outlets will be at a competitive disadvantage.

Anti-Drunk-Driving Campaigns

In recent years there has been a gradual stiffening of laws related to drinking-driving. As of the end of 1985 (Lewis, *Alcoholism Report,* Jan. 17, 1986), twenty-five states used roadside breathalyzer tests as at least preliminary evidence of impairment; forty states mandated that a blood alcohol level of .10 percent or even lower is illegal per se; twenty-one provided for administrative suspension of drivers' licenses for those with an illegal BAC (blood alcohol level); nineteen had laws against opened alcoholic beverage containers; and thirty-three states prohibited alcohol consumption in automobiles. Most states are scurrying to adopt the twenty-one-year rule because Congress in 1984 mandated a cut in federal highway funds for states not soon in compliance. Anti-drunk-driving groups say that uniform adoption of this rule will eliminate "blood borders" between states that differ in their age rules and consequently have many drunken accidents at the borders (McGinley, 1986).

However, progress in reducing drunk driving is still uneven and limited. As a number of the papers presented in *Injury in America: A Continuing Public Health Problem* (National Research Council and Institute of Medicine, 1985) and in a recent NIAAA-sponsored Berkeley conference on the prevention of alcohol-related injuries (Prevention Research Center, 1986) have emphasized, it is not so much the severity of prescribed punishments for alcohol-impaired driving that will reduce drunk driving as it is the certainty and swiftness of some form of punishment. That certainty is now lacking. Wagenaar, in a brief review of "Youth, Alcohol, and Traffic Crashes" (1986), says that the usual state legislative approach to deterring alcohol-impaired driving is to increase the penalties and put on additional enforcement efforts. But, citing evidence presented by Ross (1982), he argues that the deterrent effect of threats of severe punishment *if* convicted is minimal because, on the average, only one out of every 500 to 2,000 intoxicated drivers on the road will be stopped by police for violating the law; and many who are arrested will escape punishment through invoking legal technicalities.

Wagenaar recommends a whole series of difficult legislative and enforcement steps that need to be invoked together in order to reduce drinking-driving on a consistent basis. These include making driving with a blood alcohol level of .10 percent a per se violation; use of portable breath-testing equipment to provide immediate evidence; use of car-stopping check lanes to increase the public's perception of high likelihood of detection; swift adminis-trative suspension of driving licenses rather than through lengthy court battles; and elimination of plea bargaining. Improving the *consistency* of punishment also is needed to build better respect for drinking-driving laws. A recent seven-county pilot study by California's Department of Motor Vehicles found that in one county about 95 percent of first-time offenders received jail terms, while in another county only about 18 percent received similar treatment (Capps, 1986). Also, among those who were driving with suspended licenses (about 9 percent of those arrested), only 20 percent were convicted of driving with a suspended license.

Another recent drinking-driving research review, by Andrew Clayton (1986), reaffirms the importance of certainty of punish-ment. As Clayton shows, the general public has very little knowledge of the laws on alcohol-impaired driving and of the amount of alcohol it takes to reach a law-breaking level.

Many of those recommending a tougher, more comprehensive "systems" approach in coping with drunk driving have been very disappointed by what they consider the shallow recommendations of President Reagan's Presidential Commission on Drunk Driving. Although it was launched with much fanfare, its membership consisted largely of old-line NCA stalwarts or politicians and included two representatives of the alcohol industry itself. Predictably, therefore, it failed to recommend many new or stringent approaches. One reviewer (Mosher, 1985a, p. 239) said:

> The Report, despite the wide support and publicity that it generated, is seriously flawed. It relies primarily on strategies that are directed at individual behavior change—e.g. education, deterrence, treatment, and publicity campaigns. Research shows that these strategies, standing alone, have only a minimal long-term impact on the drunk driving problem. The Report fails to consider important new research on environmental factors affecting drunk driving, notably alcohol availability, price and tax policies, server intervention programs, alcohol advertising and transportation policies. These environmental strategies are a critical part of a comprehensive prevention policy and can greatly enhance the individual-based strategies relied on in the Commission Report.

Prevention Through Tax Increases and Marketing Controls

Much of the case for increases in alcohol taxes as a means of reducing alcohol-related problems has been presented in the preceding chapter, along with counterarguments from the alcohol industry that such increases would not accomplish their stated purpose, would be harmful to legitimate business interests, and would result in loss of tax revenues. Mosher and Beauchamp (1983) provide a summary of state-by-state tax rates for beer, wine, and liquor, which shows that the rates vary widely and inconsistently. From reviewing their own research and other studies, they recommend the following actions: (1) federal excise alcohol taxes should be raised substantially, with a doubling of the federal tax on distilled spirits; (2) beer and wine taxes should be raised to the same level as spirits (currently they are taxed at about 30 percent and 5 percent, respectively, of the tax on spirits); (3) tax rates should be indexed to the inflation rate, so as to keep the cost of alcohol at a constantly high level in relation to other goods; (4) state taxes on all alcohol should be raised substantially to compensate for a drop in state taxes of nearly 50 percent during the last thirty years in terms of real dollars; (5) there is little evidence that, for the vast majority of states, price competition across state borders is any serious threat to overall revenue and public health gains brought about by higher alcohol taxes, but states should coordinate their tax schedules to be as uniform as possible; and (6) the practice of setting low prices for alcohol on military bases (with large populations of potentially heavy-drinking young men) should be abandoned. They contend that these tax increases would cut consumption enough to reduce drinking problems and also would be equitable, because the primary burden of the raised taxes would fall on the approximately 9 percent of the drinking-age population that is now consuming fully two-thirds of the alcohol.

The alcohol lobbyists naturally are fighting any threatened increases in taxes as hard as they can. Whether their lobbying connections and substantial war chests can prevail over recent intensification of tax demands by private citizen groups remains to be seen. One group lobbying for taxes, the National Alcohol Tax Coalition, recently called on Congress to enact increases on alcohol excise taxes, which it said would generate $12 billion in new revenue, reduce consumption by an estimated 14 percent, and decrease the cost of alcohol problems by about $16.4 billion (Lewis, *Alcoholism Report,* Sept. 30, 1985).

Another such lobbying campaign goes by the acronym of SMART (Stop Marketing Alcohol on Radio and Television). The Center for Science in the Public Interest (CSPI) is spearheading this drive to ban all alcohol broadcast advertising or to require equal time for health messages. The *Newsweek* story summarizing some of these lobbying efforts was aptly named "Alcohol on the Rocks" (Poltz and others, 1984) because the last decade has seen a drop of more than 11 percent in liquor consumption and a consequent drop in profits. This article—like many others—pays tribute to the dramatic lobbying carried on by MADD (Mothers Against Drunk Driving). Of course, the alcohol industry is not yielding readily to these pressures: the same *Newsweek* article quoted a vice-president of Miller Brewing as saying, "There is no link whatsoever between advertising and alcohol abuse. They are just tilting at windmills" (p. 53).

However, the current pressure toward greater regulation of alcohol seems to be gathering strength as it goes along. A recent *Business Week* article (Moskowitz and Pave, 1985) concludes that Americans have overcome their postprohibition distaste for controlling other people's personal behavior. The article quotes Sanford Schwartz of the University of Missouri as saying, "I don't think the drinking-and-driving problem is significantly more serious than it was a decade ago. We're just wearing different spectacles. Society is saying, 'Hey, we're tired of getting killed by drunk drivers'" (p. 112). He added that business is losing patience with alcohol-caused losses in productivity and that the ordinary citizen's rising medical insurance costs can be blamed to a large extent on excessive drinking. The article also cites a national Harris Poll, which found that the proportion of those who supported raising the drinking age to twenty-one had risen in just two years from 70 percent to 85 percent, that some 65 percent would jail a drunk driver even if he caused no accident, and that 89 percent would lift the driver's license on the second arrest.

A recent World Health Organization study (Farrell, 1985) has compiled data from many Western countries indicating that increasing the price of alcohol relative to other consumer goods appears to reduce traffic injuries and deaths and cirrhosis deaths; increasing the minimum legal drinking age is associated with a reduction in traffic accidents, injuries, and deaths; and restricting the distribution of alcoholic beverages is accompanied by marked reductions in public drunkenness, alcohol-related violence, cirrhosis deaths, and alcohol-related hospital admissions.

Persistent Obstacles to Primary Prevention

There may be a general trend emerging toward public approval of increasing constraints against behavior that puts the general public at risk of financial loss and physical or emotional harm. Instances that come readily to mind include antismoking campaigns to protect nonsmokers from the harm or annoyance of cigarette smoke, and laws requiring cyclists to wear helmets and motorists to wear seat belts (and requiring special safety seats for infants in some states), so that there will be fewer accidents entailing high medical costs which are passed on to the general public. Certainly, people have strong feelings that drastic action should be taken against drinking drivers, to prevent them from injuring other people or themselves in costly accidents. Growing public awareness about the mounting costs of medical care may well serve to encourage future demand that the government "do something" to get those with alcohol problems earlier and more effective treatment.

Logically, public anxiety about drinking-driving and other alcohol problems, and about the mounting cost of medical care, should lead to a public demand for more and better primary prevention programs. However, prevention programs will continue to have hard sledding in America. Not only are we still very individualistic and thus prone to react strongly against any fancied incursions on our "right" to buy our favorite beer, wine, or liquor at what we consider reasonable prices, but the effectiveness of prevention programs is very hard to prove because there are so many conflicting variables that affect drinking behavior and thus have to be kept under control.

Further, primary prevention is not very appealing emotionally. We can understand the necessity of trying to save the lives of the very sick alcoholics in our midst. But it is hard to prove that a combination of controversial control measures has kept a countable number of potential victims out of trouble from alcohol. It is easy to count the numbers we have pulled out of the stream, but it is hard to count the numbers who would have fallen in if more effective control programs had not been adopted. Probably the most effective strategy for the advocates of control is a "salami" approach—keep slicing away slowly but steadily, never letting up on the pressure but not slicing away people's privileges so rapidly as to cause the type of counterreaction that led to repeal as a response to the excesses of prohibition.

At this time it is hard to predict whether the current good-health movement will continue to contribute to the effectiveness of primary prevention of alcohol problems. Certainly, its emphasis on adequate exercise, proper diet, sufficient rest and exercise, and avoidance of smoking is consistent with moderation in the use of alcohol. Unlike some other prevention programs, which stress sacrifice or deprivation, the good-health movement has the advantage of being positive in tone, with its emphasis on feeling good and being sexually attractive. This may help to counteract the seductive pressures in alcohol advertising to "go with the gusto" of hasty guzzling. But whether the government and the much-vaunted "private sector" will try hard enough to compete with the alcohol industry by launching effective good-health-oriented information and education campaigns long enough to make a real difference in values and lifestyles remains to be seen. The industry has the financial motivation to spend the money and exert its political clout to succeed in its marketing objectives, and at present the forces advocating stronger alcohol controls and primary prevention campaigns have little political backing. Again, it will take strong leadership, political organization, and dramatization of the tragedies and suffering caused by misuse of alcohol—such as high drinking-driving death rates—to win the wholehearted, long-term moral and financial support that will be needed to make a material improvement in the drinking behavior of the American public.

7

ⱲⱯⱲⱯⱲⱯⱲⱯⱲⱯⱲⱯ

How Well Do Alcohol Treatment Programs Work?

As we have seen in the preceding chapters, this last generation has witnessed a tremendous amount of activity in the cause of bringing the alcoholic into treatment and getting him or her more humane and effective care. Many more alcoholism clinics than ever before have been subsidized through state and federal funds. The concept of alcoholism as a disease has been sold to Congress and most courts, the medical profession (Niven, 1984), and the general public. These activities have led to a decriminalization of public drunkenness in many jurisdictions and evidently some reduction of the stigma attached to alcoholism. And most states now encourage insurance coverage for treatment of alcoholism. But still there remain the nagging questions: How well do alcoholism treatments work? Do they *really* work at all?

Diagnostic Criteria

Passing over the continuing disagreement in alcohology circles over whether alcoholism is a disease or a behavioral problem (as discussed in Chapter One), many will at least agree with

126

Schuckit (1973, p. 157), that "Alcohol abuse may become a primary illness, alcoholism, or a complication of other psychiatric processes, such as sociopathy. It is necessary to distinguish between the alcoholic who engages in a limited sphere of antisocial acts and the sociopath who abuses alcohol as part of his antisocial behavior, because the process and prognosis of these different varieties of alcoholism may be distinct." Pattison (1974) elaborates on the same theme by distinguishing five types of alcoholics: those of high social and psychological competence may benefit from psychotherapy; those of high social and psychological competence and high field dependence (susceptibility to immediate influences) should profit from AA; those with high social but low psychological competence may respond to supportive medical regimes; those of low social and high psychological competence may benefit from a combination of AA and social and vocational rehabilitation; but those of low social and psychological competence will probably require continuing supportive services and may not respond well to AA or to medical or psychological treatment. Straus (1983) stresses the need for a better understanding of how to distinguish between physiological and psychological dependence in the treatment of alcoholics: "Strategies are needed that give greater recognition to the unique combinations of biological, psychological, and sociocultural factors that are associated with an individual's problem drinking" (p. 16).

On the issue of deciding what patients will benefit from treatment, one special clinical problem in treating alcoholics is the "silting-up" phenomenon described by Richman (1978). That is, an alcoholism clinic starts out with a brand-new staff of physicians, nurses, and counselors with usually high morale; but after a few months, the clinic's limited facilities become "silted up" through repeated admissions of the same set of chronic alcoholics. This prevents admitting other patients who might benefit from treatment, and it occasions a rise in guilt and failure feelings on the part of the staff. A related difficulty in keeping staff efficiency and morale at a high level, Richman points out, is that "New programs are most successful in the hands of their innovators" (p. 10). The reformer's zeal soon wears out because of burnout when the clinic continues to be confronted by the failures who return home to roost until they are pushed out again.

Models of Treatment of Alcoholism

Kissin (1977) identifies five general models or types:

1. The medical model assumes that alcoholism is a disease and as such is most appropriately treated by a physician. Kissin's discussion of this model emphasizes the physician's use of tranquilizers or other medication.

2. The behavior modification model can involve aversive techniques (such as emetine given concurrently with alcohol to induce vomiting, with intent to get the patient to associate alcohol with nausea; or electric shock when drinking; or aversive-imagery retraining), or positive reinforcement techniques (including rewards through compliments or status enhancement of the patient upon refusal of alcohol). Kissin also mentions "systematic desensitization" as a behavior modification objective; in this approach relaxation or hypnosis is used to reduce the anxiety that is presumed to be conducive to drinking. Of the newer desensitization techniques—including transcendental meditation, yoga, acupuncture, biofeedback, and muscle relaxation—Kissin says, "The rationale and the possible mode of actions of these therapeutic modalities remain to be clarified" (p. 35).

A more recent discussion of behavior modification methods in the treatment of alcoholism by two specialists experienced in applying them (Miller and Hester, 1986c, p. 183) makes a good case for the application of covert sensitization (pairing aversive drinking scenes with imagery of one's own drinking) and community reinforcement (restructuring family, social, and job-related supports for controlled drinking or abstention).

The principles of reinforcement or operant conditioning would not be difficult for most of us to accept if we gave up our "free will" hangup that anyone with any moral fiber ought to be able to straighten up and fly right and quit harmful drinking once the damage is pointed out to the culprit. "Operant conditioning" simply means that immediately reinforced behavior tends to be repeated, whereas behavior that is rarely reinforced becomes extinguished over time. Albert Bandura's classic *Principles of Behavior Modification* (1969) describes the implications of operant conditioning theory for more effective treatment of alcoholism.

Specifically, alcohol acts as a reinforcer when it "solves" the drinker's problems. For example, social supports wither away because of the drinking; the drinker therefore resorts to more drinking to forget the loss of social supports and also seeks out other heavy drinkers for social reinforcement. Under such circumstances it is often more fruitful to find a way to intervene with immediate reinforcers (either positive ones such as praise, or negative ones such as electric shock) to break the cycle of injurious drinking than to try to find its real "cause." In any case, as Marlatt and Gordon (1985) have documented so abundantly, those who deal with alcoholics can expect frequent relapses into injurious drinking; it usually takes a great deal of patient, consistent application of social and other environmental supports to achieve consistent sobriety.

3. The psychological model, in Kissin's view, implies the standard psychotherapeutic techniques traditionally used to treat anxiety, depression, and inadequate personalities through psycho-analysis, group discussions, and social rehabilitation through reeducation.

4. The social model, in which social environments are seen as the primary influence in inducing alcoholism, emphasizes remedial measures that seek to bring about changes in the patient's environment.

5. The Alcoholics Anonymous model, as Kissin describes it, is very effective when it draws the recovering alcoholic into a single homogeneous social and cultural support group. It is also an experience in existential psychology, entailing confrontation, acceptance of reality, and emphasis on openness and honesty; and it also has many elements of the social model. Its main shortcoming is that its nonprofessional approach may neglect the individual's biomedical and psychological needs.

Most large-clinic treatment programs in America make use of many of these models. A physician ordinarily monitors the detoxification process; psychologists or psychiatrists may be called on to check for psychiatric or personality disorders that might need to be taken into account in treatment; and social workers may try to help the patient rebuild or modify his social or work environ-ment. And almost always, AA is on the scene to offer moral support and a fellowship that will attempt to help the patient maintain sobriety.

Ordinarily, any inpatient treatment will be limited to a few days unless there are unusual medical complications; and any outpatient treatment (usually in the form of attending counseling sessions) is ordinarily limited to six to eight weeks (this is about the maximum that will be paid for under insurance plans). Most of the outpatient treatment (if any) will be of a nonmedical counseling variety and primarily in the hands of paraprofessionals, such as AA members. Esther Walcott and Robert Straus discovered more than thirty years ago in a study of New York clinics that "the outstanding factor correlated with success was . . . the duration of the patient-clinic contact" (Walcott and Straus, 1952, p. 60); and a follow-up of about 474 patients from a Connecticut clinic showed improvements in the condition of nearly four-fifths of the patients who had made at least eleven outpatient visits or were still going to the clinic (p. 76). But Miller and Hester (1986b, p. 794) point out that length of stay can be influenced by many hard-to-control variables, such as the client's motivation, severity of the problems, socioeconomic stability, coercion, or appropriateness of the match between the client and the treatment. In other words, knowing that there is improvement with continued counseling is like knowing that birds are easy to catch if one sprinkles salt on their tails: the rub is that if a bird will sit still until its tail gets salted, that bird automatically will be easier to catch.

Measuring Effectiveness of Treatment

As Miller has pointed out (1986), alcoholism treatment in America today is dominated by the following assumptions: that alcoholism is an irreversible disease; that the only hope for an alcoholic is total and permanent abstinence; and that the most effective way to treat the disease is through the fellowship of AA, although group therapy and the use of disulfiram (Antabuse) are also assumed to be helpful. In the same article, Miller provides considerable documentation that *none* of these assumptions has been proved. He also notes (p. 113) that these assumptions are not shared in Europe, where a much greater emphasis is placed on psychosocial determinants of alcoholism.

Miller, editor of one of the most comprehensive recent reviews of research studies on the effectiveness of treatment (Miller and Hester, 1980), summarizes some of the findings he has made with Hester in a later publication (Miller and Hester, 1986a). They encountered many surprises in their review, centering around the fact that a great deal of research on effectiveness has been done but is being ignored in general treatment practice in America. Their review covers treatments based on the following principal components:

Pharmacotherapy. Much of the evidence they found difficult to evaluate, although antidepressants appeared to be helpful in recovery. They recommend against the routine imposition of disulfiram by alcohol offenders who come before the courts.

Psychotherapy and counseling. They found little or no evidence that these have a specific long-range impact on drinking behavior, perhaps because most such studies have not been well controlled.

Confrontation of alcoholics about their denial of problems. Found sometimes to produce negative results, such as resumed drinking or withdrawal from treatment, but useful when focused specifically on the client's health risks from drinking.

Alcoholics Anonymous. Little solid scientific evidence of effectiveness has been as yet uncovered, largely because hardly any well-controlled studies have been done on AA.

Marital and family therapy. "Mostly encouraging results."

Aversion therapies. Mixed results. Although there is some evidence that drug-induced nausea paired with drinking alcohol can be effective, it can raise ethical problems if done without appropriate informed consent.

Electric shock. Mixed results. It appears to be more effective in reducing consumption than in inducing abstinence.

Covert sensitization (pairing the showing of aversive scenes with imagining that one is drinking). Considerable evi-

dence of effectiveness in reducing drinking and promoting
abstinence. "With continued refinement in procedure, it
seems likely that aversive counterconditioning will
remain a valuable modality for inclusion in alcoholism
treatment programs" (p. 144).

Hypnosis. Hard to judge its effectiveness at present because
of lack of standardization of either the way it is administered or how the studies are conducted.

Regarding treatments with the objective of inculcating
controlled drinking, through training in behavioral self-control,
Miller and Hester report (1986a, p. 148) that "Controlled drinking
appears to be an attainable and successful goal for problem drinkers
who have not established significant degrees of dependence."

Many *broad-spectrum* approaches (including social skills
training, stress management training, and community reinforcement designed to restructure family, social, and vocational
reinforcements) proved to be effective. Of the community reinforcement approach, Miller and Hester say (p. 152): "If one were to judge
the effectiveness of alcoholism treatment methods based on the
strength of scientific support available for them, the community
reinforcement approach (CRA) would surely be at the top of the list.
A series of well-controlled studies have provided strong evidence
that this intervention has a powerful impact on alcohol use and
general adjustment. Yet the community reinforcement approach
remains little known and seldom used." This neglect of community
reinforcement is understandable in view of many therapists'
aversion to getting involved with a wide network of clients' families
and associates, who may be largely beyond the therapist's control
and who can require much unpaid time and effort to track down
and to enlist their cooperation.

In summing up their review of the effectiveness of treatment,
Miller and Hester (1986a, pp. 162–163) say: "American treatment of
alcoholism follows a standard formula that appears to be imper-
vious to emerging research evidence, and has not changed significantly for at least two decades"—the standard practice of treatment
being AA, alcoholism education, confrontation, disulfiram, group
therapy, and individual counseling. But they point to a rather

different set of practices as being of demonstrated merit: aversion therapies, behavioral self-control training, community reinforcement, marital and family therapy, social skills training, and stress management. They end their review chapter as follows (p. 163):

> In conclusion, we offer three basic principles as prudent guidelines in designing future alcoholism treatment programs. First, treatment programs, both voluntary and involuntary, should be composed of modalities supported by current research as having specific effectiveness, and consideration should be given to preferential funding of programs so constituted. Second, the first interventions offered should be the least intensive and intrusive, with more heroic and expensive treatments employed only after others have failed. Third, as research warrants, clients should be matched to optimal interventions based on predictors of differential outcomes. Clients should be informed participants in their own treatment planning process, and should be offered a range of plausible alternatives along with fair and accurate information on which to base a choice.

Two Classic Controversies on Treatment Effectiveness

In the 1970s the NIAAA attempted to assess the effectiveness of some of the alcoholism treatment programs that it sponsored directly, not only because it wanted to learn whether certain types of treatment work better than others but also because it wanted to show Congress that the expenditure of fairly substantial sums in treatment at NIAAA-sponsored clinics was paying off in relation to restoring people to productivity and in reducing medical and welfare costs in the long run. The NIAAA also gathered and publicized statistics prepared by organizations interested in establishing that their Employee Assistance Programs were cost-effective. Some of these indicated that up to 75 percent of employed persons who were treated under employee assistance insurance plans returned to normal productivity, at least for a time (Spicer and

Owen, 1985). However, these studies should be evaluated with skepticism because they were based on special populations of problem drinkers. These drinkers were still employed and thus had something to lose by not accepting management-recommended treatment. Moreover, they were hand-picked by employers who simply fired the worst risks and offered treatment for the best risks and most valued employees, or by employers who had above-average effectiveness in maintaining a work atmosphere and moral supports conducive to continued sobriety.

After the NIAAA had set up an elaborate system for reporting patients' status at intake and some time after treatment, it funded two large-scale studies of treatment effectiveness. The first contract, with Stanford Research International, called for a follow-up study of samples of clients from eight treatment centers funded by the NIAAA, interviewed eighteen months later. The Rand Corporation analyzed the data for the first report and then conducted the second follow-up four years after entry into treatment.

The first Rand report (Armor, Polich, and Stambul, 1976) was a *cause célèbre* throughout the world of alcohology, probably setting off more polemic fireworks than any other research report of its generation. Many detailed criticisms of this report were duly published in journals some time later (Roizen, 1977, 1987; Cahalan, 1977; Emrick, 1976; Peele, 1984). But the most bitter, immediate attacks on the report arose out of its clash with the ideological principles of the traditional alcoholism treatment establishment.

The major shock to hopeful readers of the initial Rand report was induced by the finding that a number of clinically defined alcoholics eighteen months after treatment had returned to what was represented by the authors as "normal drinking" without apparent medical or social consequences! This finding, which immediately drew a storm of protest from the NCA and allied groups, directly contradicted the central AA tenet that the true alcoholic never can resume "normal drinking." The report even used the term "remission" from alcoholism. (NCA/AA doctrine says that alcoholics may *appear* some of the time to be in remission but that they are never cured: "Once an alcoholic, always an alcoholic.")

After valiant year-long attempts by prominent NCA members to have the report suppressed altogether or drastically revised in its findings, it was finally released by Rand in June 1976 at a press conference. The report was greeted immediately by a ringing chorus of official denunciations from officers of the NCA at meetings and press conferences. NCA officials offered many criticisms of the research methods, including valid complaints about unrepresentative samplings of treatment agencies, use of insufficiently trained and supervised interviewers, and reliance on self-evaluation by alcoholics, whose memories are traditionally poor. They also charged that in measuring "improvements" Rand had settled for unacceptably high drinking levels; and they contended that the data provided no basis for claiming that alcoholics who were drinking socially were no more likely to relapse than those who were abstinent.

The NCA's major press conference criticizing the report revealed a level of anxiety and anger much higher than ordinary concern about fairness and balance in scientific reporting. NCA officials charged that many alcoholics would be "dying in the streets" as a direct result of the publication of the report, because it provided a graspable excuse for the alcoholic to resume drinking. A director of the community services department of a large labor union was even quoted in a press release as saying, "We feel that scientific speculation about tentative findings should be confined to scientific seminars and professional journals. . . . After all, the people's right to know does not mean the people's right to be confused— especially when it is a matter of life and death" (Cahalan, 1977, p. 18).

Embarrassed by the controversy (though privately pleased that the first Rand report had found a 70 percent "improvement" rate in treated alcoholics), NIAAA officials anxiously awaited the outcome of the second Rand report, on the status of alcoholism clients four years after treatment (Polich, Armor, and Braiker, 1980). The Rand social scientists in their follow-up study mended some of the conceptual and communication flaws in their first survey; and the questions about drinking behavior concentrated more heavily on the alcoholism establishment's criterion of "dependence." In addition, former patients were questioned about drinking during a longer period (six months, as against one month in the first study).

This tightening up of criteria of improvement reduced the figure on improvement from the 70 percent of the first study (conducted eighteen months after initiation of treatment) to below 40 percent showing no symptoms, consequences, or heavy drinking. Only 7.5 percent of the subjects said that they maintained abstinence for the whole four-and-a-half-year period; 51 percent had been back for treatment again at the same center, and 24 percent (partially overlapping the 51 percent) had received alcoholism treatment elsewhere.

As reported by Room in his succinct review of the second study (1980, p. 356):

> The picture of the "natural history" of a treatment cohort which emerges is much sadder and wiser than in the earlier Report. The earlier Report had concluded that "clients of NIAAA treatment centers show substantial improvement on a number of outcome indices. The relative rate of improvement for males is about 70 per cent for those outcomes most closely tied to the alcoholism syndrome." The new Report notes that "although there is frequent improvement, there is also frequent relapse and much instability." While a considerable improvement is still found between the clients' condition at admission to treatment and at any point thereafter, the improvement is regarded in a much more skeptical light. It is possible that the period before admission to treatment was a time of extreme drinking problems for many of the alcoholics in the sample. If so, one would expect those alcoholics to improve substantially at any later follow-up, simply because of natural fluctuations or statistical "regression to the mean."

Another study on the effects of treatment (Sobell and Sobell, 1972) was to cause great confusion and resentment among adherents of the AA principle that alcoholics never can resume normal drinking. It was reported at about the same time as the initial Rand survey, although, unlike the response to the Rand reports, the furor occasioned by the findings has not as yet died down.

The Sobells, then graduate students, compared the effects of two treatment modalities on alcoholism patients at Patton State Hospital in Southern California. One group of twenty patients received the standard AA-oriented treatment, which emphasized total abstinence; another group went through a behavior modification program in scheduled drinking sessions involving mild electric shocks if they drank more than a prescribed "moderate" limit. Patients in the controlled-drinking group were found to function with fewer problems than those in the traditional abstention-advocating treatment group. This finding was very upsetting to AA adherents, particularly since there had been a mounting tide of journal articles (as summarized by Roizen, 1987) citing largely anecdotal evidence, much of it from outside the United States, indicating that a small but significant number of those treated at alcoholic clinics were later able to resume apparently normal drinking.

Mary Pendery, an alcoholism counselor in San Diego and a strong advoacte of abstinence consonant with AA teachings, and Irving Maltzman, her former psychology professor at the University of California at Los Angeles, tried in 1973 to get access to the records of the former patients in the study. The Sobells refused to reveal the names of the subjects on ethical grounds. The conflict dragged on for several years, and finally Pendery gained access to the hospital files without the Sobells' consent and conducted interviews with the former patients in the controlled-drinking group (she did not follow up those in the traditional-treatment group). Her findings, finally published in the prestigious journal *Science* (Pendery, Maltzman, and West, 1982), were that "most subjects trained to do controlled drinking failed from the outset to drink safely. The majority were rehospitalized for alcoholism treatment within a year after their discharge from the research project" (p. 169).

The conflict between the Sobells and Pendery, Maltzman, and West fast escalated into a television and newspaper brouhaha, which culminated in allegations and counterallegations that have not fully subsided at this writing, five years after the *Science* article.

In the interim, at the behest of the Sobells, the Addiction Research Foundation of Toronto (where the Sobells are now working) appointed an outside panel of investigators, who, after examining the available evidence, concluded that there was no reasonable doubt concerning the Sobells' scientific or personal integrity (Dickens and others, 1982). Several psychologists or sociologists (notably Marlatt, 1983; and Roizen, 1987) have drawn very much the same conclusion: that, while there were methodological flaws in the Sobells' work, it was legitimate for them to try to find a means of possible improvement of the lot of the many alcoholics who just will not accept the traditional total-abstinence treatment methods.

For more details on the Sobell/Pendery controversy, the reader should turn to the Marlatt and Roizen reviews mentioned above. The conflict has been a most unseemly one because of the personal level of the attacks and counterattacks and because this emotional washing of alcoholism treatment linen in public has been the wrong kind of embarrassment to the whole field of alcoholism treatment research.

The field of alcohology *deserves* to be embarrassed—over the failure to insist on more demonstrably effective methods of treating alcoholics and to establish commonly agreed-upon standards of assessing the effectiveness of treatment. Some of the problem arises because there is no agreement in all quarters on what "alcoholism" really is. We can all agree on what constitutes cancer or tuberculosis, or even depressive or manic-depressive states; but experts are still arguing over what exactly alcoholism is and how it might be treated. And much of the problem stems from a personal emotional attachment to a particular point of view.

For example, the Pendery, Maltzman, and West team was so strongly convinced of the essential evil in conditioning alcoholics to drink moderately, rather than abstaining altogether, that they could not see the Sobell study as being other than an outright fraud (as Maltzman charged in a *New York Times* interview, June 28, 1982). And the Sobells—as members of the liberal 1970s youthful, enthusiastic reference group of behavioral psychologists—were so eager to try out their techniques on a group of unfortunates who seemed unable to adhere to the stringent demands of a total-abstinence regimen that they too quickly accepted temporary improvements as evidence of more long-lasting behavior changes. Of course, hindsight achieves the 20-20 level more often than foresight; so it is easy to say that the Sobells "should have known" that chronic alcoholics from a state hospital are extremely poor risks for successful treatment of any variety, because they would have used up all their social and financial resources before they arrived at Patton State Hospital.

Abstinence Versus Moderation: Attempts to Bridge the Gap

A number of clnical psychologists are beginning to bridge the gap between the clinicians who are tolerant of controlled drinking, as an interim option for those who will not accept immediate total abstinence, and those who adhere to the more traditional AA model of insisting on total abstinence. Notable among these are the authors of the five papers comprising Volume 1, No. 4, of the new journal *Drugs and Society*.

Nathan and McCrady explicitly state that "behavioral treatment methods with abstinence as a goal and behavioral treatment methods with moderation as a goal share important theoretical, historical, and methodological assumptions, even as they differ in strategy, tactics and ultimate goals" (p. 110). They also emphasize the desirability of social support systems such as AA: "Any client can access this system, which is constructed to provide 24-hour support, on an individual basis. The client attempting to abstain from alcohol use will be strongly reinforced for each day of success, will be exposed to powerful peer models of success, will be given advice from peers on how to think, feel, and behave in a variety of alcohol-related situations, will have the opportunity to make friends with non-drinkers, and will have the names and phone numbers of people who can assist in crises, whenever they occur" (p. 127). They also mention therapists' self-interest in promoting abstinence: "The therapist who works with a controlled drinking goal might be liable to civil suits were the client to be injured or injure someone else as a result of continued drinking" (p. 124).

In this same issue of *Drugs and Society*, Mark and Linda Sobell, in spite of their controversial behavior modification experiments to induce moderate drinking in chronic alcoholics, clearly recommend that abstinence should be the primary goal of treatment: "A robust rationale [for abstention] would involve the belief that control *is possible,* and that the reason for not drinking is that there is inordinate risk, assuming the client's history justified that conclusion, that the drinking might get out of hand and result in serious health or social problems. . . . If the treatment goal is to be abstinence, clients should be encouraged to develop a belief system that can accommodate and rationalize the control that at times they may manifest over drinking and can serve simultaneously to motivate them to continue to be committed to achieving abstinence" (p. 27).

Another plea for abstinence as a goal, and for more social reinforcements for recovering alcoholics, is made in this same issue by Foy and Rychtarik, reporting the results of ten years of working with severely dependent alcoholics in VA hospitals. None of their subjects who were drinking moderately at the end of the first follow-up year was able to maintain moderation over five or six years. They believe that lack of planned aftercare and follow-up after the first year may have been an important influence in this negative outcome.

In his methodological article in the same issue, John Taylor reviews various studies which warrant the conclusion that at least some alcoholics can achieve the goal of moderate drinking. However, he emphasizes that the preferred goal should be abstinence, so that the therapist can avoid personal responsibility for the consequences of drinking, which might have been avoided if the patient had been abstinent, and for ethical reasons: "There are few treatments in medicine in which a treatment is undertaken simply because the patient doesn't like the alternative, but preferred, treatment" (p. 91).

Miller agrees that abstinence might well be the wisest ultimate goal for chronic alcoholics, but he draws our attention to the fact that a great many alcoholics may never seek out treatment because they are given no alternatives to cold-turkey abstention: "Clients coming to our controlled-drinking clinics have frequently told us that they had never sought prior treatment because they knew they would be told they had to abstain, and that they were relieved to learn of a clinic where goal options were considered.

Despite this entry bias, the vast majority of our clients have chosen for themselves (from among options) a treatment goal that states, 'I think that total abstinence may be necessary for me, but I am not sure. If I knew that controlled drinking were impossible for me, then I would want to stop drinking completely'" (p. 139). In Miller's long-range follow-ups, about the same number of his clients wound up abstaining as continued to drink in reduced fashion (about one-third each); and the abstainers often said that their experience in the controlled-drinking program made them aware of the seriousness of their alcohol problems and ultimately of their need to abstain.

Miller's article ends with a plea for tolerance for both controlled drinking and abstinence as treatment goals (p. 147):

> In the heat of "abstinence versus controlled drinking goal" debates it is easy to lose sight of the fact that our ultimate goal is always the same: to alleviate problems and suffering related to alcohol use, and to prevent such problems from reemerging. No one approach can truthfully claim preeminence as a means to this end. Both abstinent and problem-free drinking outcomes occur (with and without intervention), and both are to be regarded as successful realizations of the common goal. A worthy search now is for greater knowledge of what methods work best with which individuals, and for better methods to motivate at-risk drinkers to alter their hazardous use patterns before inflicting greater damage upon themselves and others.

These overtures from behavioral psychologists for a continuing dialogue and reconciliation of perspectives on goals for treatment of alcoholics are healthy signs. They should be tolerated by those who now insist that abstinence should be the only goal; otherwise, those who are now staying away because immediate abstention is demanded may never be brought into treatment. Fortunately, some abstentionist AA-oriented therapists are also showing more flexibility concerning the need for more research on

how best to bring about recovery from alcohol, as reflected in
Stephanie Brown's *Treating the Alcoholic* (1985). But there is still
a great need for the various types of professionals and paraprofessionals involved in alcoholism treatment—physicians, nurses,
social workers, psychologists, counselors, and others—to learn how
to work together to provide the right kinds of reinforcements for
their clients' recovery from alcoholism. Necessary steps in the
integration of treatment teams are discussed in Chapter Nine.

Treatment Effectiveness and Social Supports

In answer to our question "How well do alcohol treatments
work?" most therapists will agree that there are no quick routes to
recovery from alcoholism; and most effective teatments today offer
very similar combinations of detoxification (where necessary),
preliminary counseling, and involvement of the client's family in
the recovery process. But it also can be said that apparently *any* type
of treatment works to *some* extent; and often the sufferer works his
or her way out of drinking problems without *any* formal treatment.
One can get "improvement" rates varying from 5 to 80 percent,
depending on the criteria for improvement (for example, long-term
abstention or improved work performance),whether the treatment
was actively sought by the client or administered under duress, and
the consistency and quality of the social supports provided during
the rehabilitation process.

Earlier, I cited Miller and Hester's finding that the most
effective reinforcements for either abstention or moderation in
drinking are *social* reinforcements—including the approbation and
good will of loved ones and associates. After all, drinking is very
"social" in that society has enjoyed and endured it for a very long
time; and Roizen (1981) has found that people in various subcultures have very definite opinions about what is (or is not) appropriate drinking behavior to be tolerated or reinforced. AA itself
concentrates almost exclusively on social reinforcements. AA
adherents insist that their mutual caring for each other and
watching over each other is what keeps them from drifting back into
drinking. Thus, in all alcoholism treatments, we should be using
the same firm yet kindly social reinforcements that the recovering

problem drinker can get from his or her family or friends; but how long will it take us in America to learn how to do this right?

As discussed in the next chapter, the costs of treatment for alcoholism have skyrocketed along with the general escalation of medical costs attributable to high inflation in the 1970s, public expectations of being insured against any misfortune that might befall, inflated expectations of what the medical profession can cure readily, and a tendency to sue if anything goes wrong—with consequent practice of "defensive medicine" by physicians and hospitals through overprescribing expensive tests and overlengthy periods of hospitalization. The cost squeeze on alcoholism treatments, now finally being applied by the government and by corporations concerned over their insurance costs, is causing considerable distress within the treatment confraternity and resulting in inadequate treatment in the short run. However, the squeeze may well result in improvements in the long run. In order to stay in business, care providers will have to learn how to channel clients more effectively into the types of treatment needed and how to develop ethically responsible outreach methods that will bring clients into treatment before they have lost all their social and economic supports. And above all, those who treat alcoholics will have to learn how to put together treatment teams that use the skills of physicians, psychologists, nurses, social workers, and counselors cost-effectively while still providing the compassionate human caring essential for recovery from alcoholism. These issues will be discussed further in Chapter Nine.

8

Economics and Management
of Treatment

Great confusion and uncertainty about the funding of alcoholism treatment still prevails several years after the federal government imposed its new Medicare guidelines in an attempt to control skyrocketing costs. Leonard Saxe of Boston University, senior author of the Office of Technology Assessment (OTA) report summarized later in this chapter (Saxe and others, 1983), said a couple of years later (Payer, 1985) that the proposed prospective payment system in Medicare is "potentially disastrous for alcoholism." He went on to say that, although the proposed prospective payments for the diagnosis-related groups (DRGs) under which alcoholism falls were intended to reduce unnecessary health care costs, they were actually creating confusion and hardship without necessarily saving money in the long run. In Saxe's view, the DRG approach, which is organized around the treatment of one episode of one disease, is not well adapted to alcoholism because patients readmitted to the hospital within six months would have to be treated without further payment to the hospital; as a result, many alcoholics would be turned out on the streets again. Moreover, although the basing of DRG payments on the average length of stay for a certain type of ailment might work well enough for suburban hospitals, whose patients are living in an atmosphere of some social

144

stability, it would not work at all for inner-city hospitals with a much more unstable alcoholic population in their catchment area.

Both profit and nonprofit private alcoholism treatment providers, according to Korcok (1985b), were up in arms over what they regarded as an arbitrary imposition in 1983 of DRGs on hospital care for alcoholism by the Health Care Financing Administration (HCFA), which relied primarily on Medicare data more appropriate for short-term detoxification than for longer-term rehabilitation. The HCFA imposed DRG 436 (alcohol dependence), which carried a geometric mean length of stay of only 8.1 days, whereas most treatment providers held out for a more costly 28-day regimen. Intensive lobbying by a combination of nonprofit and for-profit treatment centers forced the HCFA to extend the alcoholism treatment exemptions for one more year, to the fall of 1986; and then again to October 1987; and the battle for reimbursement for longer-term treatment is still continuing.

At this writing, the hassles concerning Medicare and Medicaid funding for alcoholism treatment still have not been resolved; and since payments under these systems are likely to set a standard for all types of payments for alcoholism treatment, such federal funding inevitably becomes a source of real concern, not only to the alcoholics and those responsible for them but also to every taxpayer. Joseph Califano, Jr., secretary of health, education and welfare under President Carter and one of the chief architects of Medicare, has many scathing (but constructive) comments about our American health care nonsystem. These comments, which are immediately relevant to the field of alcohol treatment, appear in his book *America's Health Care Revolution* (1986).

He believes that the initial Medicare plan led to runaway costs because of lack of incentives for cost containment; that the DRG system of prospective payments does cut costs and has the serious limitations and inequities pointed out in the OTA report; and that the health maintenance organization (HMO) approach, which pays HMOs on a yearly basis for all medically related care, is the right way to go. HMOs are supposed to be paid to keep people well, rather than concentrating only on those ailments for which the DRG system pays the most money. But, as discussed later,

HMOs are not as yet generally effective in offering alcoholism treatment.

Califano's views on the whole health care system are worthy of close attention because of his candor about federal programs that he initiated and his forthrightness in telling how he has managed to bring down the Chrysler Corporation's employee health care costs drastically within a very short time. At this point let us look at just one of his comments about alcoholism and other addictions (p. 70):

> *Addiction* is one of America's overarching health problems, yet it's hard to find out much about it in medical school classrooms. Fifty million Americans are hooked on cigarettes, 3.5 million of them under the age of 17; 13 million are addicted to alcohol or abuse it; millions more are addicted to heroin, cocaine, marijuana, tranquilizers, barbiturates, sedatives, and a variety of other pills. . . .
>
> Alcoholism and alcohol abuse together are the number-four disease in America, right behind the big three of heart and circulatory diseases, cancer, and respiratory diseases. If current trends persist, alcoholism and alcohol abuse will outpace the others at the turn of the century. In most large cities, up to 40 percent of hospital emergency-room admissions and 25 percent of inpatient admissions are alcohol-related. Alcoholism has been an enigma for medical research, but we know two things for sure: prevention is the most effective cure, and the earlier alcohol abuse is detected, the greater the likelihood of arresting the disease. Yet most medical schools devote less than 1 percent of classroom time to prevention and treatment of alcoholism over the four-year curriculum, and medical training tends to neglect teaching doctors how to spot alcohol abusers.

Third-Party Payments for Treatment

A Booz, Allen, and Hamilton 1978 report revealed (p. 70) that in 1977 governments (federal, state, and local) provided two-thirds of the money spent on alcoholism treatment. Private third-party payments, insurance, and donations provided for 22 percent; and client fees and miscellaneous sources accounted for 11.3 percent. Thus, only a small amount of the alcoholism treatment of record is being paid for on a direct fee-for-service basis by patients or their families. These figures help us understand federal concern about the need to do a better job of containing alcoholism treatments costs.

In setting up the new Medicare guidelines, the federal government attempted to tighten the criteria for reimbursement for medically based inpatient services while increasing the availability of reimbursements for outpatient treatment in hospitals and free-standing clinics. In their discussion of these guidelines, the OTA analysts (Saxe and others, 1983) recommended that the alcoholism treatment field come up with more systematic specification of what types of patients would be best served by which of the available treatment modalities.

Specifically, they pointed out that, under Medicare, alcoholism—when treated as (or in conjunction with) a psychiatric disorder—would warrant payment for up to ninety days' hospital care in each benefit period, with $304 deductible and 25 percent copayment after sixty days as well as a lifetime reserve of up to sixty days with a 50 percent copayment. Supplementary medical insurance under Part B of Medicare provided partial coverage for outpatient services, with no limit for physicians' services performed while a patient was in the psychiatric ward of a general hospital. The Medicare program at that time funded only health care providers who were physicians or other health care professionals under the direct supervision of a physician; therefore, many non-acute-care facilities and treatment centers offering non-physician-based alcoholism treatment were not eligible for reimbursement under Medicare. (The NIAAA had been funding these directly until treatment funding was turned over to the states through block grants in the early 1980s.)

Most medical care administrators will agree in principle that some form of maximum prospective payments is necessary if costs are to be kept within any limits at all. The DRGs have been in a continuous state of overhaul in recent years, because of scientific differences of opinion on its conceptual underpinnings and because

of complaints that some features are unfair or arbitrary. Development of the DRGs for alcoholism has been influenced by the
National Council on Alcoholism's successful attempts to get alcoholism accepted as a disease (Criteria Committee, National Council
on Alcoholism, 1972) and the American Psychiatric Association's
attempts (1980) to get alcoholism included in the health care system.
The DRG system was developed to set payment rules for all varieties
of conditions treatable under Medicare.

An excellent history of the evolution of the federal DRG
prepayment principles and rules for medical care in general appears
in a lengthy *Newsweek* article by Easterbrook (1987). A fair amount
of clinical research and assessment of medical opinions has gone
into the evolution of the DRG system over the years (Guze,
Goodwin, and Crane, 1969; Edwards and Gross, 1976). The history
of the DRGs for alcoholism is reviewed in detail by Jacobson (1983),
who emphasizes the need for a continuing evolution to meet
criticisms. Halikas (1983) agrees with Jacobson, saying, "His
appropriate caution is that we, the investigators in the field, have
allowed a theoretical concept, that alcoholism is a disease, to
become fossilized and axiomatic prematurely" (p. 374). "It may be
of secondary importance, or even of no importance, whether there
is one, two, three, a hundred, or no 'alcoholisms' as separate
definable diseases. What is of practical importance is the ability to
characterize specific conditions in describable, reproducible behavioral terms that communicate clearly what population is being
spoken of" (p. 373).

The origins and evolution of medical definitions of alcoholism are discussed in detail in two papers by Caetano (1985 and
1987a). As he reports, there is still controversy over the formulation
of criteria for alcoholism—in particular, whether to include signs
of social and occupational malfunctioning in addition to symptoms
of withdrawal or physiological tolerance. But, at present writing,
the federal DRG rules still include both sets of criteria—thereby
conforming pretty closely to the Jellinek definition of gamma
alcoholism, which has been advocated by the NCA for years.
However, because of pressure from government funding sources to
limit payments for treatment, as well as continuing scientific
disputes over the disease status of alcoholism, the DRG criteria

probably will be narrowed and sharpened in the near future, to rule out other than physiologically based symptoms.

Taube, Lee, and Forthofer (1984) believe that the DRGs' limiting of Medicare payments for alcoholism will need to be modified to enable psychiatrists to participate effectively. Another hotly contested issue is the extent to which payments for alcoholism treatment would give priority to in-hospital as against free-standing (independent) facilities (Lewis, *Alcoholism Report,* March 31, 1985).

In the *Federal Register* for June 10, 1985, the goverment published a new set of proposed rules for Medicare hospital prospective payments. Although, according to a 1985 survey, most alcohol and drug agencies regarded the DRG approach as a step in the right direction, there was much criticism of specifics (Lewis, *Alcoholism Report,* July 16, 1985). The National Association of Alcoholism Treatment Programs, contending that Medicare over-paid detoxification services and underpaid rehabilitation, asked for more cost-benefit studies. Concerned about potential cuts in funding of alcoholism treatment, the Alcohol and Drug Problems Association, the Comprehensive Care Corporation (which was against the original DRGs in August 1983), the NCA, and the National Association of State Alcohol and Drug Abuse Directors (NASADAD) all contended that the application of DRG plans to alcoholism probably would lead to less effective treatment. Typical was the NASADAD view (expressed by Lewis, *Alcoholism Report,* July 16, 1985, p. 22): "As now proposed, the DRGs could lead to the closure of rehabilitation services units and to the opening of units that provide only detoxification services. . . . This would keep open a revolving door for alcoholics and would also be very costly in the long run."

Serious conflicts over the way in which treatment of alcoholics is to be paid for are bound to continue for a long time, not only because a great deal of money is at stake but also because the presently planned DRG prospective payment approach probably will intensify the competition among the various treatment providers (physicians as against psychologists and other types of counselors, hospitals against nonhospital settings). The situation is further exacerbated by the fact that there is as yet no unanimity concerning the definition of alcoholism and how it is to be treated.

Strong pressure by the NIAAA in the 1970s led to the rapid growth in third-party payments for alcoholism treatment. As of June 1986, thirty-seven states had legislation either mandating or permitting alcoholism coverage for employees by their organizations (Butynski, telephone communication, June 18, 1986). The case for occupational alcoholism coverage as being cost-effective was covered at a fairly early stage by the pioneering book *Spirits and Demons at Work* (Trice and Roman, 1972). Schramm and Archer (1982) have reviewed three types of evaluations that have been made of employee assistance programs: outcome assessments, monitoring studies, and evaluations of economic efficiency. They report that "The vast majority of impact evaluations conducted to date have reported high rates of success attributable to occupational alcohol programs, on a wide range of outcome criteria" (p. 203). They summarize the results of many outcome studies as follows (p. 205):

> In general, companies that have adopted alcoholism programs have reported success rates ranging between 50 and 70 percent, with an average success rate of 66 percent for industry nationwide. . . . By contrast, a review of 22 evaluative studies of alcoholic treatment in nonwork settings revealed success rates ranging from 4 to 75 percent, with the majority of programs (interquartile range) averaging from 18 to 35 percent. . . . If success is measured by rehabilitation (rather than simply job retention), it would appear that company programs have success rates of about 50 percent, compared with 20 percent for State hospital programs, and 10 percent directed at police-court inebriates. Moreover, compared with patients referred through other types of mechanisms, occupational alcohol programs tend to refer problem drinkers at earlier stages in the course of their problem, as evidenced by shorter treatment history, younger age at referral, lower levels of impairment at intake, and greater social and economic stability.

Another instance of successful occupational alcoholism programs is the one in Yugoslavia reported a generation ago by Vladimir Hudolin (1969) at an international alcoholism conference in Washington. Yugoslavia applied an all-encompassing program in which an alcoholic's workmates, supervisors, and family worked together in a concerted effort to modify the alcoholic's environment and attitudes, in order to reduce temptations to drink. The alcoholics themselves held frequent therapeutic meetings "where the alcoholics function as equal members with therapeutic team members, including a general practitioner, psychiatrist, psychologist, social worker, and nurse. . . . It seems to us that this particular method of treatment—clubs combined with group treatment methods in a therapeutic community—contributes essentially to further progress in this field." This sounds exactly like a synthesis of AA methods plus the more intensive kinds of psychiatric/psychological treatment—a combination still relatively rare in American practice.

The Social Treatment Model

The "social model" is based largely on the traditions of the halfway house movement. It appears gradually to be coming into its own in the field of alcoholic rehabilitation, despite considerable opposition by for-profit hospitals. As popularized at several locations in California, notably by Robert O'Briant, M.D., at Stockton (O'Briant and Lennard, 1973) and later in San Francisco, the social model consists essentially of detoxification and extended care in a residential setting—usually a large, old-fashioned home with rooms for fifteen to twenty-five people on a sometimes crowded basis, several rooms quiet enough to facilitate detoxification without undue risk of DT seizures, and a living room large enough to hold discussion meetings. Clients usually are scheduled for a four- to six-week stay. There is usually a nurse in residence and a physician on call for emergencies. Most of the counseling is performed by AA members; in addition, a client who is on his way to recovery may help newer clients by sharing his experiences with them.

One signal advantage of the social treatment model is its relative inexpensiveness compared to in-hospital detoxification. In a recent demonstration conducted by the NIAAA and the Health Care Financing Administration in six states involving some 110 nonhospital providers, inpatient detoxification costs averaged $88.41 a day, compared to several hundred dollars in regular hospital settings (Lewis, *Alcoholism Report,* Oct. 31, 1985). Figures on San Diego County detoxification costs in a new demonstration showed an average cost of $336 per day in hospital settings, in contrast to $52.86 in social model residential settings; and costs of inpatient rehabilitation after detoxification ran $262 a day in the hospitals, as against $16.59 in social model settings (Zimmerman, 1986).

Closely allied to the social treatment model is the "community model," which has primary prevention implications as well as emphasizing the early identification of alcohol problems. In the alcohol programs directed by Al Wright in Los Angeles County, in San Diego by Robert Reynolds, and in Salinas by Martin Dodd, staff workers go out into the community to work with the agencies (including the schools, churches, health and mental health agencies, voluntary organizations, and the police and courts) that are in a position to influence community attitudes and practices and that come into daily contact with those who are high-risk candidates for drinking problems. Wright and Dodd reason that this kind of outreach to get the community actively involved in prevention is the only way to begin coping with our society's creation of new alcoholics faster than they possibly can be treated.

At a San Diego meeting held in February 1986 under the auspices of the University of California, San Diego, Daniel Lettieri, research psychologist with the NIAAA, spoke of the social model recovery process as "the wave of the future," in line with the report of the congressional Office of Technology Assessment (OTA), which concluded that hospital treatment for alcoholism showed no more effectiveness than any other kind of treatment (Saxe and others, 1983). This conclusion is consistent with the more recent extensive analysis of treatment effectiveness by Miller and Hester (1986b). The conclusions in the abstract of the Miller-Hester article (1986b, p. 794) are sweeping ones:

Although uncontrolled studies have yielded mixed findings, 26 controlled comparisons have consistently shown no overall advantage for residential over nonresidential settings, for longer over shorter inpatient programs, or for more intensive over less intensive interventions in treating alcohol abuse. Predictor data suggest that intensive treatment may be differentially beneficial for more severely deteriorated and less socially stable individuals. The outcome of alcoholism treatment is more likely to be influenced by the content of interventions than by the settings in which they are offered. Third-party reimbursement policy should discourage the use of intensive residential models for addressing alcohol abuse when more cost-effective alternatives are available, and should reinforce the use of research-supported treatment methods regardless of setting. Such policy priorities run directly counter to the current practices and financial interests of many for-profit providers.

Another comparison, of alcoholics randomly assigned to either extended inpatient hospital treatment or brief hospitalization for detoxification and then outpatient counseling, found little difference in health, abstinence, and job losses for the two groups after one year. Understandably, costs for the group with a brief hospital stay were significantly lower (McCrady and others, 1986).

At the February 1986 San Diego meeting, Ripley Forbes, staff member of the House Subcommittee on Health and the Environment, said that the cost squeeze under the Gramm-Rudman-Hollings bill underscores the importance of the potential contribution of social model detoxification and rehabilitation to cost containment. Commenting on the rise in numbers of for-profit hospitals (which are aggressively going out after the alcoholism treatment market) from 420 to 890 between 1977 and 1984, Forbes advised those advocating social model treatment, "If you think the federal government can set precedents, can set trends, and if you think the spread of social model programs can be enhanced by the federal government recognizing those programs for purposes of Medicare, I urge you to get involved in that process—and not get involved as partners to the hospitals" (quoted in Zimmerman, 1986, p. 12).

Trends in Alcoholism Treatment Economics

For-profit hospitals have more than doubled in numbers in the last decade, with important implications for the treatment of alcoholism. While the number of alcoholism treatment units and the number of patients served actually decreased just prior to 1983, in three years there was a 48 percent growth in the number of proprietary units run on a profit-making basis (National Institute on Alcohol Abuse and Alcoholism, 1983/84). The growth of for-profit treatment centers is likely to bring its own mix of merits and demerits. On the one hand, the strong advertising and publicity programs of for-profit establishments are likely to bring more alcoholics into treatment. On the other hand, a three-year inquiry by a special committee appointed by the Institute of Medicine (1986) warns that for-profit centers may need new safeguards to protect the patients from the business self-interest of physicians who might cut corners on treatment to increase their share of the profits.

Private health insurance payments for alcoholism treatment increased 106.8 percent between 1979 and 1982. The increase probably is caused by the increasing availability of third-party payments as more states have continued to make insurance for alcoholism treatment mandatory (National Institute on Alcohol Abuse and Alcoholism, 1983/84). Korcok (1985b) tells of a report prepared by John Noble of the NIAAA for a meeting of state alcoholism and drug abuse directors. Noble cited American Hospital Association survey figures of a 99 percent expansion in private, not-for-profit beds allocated for alcoholism/chemical dependency patients between 1978 and 1983, and a 386 percent increase in bed capacity in *for-profit* hospitals during that span.

For-profit hospitals have increased their alcoholism treatment revenues sharply by a combination of improved organization and marketing and aggressive advertising in television, radio, and print media. An article in *Esquire,* "Alcoholics Not So Anonymous" (Kagan, 1985), focuses on Comprehensive Care Corporations (CompCare), which offers packaged CareUnits to community hospitals as outside contract programs. The units provide the treatment staff of counselors, psychologists, a program manager, and a medical director (M.D.); and the hospital provides the beds, nurses, and other services. CompCare pioneered in marketing directly to alcoholics and their families. Its principal competitors (Hospital Corporation of America, Charter Medical Corporation, Raleigh Hills Hospitals, and Recovery Centers of America) are now following similar organizational and marketing strategies.

Modern marketing methods are also being adopted by some of the smaller recovery homes. One instance is Vista de la Vida, a posh residence in the rolling hills of Marin County, California, which provides a social/medical treatment program for alcoholism and chemical dependency (Watson, 1986). The owner/manager, Ron Brandes, himself a recovering alcoholic who had been a general manager of a chain of hotels, has as clients such major West Coast corporations as Bank of America, Wells Fargo, Bechtel, Chevron, Lockheed, and TWA, who send patients to him under their third-party insurance programs. Brandes has a staff of ten, including two M.D.s, one registered nurse, and two counselors. In 1985 they treated sixty-five patients, 93 percent of whom were men, of an average age of forty-seven. Average length of stay was twenty-eight days, and the average cost $7,000—which Brandes claims is as much as 50 percent below hospital treatment costs; and he says that one of his clients, "a major company in the Bay Area, figures that for every dollar it spends on executive treatment it recovers $10 in lost time" (p. 29).

As Califano says in his book (1986), corporations and government units are getting increasingly restive about the costs of alcoholism treatment, and the treatment facilities very soon will have to modify their practices drastically to stay within the new cost constraints. Many kinds of innovations to meet this need are in the pipeline. One is the Oregon law in effect since July of 1984, which provides insurance benefits for the first time for residential and outpatient mental health and chemical dependency services (Korcok, 1985c). The bill stipulates that policies must include at least $1,500 in outpatient coverage and $3,000 in residential coverage over a twenty-four-month period. Under this plan more people are being treated than ever before; and the greater emphasis on outpatient and residential services is resulting in substantially lower costs.

What is likely to happen within the next ten years in the rapidly changing health care field is predicted in the summary of a survey of 125 health care experts conducted by the consulting firm Arthur D. Little for the Health Insurance Association of America ("The Health Care System in the Mid-1990's," 1985). One prediction is that the complexity and rigidity of the DRG system "will probably lead to their replacement by a wholly or primarily capitation-based reimbursement system" (p. 2) and that "HMOs [health maintenance organizations] and other capitation arrangements will experience explosive growth. By 1995 HMO penetration is expected to have increased from the present 6 percent of the population to 25 or 30 percent or more. Major areas of growth will include investor-owned HMOs, HMO networks or chains providing nationwide coverage, and 'competitive medical plans' servicing Medicare beneficiaries" (pp. 4–5).

An earlier study, conducted by the Group Health Association for the NIAAA (Boyajay, 1978) within three HMOs (in Phoenix, Detroit, and Portland, Oregon), found that this type of health service bears considerable promise of being cost-effective. This demonstration project had the limitations of a rather brief period (four years) and a lack of comparison groups, but it did indicate that those HMOs' treatment of alcoholics resulted in distinct improvements in job retention and reduction in alcohol consumption, as well as reduction in other health care costs on the part of the alcoholics' families.

Ideally, HMOs should one day become a leading mechanism for primary, secondary, and tertiary prevention and treatment of alcoholism if they learn how to accomplish their mission of providing comprehensive health care. The concept back of the HMO is that, through client education and screening, ailments will be detected and treated cost-effectively at an early stage, thus fulfilling the claim that the HMO is paid to keep the client well. Henrik Blum, a specialist in health care administration in the

School of Public Health at the University of California, Berkeley, sees the HMO of the future as holding great promise for effective prevention and treatment of alcoholism at costs that are more reasonable than fee-for-service medicine, which may involve incentives to recommend unnecessary or expensive treatment (Blum, personal interview, Sept. 10, 1986). However, he cautions that the HMOs will need to be encouraged by their client institutions or corporations to offer more comprehensive prevention, early identification, and treatment services at reasonable costs. In other interviews several leaders of national nongovernmental groups concerned with the alcoholism field agreed that the HMOs have potential future promise but cautioned that the HMOs—like most health care organizations or individuals—need much additional education and training on how to deal with alcohol problems.

To be able to cope with alcoholism effectively, the HMOs need to develop flexible service teams with the right mix of physicians, nurse practitioners and nurses, social workers, sociologists and anthropologists, and psychologists to meet the need for both prevention and treatment. Olive Jacob, who recently interviewed thirty-five representatives of alcohol-concerned national or state organizations, governments, treatment organizations, and consultants about alcoholism insurance coverage and treatment issues, ends her NIAAA-sponsored report with these treatment comments and questions (Jacob, 1985, p. 33):

The EAPs [Employee Assistance Programs] and the service system are clearly unprepared for an environment in which 20–25 percent of the population may become enrolled in HMOs, especially if significant percentages of Medicaid recipients and the poor are included.

Because few incentives exist for the new or restructured HMOs to become Federally qualified, we need studies on HMO provision of, or payment for, alcoholism and drug services: Are they providing care? If so, is such care comprehensive, effective and of

acceptable quality? Are the HMOs changing their
pattern of referrals? Are HMOs sending clients to
alcoholism and drug programs without covering the
cost of care? How do HMOs relate to EAPs? Do they
exhibit prudent buyer practices in selection of, and
referral to, treatment resources? Do the HMOs control
utilization so tightly they cannot reasonably expect
positive outcome?

Technical assistance should be provided to
alcoholism and drug [treatment] providers in order to
enable them to deal effectively with the HMOs.
Should programs ever accept HMO referrals without
payment? How does one encourage HMOs to purchase services from existing providers? How can
programs provide training, consultation, and technical assistance to HMOs about alcoholism and drug
abuse? How should programs respond when offered a
risk-sharing (capitation) contract?

If treatment facilities are to expand, in order to serve a larger
number of alcoholic patients and serve them more effectively,
government officials recognize that more stringent standards will be
needed for the treatment facilities and for treatment staffs—
particularly since today's more aggressive marketing of treatment
services increases the risk of charlatanry. Thus, the Joint Commission on Accreditation of Hospitals (JCAH) is adapting its standards
to make hospital-based programs conform to those for acute-care
hospitals by 1987 (Korcok, 1986). And a competitive agency, an ad
hoc Commission on Accreditation of Rehabilitation Facilities
(CARF), is also planning standards for treatment programs as an
alternative to the JACH standards, so as to give more emphasis to
nonhospital care. According to Lewis's *Alcoholism Report* (June
30, 1985, p. 1), this competitive "development followed increasing
dissatisfaction among segments of the treatment sector with the
JCAH accreditation process. Specific alcoholism program accreditation was initiated in 1975 by JCAH under contract with NIAAA,
but, in the years since, alcoholism program identity has become

increasingly diffused, first subsumed under psychiatric standards and now in danger of being absorbed under JCAH's general Hospital Standards." And thus another turf battle continues—which may be healthier for the patients and their pocketbooks in the long run.

9

What Helping Professionals Can Do

The previous chapter provided abundant evidence that health care services today are changing rapidly in coverage and funding, so that the professions involved in the treatment of alcoholism must learn to adapt in order to be effective. The day of the free-standing professional who can offer his or her services to the individual client on a direct fee-for-service basis is almost over. We are seeing the rapid rise of health maintenance organizations (HMOs) and other packaged services, which necessitate the working together of a variety of professionals and paraprofessionals in the delivery of alcoholism treatment to meet the standards of economy and efficiency demanded by increasingly cost-conscious public and private funding agencies. The new situation is putting new stresses on the relationships among the various care-providing professions while they are learning to work together in the newer types of organizations. Those who can adapt rapidly can look forward to successful careers in treatment and counseling; but those who fail to understand the new changes in the health care field or who do not know how to market their services will lose out in the increasingly competitive environment.

If alcoholism treatment is to become more humane as well as more cost-effective, those needing treatment or counseling must be induced to seek help at earlier stages and must be encouraged by firm but compassionate and continuous social supports to assume more responsibility for their own recovery. In order to encourage those with alcohol problems to come into treatment at an earlier stage, professionals will need to deemphasize the aribtrary "either/ or" features of the disease model of alcoholism, so that the client cannot evade the need for treatment on the grounds that he or she is "not an alcoholic yet." On the other hand, the client should not be encouraged to adopt a passive "cure me, Doc!" role, but should be made to understand from the outset that he or she will have to take on the primary responsibility for recovery.

Physicians

Among all the health care professionals, physicians now have the primary responsibility for treating alcoholism. This fact stems from the greater relative prestige of the medical profession and from Medicare and insurance companies' insistence that the care providers have certification approved by the medical establishment. However, the truth is that the average alcoholic client requires very little in the way of expert medical care and is usually turned over quickly by the physician to the ministrations of counselors from AA, clinical psychologists, or social workers. In fact, according to a recent poll, the vast majority of physicians regard alcoholism as a disease entity, but only 27 percent of those interviewed felt competent to treat alcoholic patients (Niven, 1984); and in a national survey of 200 physicians (Goldsmith and others, 1984), half of them said that the medical training they had received about the recognition, prevention, and treatment of alcoholism was either "rather" or "completely" ineffective, and most of them (88 percent) felt that they needed more education and training about alcoholism and how to treat alcoholic patients. These findings fit in with a national study of medical school curricula, which showed that the average medical student gets only a few hours, at best, of any training on the clinical diagnosis and treatment of alcoholism, and usually zero training on how to prevent alcoholism (Pokorny, 1983).

A new national process for the certification of physicians specializing in treatment of chemical dependency is being sponsored by the American Medical Society on Alcoholism and Other Drug Dependencies (Korcok, 1985a). This certification procedure should be helpful in setting and maintaining standards for physicians in this field.

While a physician should be called in immediately if there is any evidence that the new client has a serious medical problem, physicians are not always the best diagnosticians; they tend to look for the strictly medical symptoms but may not see the problems requiring the attention of other professionals. (As Abraham Maslow has said, "If the only tool you have is a hammer, you treat everything like a nail.") Psychologists, social workers, and nurses should be utilized more effectively in the intake and diagnostic process, for their perspectives are needed; and they may have more experience and interest than physicians in intensive questioning of the client regarding his or her drinking history and living circumstances, which are important in determining what kind of treatment is needed.

Medicine is a stressful profession; and the ranks of practicing physicians include at least their proportionate share of practicing alcoholics. Fernandez (1986) estimates that fully 10 percent of the nearly half-million practicing physicians in the United States are alcoholics. He quotes Christine Lubinski, Washington representative of the National Council on Alcoholism, as observing that physicians who drink heavily are loath to challenge their hard-drinking patients and that they prescribe too many drugs for alcoholics. Obviously, physicians should not only set a good example for their patients but should also see to it that physicians who drink too much are diverted into rehabilitation programs.

Bissell and Haberman's *Alcoholism in the Professions* (1984) provides not only a revealing portrayal of the alcohol problems of people in the various health care professions but also a useful list of professional associations interested in improvements in the treatment of alcoholism and drug dependency.

Because of their prestige and leadership role, physicians should be able to help reduce the severity of alcohol problems by lending their support in the following ways:

1. Lobbying for curriculum changes (so that in medical training, including continuing education, more attention is given to alcohol problems) and for adequate certification (so that reasonable standards are established for physicians specializing in treatment of substance abuse).
2. Providing concerned leadership and full cooperation with other members of health delivery teams (nurses, psychologists, social workers, AA and other volunteer groups) in treating alcoholic clients with sensitivity and understanding.
3. Continuing to encourage the efforts of organizations devoted to *prevention* of alcohol problems and the promotion of good health habits (see Chapter Six). Since physicians have done much to reduce smoking among their patients and within their own ranks, they certainly can help materially in bringing about a climate of more moderate use of alcohol.

Because of a fear of financial and status losses through sharing the responsibilities for alcoholism treatment with other professionals, many members of the medical profession may be slow in accepting the role of coequals with others in the management of their clients' alcohol problems. Present insurance and funding regulations still contribute to the general insistence that an M.D. be in charge of treatment programs, even when other professionals would be as effective and certainly less expensive. However, in the long run, as treatment costs mount even higher, it is likely that the agencies paying for alcoholism treatment will insist on limiting the involvement of expensive medical practitioners and in-hospital care and will call for an increased role for other professionals with somewhat different skills.

Psychologists

Psychologists have special opportunities, and also special challenges, in helping to alleviate alcohol problems. Nicholas

Cummings, former president of the American Psychological Association, puts the problem bluntly in his article "The Dismantling of Our Health System: Strategies for the Survival of Psychological Practice":

> Psychology is particularly vulnerable because corporate American does not understand psychological services. They think that psychologists are those ethereal social scientists who talk about the human potential movement and self-realization, and psychological concepts are viewed by businesspeople as being as valid as asking "How long is a piece of string?" They don't know when therapy begins and when it ends, what psychologists' goals are and what psychology's product is; so, they are very wary of us. They do understand hospitalization for medical reasons. They know how many days medical procedures take: an appendectomy takes so many days, a hysterectomy takes so many days, a tonsilectomy takes X number of days. With psychotherapy they're terrified that they're opening up an open-ended system. If they could somehow predict actuarially how long therapy would take, they wouldn't mind funding it. Psychologists have not helped them in this task. Psychologists are going to have to market their services. It's that pure and simple [Cummings, 1986, p. 427].

Much the same concerns are being voiced within the inner councils of the American Psychological Association (APA). A recent nationwide teleconference in twenty-one cities, exploring how to set up "preferred provider organizations" (which include HMOs and other health care groups), resulted in a consensus that psychologists must adapt to demands by companies and public funding agencies for services that are convenient and cost-effective and that provide quality care (Turkington, 1986). Psychologists are at a real disadvantage also in a climate where the medical profession itself is advocating laws that would deny nonphysicians the right to use the word "diagnose" and to practice in hospitals (Welch,

1986a).The APA has set up a new Office of Professional Practice, which is developing model alcoholism treatment and psychotherapy packages and is helping clinicians, through legislative liaison and marketing activities, sell services to the key purchasers of health care services (Welch, 1986b).

Perhaps the best advice to psychologists in marketing their services is to get away from the traditional open-ended fee-per-visit client relationship, which reinforces an indefinite continuance of counseling as long as the client will pay the fees. In the long run, clinical psychologists interested in counseling alcoholics might be better off within HMOs, as part of a professional and paraprofessional team that is paid to maintain health rather than to treat patients only when they get ill. Through such auspices psychologists can play a significant role in planning and administering primary and secondary alcoholism prevention campaigns. Many psychologists also have the broad skills that are effective in administering alcohol and drug dependency treatment and prevention programs on the municipal, state, and federal levels. But if psychologists are to achieve their rightful roles in helping to prevent and to treat alcohol problems, they need to cultivate powerful friends in Congress and learn to justify their roles more effectively to those who are footing the health care bills.

Nurses

The 1.5 million nurses in the United States have a great potential impact on alcoholics, because they usually have the closest association with the incoming patient and are usually sensitized to detect alcohol problems of different types. Fortunately, a national nursing curriculum survey reported by Annie Carter (1983) found that most nursing schools have made considerable progress in offering instruction regarding alcoholism. However, from my own discussions with nurses in seminars on alcohol problems, it appears that the nursing schools (and the associations of nurses themselves) need to provide a much greater amount of moral support for the nurse as a member of the health care team that treats alcoholics. The nurse tends to have great responsibilities for patient care without sufficient authority to participate effectively in diagnosis and treatment. As a member of an emergent profession, the nurse who deals with many alcoholics is subject to burnout after a short time spent in trying to cope with the same alcoholics again and again as they come back in through the revolving door of the clinic. For the welfare of all in the health care system (including the clients), nurses should get the moral and material support that is necessary to enable them to cope with the situation.

Social Workers

Social workers in the United States are estimated as numbering about 350,000, including the more than 100,000 members in the National Association of Social Workers (NASW), most of whom have the Master of Social Work degree. Nancy Humphreys (1983) points out the wide range of positions that social workers fill in the alcoholism treatment field. For instance, they help in planning, program development, and evaluation in federal, state, and municipal alcohol and drug abuse agencies; and they also act as direct-service practitioners who provide counseling, psychotherapy, and advocacy services for their clients—including problem drinkers and their families. As Humphreys says, "Social workers bring a unique perspective to the alcohol and drug area. More than that of any other helping professional, the social worker's mission and practice style is to work with the person and his or her social environment. Social workers have an interest in the family, neighborhood, and community as well as in the individual alcohol or drug abuser. Social workers are as interested in preventing alcohol and drug abuse as treating it" (p. 28).

Because of the constantly growing complexity of regulations and policies governing eligibility for treatment and the need for expertise in knowing how to get clients appropriate care within the funding guidelines, there are many opportunities in health care delivery units and as administrators of employee assistance programs for well-trained social workers who know the ropes. However, as another emergent profession, social workers are in need of better recognition and compensation. Social work as a profession should profit from an informative public relations campaign to enlighten administrators and other professionals as to the knowledge and skills required of the modern social worker.

Other Professionals

Several other professionals, including pharmacists and dentists, play a significant role in preventing or mitigating alcohol problems. They can help in steering clients toward treatment and away from undue dependence on over-the-counter drugs. The NIAAA is working with its associations to keep their memberships informed about the contributions they can make through referral to treatment services of those with alcohol problems whom they encounter in their daily work.

Issues of Accreditation

The alcoholism counselors are by far the most numerous, and perhaps also the most important, figures in the alcoholism treatment process. It is the alcoholism counselor who usually makes the largest contribution in personal care and respect for the individual alcoholic over an extended period. Many alcoholism counselors are present or former AA members themselves, and caring for other recovering alcoholics is a necessary part of their own process of recovery. The dedication and zeal of AA members to help other unfortunates like themselves is a major factor in keeping the wobbly alcoholism treatment structure together; however, there is also a need for other perspectives and special skills within the ranks of day-to-day counselors, which can be provided by clergy, paraprofessionals, and others.

Despite the importance of the alcoholism counselors, they are usually the lowest paid of all the workers in the alcoholism treatment field, primarily because many of them are recovering alcoholics who were eager to come into the field at the bottom and because many of them have much practical experience but not much formal training. Fortunately, there is continuing pressure toward improving standards and training for alcoholism counselors, and toward official certification of counselors. Over the last decade, consistent with the increasing emphasis on accreditation of counselors, there also has been a proliferation of short courses or conferences or summer schools that aid in qualifying substance abuse counselors. One 1986 pamphlet, from the Alcohol and Drug Problems Association of North America, lists ninety-four conferences and summer schools, seventeen national association meetings and conferences, and twenty training and workshop opportunities. One of these is even a "Grantsmanship Center"—which is located in Los Angeles.

A report on *Credentialing of Alcoholism Counselors* (National Institute on Alcohol Abuse and Alcoholism, 1980) notes that the majority of the fifty states now have mechanisms for certifying alcoholism counselors. The report provides state-by-state specifics on certification requirements (usually a year or more of full-time employment as counselor, credit for relevant training, and a requirement of sobriety for the last year or two) and identifies the states that have reciprocity in recognizing each other's certification requirements. For example, in the Eastern Area Alcohol Education and Training Program, thirteen states, the District of Columbia, the Virgin Islands, and Puerto Rico share a reciprocal certification arrangement (Eastern Area Alcohol Education and Training Programs, 1977).

The NIAAA itself has accelerated the process of credentialing, first by its sponsorship of the Littlejohn report (Roy Littlejohn Associates, 1974) and then by its recent commissioning of the report, *Development of Model Professional Standards for Counselor Credentialing* (Shaw, Reuben, and Johnson, 1984). As summarized in a NASADAD special report (Butynski, 1984), the Birch and Davis credentialing project developed three major products: a core set of counselor job tasks, a set of required knowledges and skills expected of counselors, and guidelines for assessing the competencies of those seeking credentials (including number of years' experience, level of formal education, alcoholism recovery status, age, ethnicity, and prior certification status).

Accreditation of counselors is moving gradually toward a national set of standards mediated by United Services for Alcoholism and Drug Abuse Counselors, the umbrella organization formed by the three major associations of counselors: the National Association of Alcoholism and Drug Abuse Counselors, the Certification

Reciprocity Consortium/Alcohol and Other Drug Abuse, and the National Commission for Accreditation of Alcohol and Drug Abuse Counselor Credentialing Bodies (Lewis, *Alcoholism Report,* Jan. 17, 1986). However, agreement on a national set of standards for *treatment* programs has been going along at an even slower pace than national standards for counselors. The Hazelden treatment organization complained in its *Hazelden Professional Update* newsletter for May 1986 that there has been too much stalling about establishment of national standards for the quality of alcoholism treatment—that the disputes about whether alcoholism programs should be accredited by the Joint Commission on the Accreditation of Hospitals (JCAH) under its Consolidated Standards (for free-standing treatment programs), Hospital Standards (for hospital-based programs), or both, are resulting in considerable expense and delay. Treatment programs may also apply for certification by the Commission on Accreditation of Rehabilitation Facilities (CARF). The newsletter points out that the uncertainty about standards works a special hardship on nonhospital programs.

Korcok (1986, p. 1) notes that "NAATP [National Association of Alcoholism Treatment Programs] and JCAH have had a fractious history over the issue of accreditation standards development"; and both his article and the Hazelden newsletter reflect doubts as to whether the JCAH will go along with tailoring its standards to the specific needs of the alcoholism and drug abuse field. Since the issue of certification is vital to determining which treatment organizations get funded for what kinds of treatment, the controversies over turf (between such interests as the hospital-based programs and the free-standing programs, and among various groups of professionals caught in the middle) are likely to delay the settlement of the certification-of-facilities issue for a while longer.

Prevention Is Everybody's Business

Campaigns are needed to "sell" professional personnel on why they have a personal stake in taking an active part in primary prevention activities in their local communities, because ordinarily primary prevention is not their personal responsibility and they are paid to treat, not to prevent, alcohol problems. Reynolds (1985, p. 5) points out that professionals really have a "vested interest in creating a community environment in which clients may go to a restaurant for dinner without being badgered to order a drink." He also notes that clergy groups can influence community values without being too moralistic and that law enforcement people readily can come to understand that they have a stake in promoting consistent and realistic community standards on enforcement of laws relating to the sale and misuse of alcohol.

Professionals in the health maintenance organizations of the future will have a great opportunity for community service and enhancement of their own careers through active participation in primary prevention campaigns directed both at their own clients and at the community at large. If HMOs are to prosper through keeping their clients well, then their staffs should take an active part in preventing alcohol problems, since these are usually very expensive to treat once they have reached an advanced stage—not only because of the adverse effects of alcohol itself but also because alcoholism is often accompanied by a host of other health disorders, both in the individual patients and in their families.

HMO administrators and staffs have much to learn about how to screen clients for potential alcohol problems and to get them interested in counseling or other programs that encourage a healthy lifestyle. And since no prevention program can be effective without environmental support, professionals in the health care field should be alert to follow through on opportunities to exercise their skills in promoting more effective control over conditions within the community that contribute to alcohol problems.

10

Needed Directions in Alcohol Research

The National Institute on Alcohol Abuse and Alcoholism is the only federal agency that sponsors any appreciable amount of research on alcohol, although several other agencies (such as the National Highway Safety Transportation Board and the Department of Defense) occasionally sponsor individual research projects relevant to their specialized needs. Ever since the formula grant funds were taken away from the NIAAA and given directly to the states, research has been the agency's almost sole mission. But, as described in Chapter Three, NIAAA research is very thinly funded in comparison with money spent on other health-related federal research: the NIAAA research appropriation of $57 million for FY 1986 was only 1.1 percent of the total NIH and ADAMHA appropriation for research.

The NIAAA's research budget is stretched thin over a wide variety of basic and applied research on the causes, processes, and consequences of alcoholism and other alcohol-related problems and on how to facilitate their detection, prevention, and treatment. As described by Rosenthal (1983), the NIAAA funds its research through several types of grant and contract support, including regular project grants, Alcohol Research Center grants (described in Chapter Three), small grants, and research career scientist de-

171

velopment awards. Half of the research funds go for competitively awarded extramural research grants through regular peer reviews (primarily to scientists working in universities or other nonprofit research agencies); and approximately 50 percent of these grants are awarded for biomedical studies. The NIAAA also awards grants for the training of biomedical and behavioral scientists; but these grants have been gradually whittled down to a funding of only $1.436 million for FY 1986, enough to support only about sixty-six predoctoral and postdoctoral trainees (S. Long, personal interview, Aug. 27, 1986), although the new drug initiative bill passed in the fall of 1986 will mean a temporary increase in trainees. These programs are usually supervised by senior scientists at universities who have been directing NIAAA grants or contracts for some time.

In a 1979 article, I expressed the view that the behavioral sciences did not get their rightful share of NIAAA research grants because of the greater prestige of biomedical research generally and because behavioral science research is more controversial— especially when the research puts the politically influential alcohol industry in an unfavorable light by dwelling on the problems caused by alcohol. The Reagan administration in particular has repeatedly slashed behavioral science research funding, apparently because of the impression that most social science research is conducted by political liberals (Levine, 1981a). Not only is biomedical research considered scientifically more respectable, but focusing on long-term biomedical research that holds forth some hope for finding "a cure for alcoholism" helps to postpone conflicts.

Continuity in alcohol research planning and funding is sadly needed. This need is keenly felt at the NIAAA itself, which recently commissioned a study by a distinguished group of scientists under the aegis of the Institute of Medicine, chaired by Robert Straus of the University of Kentucky medical school, to advise the NIAAA on research priorities and opportunities (Institute of Medicine, 1987). Recommendations of this report emphasize the need for more interdisciplinary studies in which *both biological and behavioral factors* are considered—such as the interaction of changes in bodily functions and social roles in affecting drinking behavior of people as they go through various life cycles.

The Institute of Medicine report commends the general quality of the biomedical research conducted under competitively awarded NIAAA grants. Because alcohol is a pervasive drug that has marked effects on tissues and functions in all parts of the body, the report emphasizes the importance of adequate funding for biomedical research involving alcohol—not only for the NIAAA's purposes but for the research's contribution to advancement of general scientific knowledge. Included in current research grants are studies of alcohol's role in cancer, cirrhosis, gastrointestinal disorders, and the fetal alcohol syndrome; studies of alcohol's effect on cells in the heart, neural tissues, muscle, pancreas, and blood, to determine how the drug alters membrane structure; studies of tissue and subjective tolerance and dependence; and continuing genetic studies. The Institute of Medicine report also calls for more emphasis on comparative behavioral science studies of drinking behavior and laws and enforcement practices within various cultures throughout the world, so that the United States can learn from the successes and failures of other countries' attempts to control their drinking problems. In this respect the report echoes the opinions of Robin Room (1979) on the importance of long-term comparative analysis of drinking behavior and control policies and practices.

The report also focuses on the necessity of beefing up the NIAAA's scientific alcohol literature retrieval and dissemination resources under its National Clearinghouse for Alcohol Information (NCALI) services. NCALI funding is currently threatened by further cuts at the very time that—because of the massive increase in alcohol studies during the last decade (some 38,000 entries into the NCALI data base 1980–1986)—the information retrieval process must be accelerated if orderly scientific progress is to be made. Not only do scientists need ready access to relevant published information, but there are also treasure troves of alcohol data lying unused in the files of government agencies (such as the National Center for Health Statistics) and nongovernmental research agencies, which simply do not have the resources to analyze these valuable data sufficently.

Types of Studies Needed

Many needed studies of the epidemiology of problem drinking are still to be funded. Particularly helpful will be continuing trend surveys of *youth* from the ages of twelve through twenty, for these are the years in which drinking habits are usually developed and peer pressures to drink are very strong. Many of these studies of youth should cover the combined use of alcohol and other drugs. An intensive study of youths who have managed to abstain or to quit drinking to excess could be very helpful in providing insights for the planning of prevention programs. We know from our national surveys that drinking differs dramatically by age group, with the peak in alcohol problems occurring among men of about eighteen to twenty-five years old. Thus, this young-adult group is worth special attention in future research, to analyze how heavy-drinking habits develop and how some individuals in this vulnerable age group manage to avoid becoming heavy drinkers.

Not only alcohol problems but also problems with other drugs, involvement in violence, and high risk of suicide are much more common among those between the ages of eighteen to thirty-five than among older people. The period of low birthrates within the last generation (following the baby boom) and the recent increase in the proportion of the elderly are making for rapid shifts in the age distribution in the United States. Thus, studies of trends in the prevalence of alcohol problems (and related problems such as violence) always should entail holding constant for changes in the age distribution. Otherwise, there will continue to be misinterpretations if problem-drinking rates go down not because of better control over alcohol, but because of the aging of the population. Without holding constant for age, we could misinterpret the cause of a perhaps temporary improvement, as happened when crime statistics lowered appreciably in the early 1980s.

More research is needed to establish the degree to which alcoholism is attributable to *genetic* factors. Goodwin's (1983) symposium overview succinctly presents the evidence supporting the influence of genetics in alcoholism. That evidence is based largely on data from Scandinavian studies. One such study found that identical twin sons born to alcoholic parents who were later adopted out were significantly more likely to become alcoholics than nonidentical twin sons also born of alcoholics and also adopted out; another study found that children of alcoholics who were adopted out were significantly more likely to become alcoholics than adoptees of nonalcoholic parentage. Murray, Clifford, and Gurling (1983) point to methodological shortcomings in these adoption studies, as does Peele (1986), who adds that "balanced genetic models leave room for the substantial impact of environmental, social and individual factors (including personal values and intentions) so that drinking to excess can only be predicted within a complex, multivariate framework. The denial of this complexity in some quarters obscures what has been discovered through genetically oriented research and has dangerous consequences for prevention and treatment policies" (p. 63). Fillmore (forthcoming) provides additional criticism of past genetic research and also emphasizes the danger of neglecting environmental influences.

Petrakis (1985, p. 35) sums up the case for considering both heredity and environment: "The evidence for genetic mechanisms in some forms of human alcoholism is compelling. It is important to realize, however, that even if heredity is involved in alcoholism it is no cause for adopting a fatalistic attitude. Environment is also involved, and while we cannot alter our own heredity, we can alter our environments. A proper environment or an appropriate intervention can prevent milieu-limited alcoholism despite the existence of a genetic component, and even if the more serious male-limited form of hereditary alcoholism cannot be prevented, it can at least be mitigated by environment or intervention."

I would add that nobody who emphasizes the genetic factor in alcoholism has come up with any estimate of what proportion of the population becomes alcoholic primarily because of genetic factors. We need to learn much more about the potential role of genetics in alcoholism, not only to establish prevalence estimates but also to determine *how* genetic effects influence alcoholism. For example, it may be found that much alcoholism stems from the inheritance of a physical capacity or tolerance for alcohol, a "hollow leg" syndrome that facilitates excessive drinking *if* the environment is permissive.

Regardless of how much of the variance in alcoholism may be accounted for by genetic factors, it seems prudent to emphasize the manifold social, other environmental, and psychological causes of alcoholism—for these are the types of causes that hold the most immediate promise of corrective action.

Whenever *states or municipalities* are planning changes in alcohol control regulations or taxes or drinking-driving law enforcement, there should be before-and-after studies to determine the effects of such changes. States with a mixture of dry and wet counties (such as Mississippi) can provide many possibilities for demonstration research projects on how to bring about more effective alcohol control without undue infringement on moderate levels of consumption. Those under surveillance or reeducation because of drinking-driving arrests are also a population worthy of special study of their characteristics and of the events contributing to their arrest. For example, knowledge of *where* they were drinking—bars, in autos, or parties—should help in designing measures to reduce the incidence of drunken driving (Snow and Wells-Parker, 1986).

Another neglected area is the study of *organizational behavior* related to alcohol research and action agencies, including treatment facilities; federal, state, county, and municipal program administrations; and the major nonprofit advocacy associations. It is now fifteen years since the founding of the NIAAA; and many fundamental changes have occurred during those years in the incentives offered to organizations and in the way that these incentives are administered. The changes in third-party payments for alcoholism treatment and rehabilitation, as well as general changes in the overall health care delivery system, are in urgent need of realistic study if we are not merely to repeat in the 1990s the inefficiencies and disappointments we have encountered in the 1970s and 1980s.

Few penetrating studies of organizations have emerged in recent years, mainly because those most knowledgeable of what goes on in organizations are standing too close to the picture to see it clearly or are too protective of themselves and the organization to give a candid appraisal. The most valuable organizational studies would entail teamwork between innovative organizational theorists and model builders and several sets of researchers with a background in alcohol studies, who would study a variety of organizations in considerable depth, using inductive methods such as those used by Wiener in *The Politics of Alcoholism* (1981). At least some members of such research teams should come from Western European countries with long histories of dealing with alcohol problems, both to take advantage of their experience and to get an outsider's perspectives.

Out of such candid organizational studies could emerge better insight into the working of Parkinson's Law, Murphy's Law, and Machiavelli's management maxims, the role of burnout, and the operation of the law of self-preservation. Organizations deteriorate over time: like the preachers who went to Hawaii to save the natives' souls, they go out to do good, but their successors stay to do well. If we just knew more about how best to pick our ways across the mine fields of funding and coping with contending constituencies, we might be able to help ourselves—and Congress and the administration—avoid more of the costly blunders that can happen in such a controversial field as control of alcohol problems.

Utilization of Research Findings

No matter how efficiently the scientific alcohol literature is made available to administrators, practitioners, and researchers, it serves little purpose unless it is effectively utilized. And it is not enough merely to package the information neatly and distribute it wholesale. As Miller (1987) points out in his forthright article on barriers to utilization, alcohol researchers themselves often fail to use effective attitude change procedures in experiments, or to disseminate research findings, or to recognize disconfirming data, or to address the needs of decision makers. And he holds decision makers themselves responsible for much ineffectiveness because of simple inertia, ignorance, selective inattention, and biases arising from outside pressure or stubbornness. While his illustrations of poor utilization of research are drawn primarily from the treatment field, any of us readily can think of poor utilization of research findings in the priorities given in awarding of grants and in the conduct of the research itself. If a new Galileo were to arise to challenge the conventional thinking and decisions of some grant-review panels, he or she would risk being threatened with a secular form of excommunication.

What are the remedies for poor research utilization? The reforms must start at the top, in the guidelines for selecting grant-review committees and in the guidelines on how they must operate. Most grant-review committees cannot be faulted for not working hard enough; in fact, the members usually have thousands of pages of grant proposals sent to them on the very eves of their meetings, so that they have no time even for thorough reading of the material, much less the time to think it through. This situation is hardly conducive to an evaluation that takes into account alternative research approaches and considers how the research might fit in with some master plan for its ultimate utilization.

The overloading of grant-review panels can be reduced materially if the NIAAA is given more money and personnel to speed up the paperwork and broaden the searches for appropriate reviewers for specific proposals. The present time pressures inevitably result in falling back on old-boy networks in order to meet deadlines.

Much needed is an increased emphasis on setting up long-term study groups to review the state of knowledge in specific fields. Such groups should be given sufficient staff resources to help in compiling and evaluating past research findings, so that the study group members can spend more time on preparing recommendations for policies and priorities. Commendably, at present the NIAAA and some state alcohol agencies commission a fair number of state-of-the-art papers and three-day conferences on specific topics. However, in view of the growing mountains of alcohol research literature to be evaluated, longer-term study groups should get a higher priority. Such groups should be reinforced for recommending ways to improve research methods and research utilization, rather than pressured to come forth with conventional wisdoms. Membership of such study groups should be carefully selected to include not only some recognized experts in the relevant field but also outstanding scientists and administrators from other fields, chosen for a balance between scientific rigor, creativity, and hard-headed practicality.

Withal, the field of alcohol research has made a remarkably good beginning during the last generation. As Straus has observed (1986, p. 1), forty years ago "Alcoholism was assumed to be primarily a problem of homeless derelicts, disturbed persons, or the jail population of repeatedly arrested inebriates"—and a problem of middle-aged men rather than of the young. Much has been learned about the metabolism of alcohol and its potentially deleterious effects on unborn children. Through comparative studies of alcohol control measures in other countries, we are beginning to get a better handle on how to minimize the problems created by alcohol while not unduly interfering with its moderate use.

But certainly, in view of the high costs of alcohol problems and in light of the progress that has been made during the last generation in research on alcohol's effects and their mitigation, a quadrupling of the NIAAA research budgets to help prevent such problems is warranted. Yet whatever the size of alcohol research budgets, in order to consolidate the gains that have been made recently, we need to have much more interaction between those who do basic or applied research and those interested in translating that research into action on problems related to excessive use of alcohol. In this interaction all the health care professions discussed in Chapter Nine have an obligation—and an opportunity—to help in applying new research knowledge in effective prevention and treatment of America's alcohol problems.

11

Steps
Action Agencies
Can Take

Review of the history of alcohol programs in America indicates that no amount of dedication and hard work in trying to control drinking problems can be effective unless and until the people of the United States, through Congress and the Executive branch of the government, make up their minds that they really *want* to see an effective control program carried out. This book has presented much evidence on the fragmentation of responsibilities and conflicts of interest among the federal agencies involved with the marketing, taxing, and control of alcohol. There are many grounds to recommend more centralization of authority and responsibility, as in the Scandinavian countries. For example, in Finland *one central agency* sets standards and issues licenses for production; produces or purchases alcoholic beverages for sale in state-licensed on-premise and off-premise outlets; establishes tax levels; and makes recommendations to the legislature for laws and regulations governing such matters as drinking-driving, minimum age of purchasers, and hours and conditions of alcohol sales. The same centralized agency conducts research on alcohol-relevant consumption statistics and consumer attitudes (Osterberg, 1985). Very similar

180

controls also prevail in Sweden. These arrangements have cut down on the potential overlapping, duplication, and buck-passing among agencies.

These Scandinavian government semimonopolies of alcohol marketing were set up to reduce the profit pressures and lobbying activities of the alcohol industry and to put the primary emphasis in alcohol marketing upon promoting public health and preserving order. While Scandinavian legislators must remain vigilant lest government agencies overemphasize sales for the purpose of increasing tax revenues, these objectives appear to have been met fairly well in practice.

It is true that the Scandinavian countries have much more homogeneous cultures and greater respect for laws and regulations than is true in multicultural America. However, we surely could benefit if we drew on Swedish and Finnish experience and insisted on a single national alcohol control authority instead of the present confusing welter of overlapping agencies. The notion of having one central federal authority over alcohol in the United States is, of course, a pipe dream as long as government regulatory bodies are heavily influenced by commercial interests. The present administration views the country as a confederacy rather than a centralized union and is doing its best to dismantle federal agencies and to return more controls to the individual states. Also—even without the help of the all-powerful wine, beer, and liquor lobbies, which are adept at playing one agency off against another—entrenched bureaucracies in several departments—Treasury, Justice, Agriculture, Commerce, Health and Human Services—would still fight hard against the loss of any of their turf to another agency. However, before settling for only as much centralization as is practicable until the present climate in Washington has changed, we should take a hard look at what might be a reasonable amount of centralization on an interim basis.

President Kennedy once said that one should not tear down a fence until after asking why the fence was put up in the first place. A conservative stance would call for using as a nucleus the agency or agencies that already seem to be representing the interests of the general public. The best agency to serve as a nucleus appears to be the NIAAA, because it still has its original charter of dealing with alcohol problems in ways that will enhance public health and welfare; it has been in existence now for almost a generation; and it has had much experience in liaison and cooperation with the alcohol control agencies in all the states and territories.

Of course, the NIAAA will not be in a position to take on more controversial functions unless it gets the strong support of important constituencies or lobbies, plus congressmen as mentors who will speak up in its behalf in the same way that Senator Hughes did in the founding of the NIAAA in 1971. In fact, since the NIAAA lost the bulk of its budget in 1983, when funds for alcoholism treatment were set aside in block grants for the states, it has been relegated to being primarily a research agency. As mentioned at the end of Chapter Three, there is serious talk of taking it out of its present ADAMHA locus and making it one of the many research institutes within the National Institutes of Health. Since the NIAAA no longer has multi-million-dollar alcohol treatment budgets to dispense, it no longer has the enthusiastic support of treatment lobbies with financial interests to protect. Thus, if the NIAAA is to take a more decisive role in control over alcohol problems, it will have to rebuild its old treatment-oriented constituencies and generate new prevention-oriented ones—in addition to shoring up its congressional supports.

If the country actually *wants* to bring about effective control over alcohol problems, a strong case could be made for making the NIAAA a special division of the Food and Drug Administration. The FDA is an agency with generations of experience in administering laws and regulations to protect the purity of foods and the safety and efficacy of drugs, in the interest of consumer protection; one of its functions is to monitor labeling and advertising. As an old-line agency, the FDA has the respect of the general public and generally enjoys much congressional support as protection against undue commercial pressures to cater to special interests. Putting the NIAAA within the FDA should signify that its true role is to protect the health and welfare of the general public through appropriate control of alcohol. If given White House and congressional backing at the outset, the FDA would be more highly motivated to nurture the NIAAA than is ADAMHA, which is a largely nonsubstantive bureaucratic umbrella organization used by the last several administrations to keep the NIAAA, NIDA, and NIMH from overvigorous pursuit of their health and safety charters whenever their activities impinge on powerful commercial interests.

The NIAAA already has had more than fifteen years' experience in sporadic cooperative relationships with other federal agencies concerned with alcohol, such as the Occupational Safety and Health Administration, the Consumer Product Safety Commission, the Environmental Protection Agency, the National Highway Transportation Safety Administration, the National Transportation Safety Board, the Federal Aviation Administration, the Federal Railroad Administration, and the Department of Defense. Such cooperative networks could be more effective if the NIAAA's charter were to provide more regulatory authority and adequate operating budgets. The same can be said for the NIAAA's long-term relationships with the individual states and territories. While alcoholism treatment funds now go directly to the states through block grants rather than through the NIAAA, cooperative NIAAA-state relationships have continued to be fostered, to the extent possible with very limited budgets, through interchange of information on matters concerned with treatment and prevention of alcohol problems and comparative data on laws, regulations, and administrative practices.

Off and on over the years, there has been talk of merging the NIAAA and the National Institute on Drug Abuse (NIDA), in the interest of closer coordination and perhaps some savings in administrative overhead. In the opinion of most specialists who have followed alcoholism treatment and prevention efforts for some years, this would be a serious mistake. NIDA deals largely with illegal drugs or normally legal drugs that are being misused, whereas the NIAAA is dealing with a legal drug marketed by a politically powerful industry. This situation calls for specialized coping behavior on the part of constituencies dedicated to solving alcohol problems—and these groups are not normally willing or able to take on responsibilities for the rather different set of problems involved with illegal drugs. In my opinion, to associate treatment and prevention of alcoholism with efforts to combat illegal drugs would result in a mixture of criminal justice and public health and welfare measures and administrative atmospheres that would be even more confusing and counterproductive than the current situation. Currently, the NIAAA and NIDA appear to be cooperating very well in exchange of information and sponsorship of joint programs (such as in alcohol and drug education) where appropriate.

However, the two agencies may be working together even more closely as a result of the current antidrug initiatives proposed by the President and passed by Congress (HR-5484) in the fall of 1986. This hastily contrived omnibus measure has not been fully implemented at this writing; but it provides for a new Office for Substance Abuse Prevention within the ADAMHA umbrella agency, which will take away from the NIAAA and NIDA their line responsibilities for prevention. It is hoped by those with much experience in alcoholism and drug abuse prevention programs that, when the new drug-initiative dust settles, the NIAAA and NIDA will be allowed to run their own programs, because it is impossible to separate primary prevention from secondary prevention and treatment.

The largely unexercised authority for control of advertising and labeling of alcoholic beverages should be taken away from the Bureau of Alcohol, Tobacco, and Firearms and given to the Federal Trade Commission or the Food and Drug Administration. The BATF consistently has shown itself to be more concerned with protecting the commercial interests of the alcohol industry than in regulating them for the general welfare. The BATF obviously has a conflict of interest because of its joint responsibility for collection of alcohol taxes (which has evolved into nurturance of the industry from which the taxes are collected) and for control over advertising and labeling (which, if exercised appropriately, would result in inconvenience to the industry and perhaps some lessening of tax revenues).

The alcohol industry can be counted on to fight against the establishment of a federal control agency with any increased power to control alcohol labeling, advertising and marketing practices, or alcohol taxes. The industry is always ready to make effective campaign contributions and to stimulate letter-writing campaigns by hundreds of alcohol outlets whenever needed to influence Congress against passing any unwanted legislation. Thus, it will take the rekindling of strongly motivated constituency groups (such as the National Council on Alcoholism and Mothers Against Drunk Driving) plus strong senatorial and White House support to bring about a centralized alcohol control agency with any real clout. This is not likely to happen until alcohol problems become visibly even worse than they are now or until another congressional knight in shining armor like Senator Hughes emerges to do battle.

The NIAAA takes credit for the following achievements during its first fifteen years: a reduction in per capita consumption of alcohol, leading to a reduction in alcohol-related problems; some increase in distilled spirits prices, expected to result in a further reduction of per capita consumption; a reduction in alcohol-related traffic fatalities and accidents; a reduction in cirrhosis rates; a reduction in daily and heavy consumption by high school seniors; and a greater awareness of risks associated with drinking during pregnancy (National Institute on Alcohol Abuse and Alcoholism, 1986a). As mentioned earlier, the NIAAA's National Plan for 1986–1995 has very ambitious objectives: to reduce alcohol abuse and alcoholism 20 percent, drinking problems among youth fourteen to seventeen years old 11 percent, alcohol-related motor vehicle deaths 19 percent, other alcohol-related accident deaths 20 percent, liver cirrhosis deaths 11 percent, and fetal alcohol syndrome 25 percent (National Institute on Alcohol Abuse and Alcoholism, 1986b, p. 7). Unfortunately, these objectives do not appear to be at all realistic in the light of the limited resources now available to the NIAAA and other federal and state and nongovernmental agencies.

Politically, the NIAAA is not in a position now to take a strong stand in favor of constraints on alcohol advertising, warning labels on alcoholic beverages containers, increases in alcohol taxes to reduce consumption, and stronger controls over alcoholic beverage outlets. Thus, it is understandable that the NIAAA National Plan bows to the current administration's party line by stating that the primary responsibility will rest on the individual states and "the private sector" and that the NIAAA's role will be that of coordinator and facilitator. But, although controls over local alcohol problems ultimately must be applied on a local level, the individual states do not have the power and the political will to apply strong controls; for the alcohol industry already has proved that it is very efficient at concentrating overpowering pressures on

almost any state or local government agency that threatens to adopt
much more stringent controls over alcohol marketing. Even the
federal government finds it politically difficult to apply stiffer
controls, but it can do much through use of its taxing and
regulatory powers if it has the will; and certainly it should expand
its leadership in setting proposed standards for controls and other
preventive and treatment programs to be administered on the state
level.

     To turn to the issue of shoring up the NIAAA's current
programs: As reported in Chapter Three, the administration's
proposed NIAAA budget for fiscal year 1987 is less than $70 million,
substantially less than the NIDA budget. The NIAAA has a staff of
less than 200 currently and is being constrained to a limited role
even in noncontroversial basic research. The political situation
systematically works to the NIAAA's disadvantage vis-à-vis NIDA
and many other National Institutes, because the alcohol industry is
a determined adversary of the NIAAA and has deep pockets for
campaign contributions and lobbying. A congressman will not lose
many votes or contributions by taking a stand against illegal drugs
or cancer or heart disease or muscular dystrophy; but the alcohol
industry can be pretty rough on any legislator who advocates higher
alcohol taxes or increased controls over alcohol advertising. Thus,
until there is a change in the federal climate, the NIAAA is unlikely
to be awarded the budgets to broaden its operations beyond its
current limited research and information functions.

Expanded Functions for NIAAA

     An agency such as the NIAAA, revitalized by a mandate and
adequate budgets from Congress to provide leadership in controlling
alcohol problems, should carry out many of the same kinds of functions as its counterparts in Scandinavia. These should include, in
addition to its present intramural and extramural research and information services, at least the following authorities from Congress:
     1. To serve as coordinator of alcohol-related activities of
other federal agencies, including the other agencies listed earlier in

this chapter, for the purpose of ensuring that the public interest is being adequately protected.

2. To set standards for purity of alcoholic beverages and for adequacy of labeling—including additives, strength, and warnings about overuse.

3. To set constraints against advertising that is misleading or otherwise injurious to the public. Some (such as the Center for Science in the Public Interest) would like to see alcohol advertising banned altogether from broadcast media, and printed advertising limited to announcements of availability of specific alcoholic beverages at stated prices; or a provision of equal time or space and prominence for warnings about the dangers of alcohol. The evolution of advertising policy will continue to be a controversial problem for any federal agency to police; but the NIAAA certainly seems to be a much less biased agency for exercising authority over alcohol advertising than the BATF, which as a tax collection agency has proved repeatedly its incompetence to serve the public interest rather than that of the alcohol industry.

4. To promote liaison with state agencies that have been set up for administration of state laws regarding control of alcohol. In keeping with the spirit of arrangements made at the time of repeal, the states should continue to have authority to control alcohol marketing and taxing within their own boundaries, consistent with overall federal laws and tax policies. However, a federal agency should have the responsibility for negotiating uniform standards in controls, particularly among neighboring states; for it is too easy to cross state lines to take advantage of lower taxes or longer hours of service. The federal agency could recommend to Congress that states which conform to certain standards of controls be rewarded by increases in grants for alcohol control and treatment of alcoholism. Other incentives for states to comply with federal standards could include such arrangements as the current tie-in of federal highway funds to states in relation to their invoking a twenty-one-year age requirement for purchase of alcoholic beverages.

5. To continue development by the NIAAA of model statutes and regulations for states' decriminalization of alcoholism, inclusion of alcoholism among treatable health conditions covered by insurance, and dram shop liability and rules for conditions of sale

of alcoholic beverages, including establishment of appropriate zoning standards for alcohol outlets.

6. To expand the NIAAA's data gathering on state laws and regulations concerning alcohol control and expenditures of federal, state, and local funds in alcoholism treatment and prevention. At present the states voluntarily submit such data at intervals to the NIAAA, primarily through the data-gathering efforts of the National Association of State Alcohol and Drug Abuse Directors (NASADAD). To be of optimum value, such data should be collected at more frequent intervals and should include more information related to program effectiveness.

7. To accord a very high priority to comparative studies of alcohol control policies and practices in other countries. In the past, NIAAA cooperation in international exchange of such information has helped us discover which types of control measures are most likely to be effective in view of the experiences of other countries with cultures similar to ours (Farrell, 1985). Many European countries and Canada have a number of experienced alcohol research agencies, whose findings can help us improve our control policies and our own research capabilities.

8. To resume some of the NIAAA's pilot grant or contract arrangements for implementing and assessing alternative modes of alcoholism treatment and aftercare. However, such pilot programs are necessarily expensive and time consuming and thus should not be implemented until a clearer consensus regarding the criteria for "improvement" and clearer standards for treatment components are established.

9. To develop pilot programs to foster improvement of primary prevention of alcohol problems on a community level. Programs could range from ambitious multimedia campaigns, coordinated with local enforcement programs designed to reduce alcohol problems, down to small-scale pilot studies on how to reduce drinking-driving accidents after high school proms.

10. To strengthen the NIAAA's information retrieval and exchange programs, which have been crippled by stringent funding limits. As discussed in Chapter Ten, the accumulation of vitally useful data on alcohol use and problems has proceeded at such a rapid pace that the NIAAA's National Clearinghouse for Alcohol

Information (NCALI) system has been hard put to cope with classifying the information and making it available for the use of administrators and researchers.

Consolidation of State Alcohol Agencies

States should be encouraged to shore up their administrative arrangements by such means as putting the alcohol control, treatment, and prevention agency and the alcoholic beverage control (ABC) agency under single offices in each state. This would parallel the recommended federal combining of most alcohol programs under a single agency (ostensibly the NIAAA) and should help to temper the tendency of ABC agencies to be unduly lenient with the alcohol industry because of the ABCs' traditional primary role of maintaining orderly alcohol markets in relation to the collection of alcohol taxes. Congress could use the power of the formula grant allocations to induce individual states to maintain reasonable uniformity of standards in their administration of alcohol control agencies.

In any event, regardless of whether it is politically feasible to merge the ABC agencies into their respective states' alcoholism and alcohol abuse agencies, steps should be taken to remedy some of the current ABC practices that Mosher (1985c) lists as being inconsistent with sound public policy. In his study of California, he concluded that local jurisdictions should be accorded more authority in deciding how many and what kinds of alcohol licenses to issue; that license fees should be increased to reflect actual administrative and enforcement costs; and that a model dram shop law should be enacted, to establish more stringent server responsibilities for denying service to underage and intoxicated patrons. The NIAAA-sponsored study by Medicine in the Public Interest (1979) had similar criticisms of ABC practices throughout the United States.

Less Fragmentation of County and Municipal Services

County and municipal agencies need to exchange expertise with state and federal alcohol agencies on how to spend alcohol treatment and prevention funds equitably and efficiently. Roizen and Weisner (1979) have provided ample evidence of the chaotic fragmentation of alcoholism services on the county level, where many diverse and thinly funded local treatment or referral agencies are at work. These agencies are either voluntary organizations (for example, local chapters of the National Council on Alcoholism, the Salvation Army, or fraternal groups) or governmental units (such as local VA hospitals, city or county hospitals, or rehabilitation or social welfare agencies). They had been working in the alcoholism field before specialized governmental alcoholism agencies—such as the NIAAA and state or city and county alcoholism program-coordinating authorities—were established. When local government umbrella organizations were set up to dispense federal, state, and local funds, much confusion resulted because the existing treatment groups were torn between maintaining their identity and their special goals and doing things differently in order to qualify for funds dispensed by the new coordinating agencies. Further, the coordinating agencies have so many demands on their limited funds that there is a temptation to dole out money very thinly among many competing treatment services. This situation has intensified the competition between private and public treatment services for public funds.

As Weisner (1981) points out in her intensive study of social agencies in a single county, an alcoholic's treatment is increasingly dependent on his or her financial status and insurance coverage. Regardless of their health care needs, poor alcoholics are much more likely to wind up in municipally run, thinly funded alcoholism services, whereas well-to-do alcoholics are more likely either to get treated ostensibly for illnesses that do not label them as alcoholics or to go to "drying-out" establishments that preserve their privacy. Patients may get quite different treatment depending on the agency that happens to be willing to accept them. Weisner found that individuals with the same problem behavior could be treated as "alcoholics" by an alcoholism program or for "family dysfunction" if treated by a social service agency; an adolescent with behavior problems might be labeled as a "teenage alcoholic" in an alcoholism treatment facility, whereas an agency with a nonalcoholism orientation might regard the same behavior problems as evidence of an adolescent "adjustment reaction." She also noted that inconsistencies in treatment often stem from the fact that alcohol-specific institutions may be staffed primarily by recovering alcoholics with an AA orientation, whereas non-alcohol-specific services are staffed largely by professional physicians, nurses, social workers, or psychologists.

Some competition and conflict between agencies on how to administer alcoholism treatment and how to handle prevention programs are inevitable; but the confusion and loss of morale of county and municipal agency staffs over contradictory guidelines and overlapping jurisdictions often result in the clients' getting the short end of the stick. This situation is not likely to get better until Medicare and Medicaid funding requirements become more equitable.

Separate Programs for Drink-Impaired Drivers

The increasing diversion by the courts of drink-impaired drivers from the criminal justice system to the alcoholic treatment system is interfering with adequate treatment for alcoholics (Weisner, 1984; Weisner and Speiglman, 1982; Speiglman, 1985). A California county alcohol program administrator has estimated that 40 percent of the alcoholism treatment budgets of some counties in California are expended in support of drinking-driving programs (Speiglman, 1985). Diversion of the drink-impaired driver does help to relieve pressure on the jails, gives an opportunity for drunk drivers to benefit from reeducation in lieu of going to jail, and provides considerable income from the fees paid by the drunk drivers. However, thus mixing the drunk drivers with the non-DUI treatment programs runs the risk of neglecting the needs of the alcoholics or turning them away because they perceive the treatment environment as punitive and hostile. Further, since Vingilis's (1983) review of the drinking-driving literature indicates that the majority of drinking drivers are not "alcoholics" in a clinical sense, they probably would benefit more from a different type of remedial program (with emphasis on the necessity of separating alcohol and gasoline) than the usual treatment for alcohol addiction. Vingilis's conclusions are also borne out by two recent studies comparing drinking-driving referrals to alcoholic rehabilitation programs to other referrals to these programs in Colorado (Packard, 1987) and Alaska (Fillmore and Kelso, forthcoming).

Weisner (1987) reminds us that the *majority* of clients in public alcoholism treatment now come from criminal justice or other coercive systems. She also provides details (Weisner, 1986) showing that compulsory rehabilitation and retraining of the drinking driver has taken over much of the alcoholism treatment agenda throughout California within the last few years. One illustration: Only 28 percent of the caseload of three outpatient programs consisted of mandatory clients in 1979–80; but that figure reached 80 percent in 1983–84, when first violators of stiffened driving-under-the-influence (DUI) laws were added to the treatment load by the courts and probation officers. Recovery homes are affected by this practice, because of the temptation to take compulsory fee-paying DUI clients rather than voluntary clients who may not have alcoholism insurance.

Weisner and Room (1984, p. 177) point out how referrals from the criminal justice system (mostly drinking drivers) have adversely affected treatment of alcoholism:

> The flood of clients referred from the courts has been accompanied by changes in treatment philosophy. The original ideology of Alcoholics Anonymous (AA) and the alcoholism movement was highly oriented toward the client's motivation and voluntary treatment. AA waited for people to come in the door. Being properly motivated and receptive to the recovery process was considered crucial to recovery. Within the space of a few years, however, the barrier between voluntary and involuntary clients dissolved. The movement's rhetoric shifted to accommodate the realities of gathering clients. Programs became expert in "breaking through denial" [of alcoholism]; indeed, the whole rhetoric of intervention revolves around the concept of denial. Public programs use the threat of jail as a therapeutic tool. . . .
>
> Ideology and rhetoric have undergone dramatic change. Treatment providers now emphasize aggres-

sive outreach and intervention; they talk of confrontation and constructive coercion as tools of a tough love which will overcome denial. The providers themselves have not changed, only the rhetoric. Some would suggest that this shift is related to a drift toward a more punitive approach in U.S. society. However, as our research indicates, the shift reflects radical changes in the size, structure, and financing of the alcoholism treatment system itself.

Regardless of the necessity of compulsory drinking-driving rehabilitation programs, there is no question that this emphasis on law enforcement and economic influences as against clinical/diagnostic considerations needs to be kept within proper bounds. Perhaps an acceptable way to accomplish this is to provide separate-track rehabilitation programs for court-referred clients, with funding earmarked so that the clinically defined alcoholic is not neglected.

Prepaid Employee Assistance Programs

The private sector is rapidly undergoing reforms in the management of health insurance, as demonstrated by Califano's cost containment activities at the Chrysler Corporation (see Chapter Eight), through which he coped with the astronomically rising costs resulting from Medicare programs that he himself had helped launch when he was special assistant to President Johnson. Similar cost containment methods for a range of other United States corporations, including General Motors, Georgia Power, Eastman Kodak, and Tenneco, are described in a *Time* article (Castro, Delaney, and Dolan, 1986). Some of the methods include having employees pay higher portions of medical bills, so that they will be more careful about running up costs; greater use of health maintenance organizations to effect economies of scale and to put more emphasis on preventive medicine; and more careful monitoring of the necessity for expensive medical tests and treatments.

Either because of moralistic sentiments or the tendency of alcoholics to relapse repeatedly, many insurance companies refuse to provide coverage for alcoholism treatment, or they provide it only under prohibitive premium costs. On the other hand, many companies will reimburse for alcoholism treatment only if it is provided by a physician—thereby encouraging expensive in-hospital treatment when, in many instances, equally good detoxification and rehabilitation services could be provided in nonhospital settings. Leadership in solving such problems ultimately will have to be exerted by Congress in establishing clearer and more equitable rules for reimbursement under Medicare and Medicaid, which usually set precedents for the terms of private insurance coverage. As Chapter Eight has noted, the evolution of HMOs and similar general health care systems, which are reimbursed for keeping their clients well instead of on a fee-for-specific-service basis, may result in better prevention and treatment of alcoholism.

Insurance commissioners should require that all employee assistance programs (EAPs) be staffed with personnel who have had professional training in the ethics of treating employees with alcohol problems. EAPs also should have review boards consisting of representatives from management, the labor union, and employees; these boards should be responsible for ensuring that employees of the organization are accorded fair treatment. The existence of such review boards not only will be good for employee morale but also will help reduce turnover and lawsuits because of unfairness or ineptitude in referral or treatment.

Finally—

The following perspectives are suggested for consideration by all agencies, public and private, concerned with the reduction of alcohol-related problems:

1. The drinking habit of the problem drinker involves many of the same powerful immediate reinforcements as the habituated smoker gets from tobacco. Tobacco and alcohol do differ in their addictive properties because smokers usually are able to smoke incessantly, whereas drinkers can hold only so much alcohol at a sitting. Further, there usually is more social pressure from one's associates to join them in drinking than in smoking. However, smoking and drinking have in common the fact that both are

powerful habits which commonly require considerable retraining to break and are readily resumed unless one makes a great effort and has the support of his peers.

2. Some problem drinkers will respond more readily to the disease model of alcoholism in learning how to break the cycle of heavy drinking. Others will respond more readily to the "strong-habit" model of alcoholism in cooperating with retraining techniques designed to limit or eliminate their drinking. Both models can coexist effectively side by side, as long as people realize that these two models need not be antagonistic.

3. If we are to be at all effective in controlling alcohol problems, we should be realistic enough to see the absolute necessity of changing the total climate in which drinking occurs. The situation since repeal in America has become a stylized exercise in self-deception. More and more marketing pressure and advertising are being permitted, intensifying an atmosphere in which alcoholic beverages are being sold as though they were especially glamorous kinds of soft drinks. Until recent years the well-intentioned leaders of the alcoholism treatment movement agreed with the alcohol industry that the problem with alcohol was in the person, not the bottle. The industry would even have us swallow its alibi that the many millions of dollars poured into alcohol advertising were not really intended to increase consumption of alcohol, but merely to increase brand share.

4. A *public health* emphasis in alcohol problem prevention is more likely to be effective than a prohibitionist, moralistic approach. This nation has tried the latter approach repeatedly and has found it wanting. The public health approach is proving effective in reducing cigarette smoking through drawing the public's attention to the dangers of smoking and requiring warning signs on cigarette packages and advertising. Project SMART, spearheaded by the CSPI and drawing the support of more than thirty-five national consumer and public interest groups, is also applying a public health approach in its lobbying for warning labels on alcoholic beverage containers. The CSPI is using the same public health approach in its advocacy of legislation to reduce drinking problems through increasing taxes on alcohol and more stringent zoning and dram shop laws to reduce the linkage between

alcohol and the automobile. But again, in order to make any dent in the rates of problems caused by alcohol, we must work toward changing the climate of alcohol marketing, so that we do not permit the alcohol industry to go on selling alcoholic beverages as though they are alluring alternatives for Seven-Up. Despite the alcohol industry's claims that its advertising is intended only to increase brand share and not to increase the total amount of alcohol consumed, it does not take a marketing genius to know that alcohol advertising and marketing efforts are designed to engineer public acceptance of the image of alcoholic beverages as completely wholesome and desirable. Warning labels will at least make the public more aware of the hazards of excessive drinking and thus less susceptible to drinking problems.

5. In relation to alcohol policy: Obviously, our state, local, and national governments are the agencies we should hold responsible for bringing about equitable relationships between the general consuming and tax-paying public, the sellers of alcoholic beverages, the sufferers from alcoholism and their families, and those who treat alcoholics. These matters are not to be left to the much-vaunted "private sector," for the laissez-faire policy vacuum and overemphasis on individualism have been largely responsible for the high level of drinking problems in our country today. We already know how to do a better job of preventing alcohol problems; therefore, we should be able to formulate a set of rules and safeguards that will be much more effective than the patchwork ones we have now. Our country has solved even worse problems before. With a little political backbone, we should be able to reduce drinking problems to a livable level without a return to prohibition.

This chronicle of America's history of alcohol problems and their control will close with this final paragraph from a recent article, "Notes on the United States," by Octavio Paz of Mexico, the poet-essayist and former diplomat. Although he is writing about our foreign relations primarily, what he says fits our alcohol control situation equally well:

> The remedy is to regain unity of purpose,
> without which there is no possibility for action—but
> how? The malady of democracies is disunity, mother

of demagogism. The other road, that of political health, leads by way of soul-searching and self-criticism; a return to origins, to the foundations of the nation. In the case of the United States, this means to the vision of its founders—not to copy them, but to begin again. Not to do exactly as they did but, rather, like them, to make a new beginning. Such beginnings are at once purifications and mutations: With them something different always begins as well [Paz, 1986, p. 93].

References

Aaron, P., and Musto, D. "Temperance and Prohibition in America: A Historical Overview." In M. Moore and D. Geerstein (eds.), *Alcohol and Public Policy: Beyond the Shadow of Prohibition.* Washington, D.C.: National Academy Press, 1981.

Albee, G. "The Answer Is Prevention." *Psychology Today,* Feb. 1985, pp. 60-62, 64.

Alcohol and Drug Problems Association of North America. *Professional Training and Educational Opportunities, 1986 Schedule.* Washington, D.C.: Alcohol and Drug Problems Association of North America, 1986.

Alcohol, Drug, and Mental Health Administration. *FY 1983 ADAMHA Data Book.* Washington, D.C.: U.S. Department of Health and Human Services, 1977.

Alcoholics Anonymous. (3rd ed.) New York: A.A. World Services, 1976.

"Alcoholism: New Victims, New Treatment." *Time,* Apr. 22, 1974, pp. 75-81.

"AMA Wants Warnings on Liquor Bottles." *San Francisco Chronicle,* June 20, 1986, p. 8.

American Psychiatric Association. *Diagnostic and Statistical Manual of Mental Disorders* (3rd ed.) Washington, D.C.: American Psychiatric Association, 1980.

Armor, D., Polich, J., and Stambul, H. *Alcoholism and Treatment.* Santa Monica, Calif.: Rand, 1976.

Atkin, C., Neuendorf, K., and McDermott, S. "The Role of Alcohol Advertising in Excessive and Hazardous Drinking." *Journal of Drug Education,* 1983, *13* (4), 313–325.

Austin, G. *Perspectives on the History of Psychoactive Substance Abuse.* Washington, D.C.: National Institute on Drug Abuse, 1978.

Babor, T., and Meyer, R. (eds.). "Typologies of Alcoholics." In M. Galanter (ed.), *Recent Developments in Alcoholism.* Vol. 4. New York: Plenum, 1986.

Bacon, S. "Classic Temperance Movement of the U.S.A." *British Journal of Addiction,* 1967, *62* (112), 5–8.

Bailey, J., and Wakely, J. *Analysis of Education Programs for Primary Alcoholism Prevention.* Research Triangle Park, N.C.: Research Triangle Institute, 1973.

Bandura, A. *Principles of Behavior Modification.* New York: Holt, Rinehart & Winston, 1969.

Baumohl, J. "Dashaways and Doctors: The Treatment of Habitual Drunkards in San Francisco from the Gold Rush to Prohibition." Unpublished doctoral dissertation, University of California, Berkeley, 1986.

Baumohl, J., and Room, R. "Inebriety, Doctors, and the State: Alcoholism Treatment Institutions Before 1940." In M. Galanter (ed.), *Recent Developments in Alcoholism.* Vol. 5. New York: Plenum, 1987.

Bellah, R., and others. *Habits of the Heart: Individualism and Commitment in American Life.* Berkeley: University of California Press, 1985.

Belloc, N. "Relationship of Health Practices and Mortality." *Preventive Medicine,* 1973, *2,* 67–81.

Bennett, L., and Ames, G. (eds.). *The American Experience with Alcohol.* New York: Plenum, 1985.

"The Best Students Money Can Buy." "This World" sec. of *San Francisco Examiner,* Feb. 23, 1986.

Bissell, L., and Haberman, P. *Alcoholism in the Professions.* New York: Oxford University Press, 1984.

Blane, H. "Education and the Prevention of Alcoholism." In B. Kissin and H. Begleiter (eds.), *The Biology of Alcoholism.* Vol. 8: *Social Aspects of Alcoholism.* New York: Plenum, 1976.

Booz, Allen, and Hamilton. *The Alcoholism Funding Study: Evaluation of Sources of Funds and Barriers to Funding Alcoholism Treatment Programs.* Washington, D.C.: U.S. Department of Health and Human Services, 1978.

Boyajay, T. *Alcoholism Within Prepaid Group Practice HMOs.* Washington, D.C.: Group Health Association of America, 1978.

Breed, W., and De Foe, J. "Themes in Magazine Alcohol Advertisements: A Critique." *Journal of Drug Issues,* Fall 1979, pp. 511–522.

Breed, W., and De Foe, J. "Effecting Media Change: The Role of Cooperative Consultation on Alcohol Topics." *Journal of Communication,* 1982, *32* (2), 88–99.

Brenner, B., Cisin, I., and Newcomb, C. "Drinking Practices and Accidental Injuries." Paper presented at conference on Alcohol Use and Accidents, sponsored by the Society for the Study of Social Problems, Miami Beach, Aug. 1966.

Bretherton, G. "Against the Flaming Tide: Drink and Temperance in the Making of Modern Ireland." In R. Room, S. Barrows, and J. Verhey (eds.), *A Social History of Drinking.* Berkeley: University of California Press, forthcoming.

Brown, S. *Treating the Alcoholic.* New York: Wiley, 1985.

Bruun, K. "The Minimization of Alcohol Damage." *Drinking and Drug Practices Surveyor,* 1973, No. 8, 15 (abstract).

Bruun, K., and others. *Alcohol Control Policies in Public Health Perspective.* Helsinki: Finish Foundation for Alcohol Studies, 1975.

Bunce, R. *The Political Economy of California's Wine Industry.* Research Paper F-88. Berkeley, Calif.: Social Research Group, 1979.

Burt, M., and Biegel, M. *Worldwide Survey of Nonmedical Drug Use and Alcohol Use Among Military Personnel.* Bethesda, Md.: Burt Associates, 1980.

Butynski, W. (ed.). *Executive Summary from the January 1984 Final Contract Report of the Development of Model Professional Standards for Counselor Credentialing Submitted to the National Institute on Alcohol Abuse and Alcoholism.* Washington, D.C.: National Association of State Alcohol and Drug Abuse Directors, 1984.

Butynski, W. *Resource Directory of National Alcohol-Related Associations, Agencies and Organizations.* Washington, D.C.: National Association of State Alcohol and Drug Abuse Directors, 1985.

Butynski, W., Record, N., and Yates, J. *State Resources and Services for Alcohol and Drug Abuse Problems: Fiscal Year 1984.* Washington, D.C.: National Association of State Alcohol and Drug Abuse Directors, 1985.

Butynski, W., Record, N., and Yates, J. *State Resources and Services Related to Alcohol and Drug Abuse Problems: Fiscal Year 1985.* Washington, D.C.: National Association of State Alcohol and Drug Abuse Directors, 1986.

Caetano, R. "Two Versions of Dependence: DSM-III and the Alcohol Dependence Syndrome." *Drug and Alcohol Dependence,* 1985, *15,* 81–103.

Caetano, R. "A Commentary on the Proposed Changes in DSM-III Concept of Alcohol Dependence." *Drug and Alcohol Dependence,* 1987a.

Caetano, R. "Drinking Patterns and Alcohol Problems in a National Sample of U.S. Hispanics." In *The Epidemiology of Alcohol Use and Abuse Among U.S. Minorities.* Rockville, Md.: National Institute on Alcohol Abuse and Alcoholism, 1987b.

Cahalan, D. *Problem Drinkers: A National Survey.* San Francisco: Jossey-Bass, 1970.

Cahalan, D. "Can Alcoholism Be Defeated?" *The Sciences,* Mar./Apr. 1977, *17,* 16–19.

Cahalan, D. "Why Does the Alcoholism Field Act Like a Ship of Fools?" *British Journal of Addiction,* 1979, *74,* 235–238.

Cahalan, D. "Quantifying Alcohol Consumption: Patterns and Problems." *Circulation,* 1981, *64* (Supp. III), 7–14.

Cahalan, D. "Studying Drinking Problems Rather Than Alcoholism." In M. Galanter (ed.), *Recent Developments in Alcoholism.* Vol. 7. New York: Plenum, 1987.

Cahalan, D., and Cisin, I. *Final Report on a Service-Wide Survey of Attitudes and Behavior of Naval Personnel Concerning Alcohol and Problem Drinking.* Washington, D.C.: Bureau of Social Science Research, 1975.

Cahalan, D., Cisin, I., and Crossley, H. *American Drinking Practices.* New Brunswick, N.J.: Center of Alcohol Studies, Rutgers University, 1969.

Cahalan, D., and others. *Drinking Practices and Problems in the U.S. Army, 1972.* Arlington, Va.: Information Systems Inc., 1972.

Califano, J. *America's Health Care Revolution.* New York: Random House, 1986.

Capps, S. "Courts Vary in Handling of Drunk Drivers." *San Francisco Examiner,* Apr. 15, 1986, p. D-4.

Carter, A. "Alcohol and Drug Abuse Training in Nursing Schools." *Alcohol Health and Research World,* Fall 1983, *8* (1), 24-25, 29.

Castro, J., Delaney, P., and Dolan, B. "Pinned Down by Medical Bills." *Time,* June 30, 1986, pp. 64-65.

Cavanagh, J., and Clairmonte, F. *Alcoholic Beverages: Dimensions of Corporate Power.* New York: St. Martin's Press, 1985.

Cherrington, E. H., and associates. "Inebriate Institutions." In E. H. Cherrington (ed.), *Standard Encyclopedia of the Alcohol Problem.* Vol. 3. Westerville, Ohio: American Issue Publishing, 1926.

Clark, W. "Operational Definitions of Drinking Problems and Associated Prevalence Rates." *Quarterly Journal of Studies on Alcohol,* 1966, *27,* 648-668.

Clark, W., and Cahalan, D. "Changes in Problem Drinking over a Four-Year Span." *Addictive Behaviors,* 1976, *1* (3), 251-259.

Clark, W., and Hilton, M. "Changes in American Drinking Patterns and Problems, 1967-1984." Unpublished paper. Berkeley, Calif.: Alcohol Research Group, 1986.

Clark, W., Knupfer, G., and Midanik, L. *Draft Report on the 1975 Survey.* Berkeley, Calif.: Social Research Group, 1981.

Clayton, A. "Attitudes Towards Drinking and Driving: Their Role in the Effectiveness of Countermeasures." *Alcohol, Drugs and Driving Abstracts and Reviews,* Jan.-Mar. 1986, *2* (1), 1-8.

Clayton, J. "City Extends Limits on Liquor Outlets in South-Central L. A." *Los Angeles Times,* May 1, 1986, Part II, p. 1.

Coffey, T. "Beer Street: Gin Lane: Some Views of 18th-Century Drinking." *Quarterly Journal of Studies on Alcohol,* Dec. 1966, *27* (4), 669-692.

Cook, P. "Alcohol Taxes as a Public Health Measure." *British Journal of Addiction,* 1982, 77, 245–250.

Cowan, R., and Mosher, J. "Public Health Implications of Beverage Marketing: Alcohol as an Ordinary Consumer Product." *Contemporary Drug Problems,* Winter 1985, pp. 621–657.

Criteria Committee, National Council on Alcoholism. "Criteria for the Diagnosis of Alcoholism." *American Journal of Psychiatry,* 1972, *129,* 127–135; *Annals of Internal Medicine,* 1972, 77, 249–258.

Cummings, N. "The Dismantling of Our Health System: Strategies for the Survival of Psychological Practice." *American Psychologist,* Apr. 1986, *41,* 426–431.

Day, N. "Alcohol and Mortality: Separating the Drink from the Drinker." Unpublished doctoral dissertation, University of California, Berkeley, 1979.

De Foe, J., and Breed, W. "The Problem of Alcohol Advertisements in College Newspapers." *Journal of the American College Health Association,* Feb. 1979, *27,* 195–199.

Dickens, B., and others. *Report of the Committee of Enquiry into Allegations Concerning Drs. Linda and Mark Sobell.* Toronto: Addiction Research Foundation, 1982.

Distilled Spirits Council of the United States. *Annual Statistical Review, 1984/85.* Washington, D.C.: Distilled Spirits Council, 1985.

Dorchester, D. *The Liquor Problem in All Ages.* New York: Phillips & Hunt, 1888.

Doroff, D. "Group Psychotherapy in Alcoholism." In B. Kissin and H. Begleiter (eds.), *The Biology of Alcoholism.* Vol. 5: *Treatment and Rehabilitation of the Chronic Alcoholic.* New York: Plenum, 1977.

"Dr. Robert Niven: Alcohol Research." *ADAMHA News,* Apr. 1985, *11* (4), 3.

Durkheim, E. *Suicide.* (J. Spaulding and G. Simpson, trans.) New York: Free Press, 1947. (Originally published 1897.)

Earle, R. "Prevention of Alcoholism in the United States and the National Council on Alcoholism: 1944–1950." *International Journal of the Addictions,* 1982, *17* (4), 679–702.

Easterbrook, G. "The Revolution in Medicine." *Newsweek,* Jan. 26, 1987, pp. 40-74.

Eastern Area Alcohol Education and Training Program. *A Manual of Accreditation Standards for Alcoholism Counselor Training Programs.* Bloomfield, Conn.: Eastern Area Alcohol Education and Training Programs, 1977.

Edwards, G., and Gross, M. "Alcohol Dependence: Provisional Description of a Clinical Syndrome." *British Medical Journal,* 1976, *1,* 1058-1061.

Edwards, G., and others. *Alcohol Related Disabilities.* WHO Offset Publication no. 32. Geneva: World Health Organization, 1977.

Emrick, C. "Review of Ruggels and others." *Journal of Studies on Alcohol,* Dec. 1976, *37* (12), 1902-1907.

Farrell, S. *Review of National Policy Measures to Prevent Alcohol-Related Problems.* Geneva: Division of Mental Health, World Health Organization, 1985.

Fernandez, E. "Who Heals the Drunken Doctor?" *San Francisco Examiner,* Mar. 16, 1986, p. S-1.

Fillmore, K. "The 1980s Dominant Theory of Alcohol Problems— Genetic Predisposition to Alcoholism: Where Is It Leading Us?" *Drugs and Society,* forthcoming, *2* (2).

Fillmore, K., and Kelso, D. "Coercion into Alcoholism Treatment: Meanings for the Disease Concept of Alcoholism." *Journal of Drug Issues,* forthcoming.

Fingarette, H. "Alcoholism—Neither Sin nor Disease." *The Center Magazine* (Santa Barbara, Calif.), May-June 1985, pp. 56-63.

Finn, P. "Decriminalization of Public Drunkenness: Response of the Health Care System." *Journal of Studies on Alcohol,* 1985, *46* (1), 7-23.

Foy, D., and Rychtarik, R. "Practical Issues in Selecting and Using Treatment Goals with Severely Dependent Alcohol Abusers." *Drugs and Society,* 1987, *1* (2-3), 69-81.

Goldsmith, F., and others. *Analysis of a Survey of Leadership Attitudes Toward Alcoholism in the United States.* Vol. 2: *Major Findings Report.* New York: Roper Organization, Aug. 1984.

Goodwin, D. "Overview." In M. Galanter (ed.), *Recent Developments in Alcoholism.* Vol. 1: *Genetics, Behavioral Treatment,*

Social Mediators and Prevention: Current Concepts and Diagnosis. New York: Plenum, 1983.

Goodwin, D., and Guze, S. "Alcoholism." In *Psychiatric Diagnosis.* (3rd ed.) New York: Oxford University Press, 1984.

Greider, W. "The Education of David Stockman." *Atlantic,* Dec. 1981, *248,* 27–40.

Gross, L. *How Much Is Too Much?* New York: Random House, 1983.

Gusfield, J. "Status Conflicts and the Changing Ideologies of the American Temperance Movement." In G. Pittman and C. Snyder (eds.), *Society, Culture, and Drinking Patterns.* New York: Wiley, 1962.

Guze, S., Goodwin, D., and Crane, J. "Criminality and Psychiatric Disorders." *Archives of General Psychiatry,* 1969, *20,* 583–591.

Halikas, J. "Overview" to Chap. 4, "Diagnosis of Alcoholism." In M. Galanter (ed.), *Recent Developments in Alcoholism.* Vol. 1. New York: Plenum, 1983.

"Harper's Index." *Harper's,* July 1986, *273* (1634), 11.

Harwood, H. J., and others. *Economic Costs to Society of Alcohol and Drug Abuse and Mental Illness: 1980.* Research Triangle Park, N.C.: Research Triangle Institute, 1984.

"The Health Care System in the Mid-1990's." Attachment No. 5 to *A Study Conducted for the Health Insurance Association of America.* Boston: Arthur D. Little, 1985.

Heath, D. "Anthropological Perspectives on the Social Biology of Alcohol: An Introduction to the Literature." In B. Kissin and H. Begleiter (eds.), *The Biology of Alcoholism.* Vol. 4. New York: Plenum, 1976.

Herd, D. "The Epidemiology of Drinking Patterns and Alcohol-Related Problems Among U.S. Blacks." In *The Epidemiology of Alcohol Use and Abuse Among U.S. Minorities.* Rockville, Md.: National Institute on Alcohol Abuse and Alcoholism, 1987.

Hilton, M. "The Presence of Alcohol in Four Social Situations: Survey Results from 1964 and 1984." *International Journal of the Addictions,* forthcoming.

Hoffman, F. *A Handbook on Drug and Alcohol Abuse: The Biomedical Aspects.* (2nd ed.) New York: Oxford University Press, 1983.

Holder, H., and Wallack, L. "Contemporary Perspectives for Preventing Alcohol Problems: An Empirically Derived Model." *Journal of Public Health Policy*, 1986, 7 (3), 324–339.

Hudolin, V. "Medical-Psychiatric Research on Alcoholism." In M. Keller and T. Coffey (eds.), *Proceedings of the 28th International Congress on Alcohol and Alcoholism.* Highland Park, N.J.: Hillhouse Press, 1969.

Humphreys, N. "Social Workers' Roles in Alcohol and Drug Abuse Services." *Alcohol Health and Research World*, Fall 1983, 8 (1), 28–29.

Hyman, M., and others. *Drinkers, Drinking and Alcohol-Related Mortality and Hospitalizations: A Statistical Compendium.* New Brunswick, N.J.: Center of Alcohol Studies, Rutgers University, 1980.

Institute of Medicine. *For-Profit Enterprise in Health Care.* Washington, D.C.: National Academy Press, 1986.

Institute of Medicine. *Causes and Consequences of Alcohol Related Problems: An Agenda for Research.* Washington, D.C.: National Academy Press, 1987.

Jacob, O. *Public and Private Issues on Alcohol and Other Drug Abuse.* Rockville, Md.: Alcohol, Drug, and Mental Health Administration, 1985.

Jacobson, G. "Detection, Assessment, and Diagnosis of Alcoholism: Current Techniques." In M. Galanter (ed.), *Recent Developments in Alcoholism.* Vol. 1. New York: Plenum, 1983.

Jacobson, M., Atkins, R., and Hacker, G. *The Booze Merchants: The Inebriating of America.* Washington, D.C.: Center for Science in the Public Interest, 1983.

Jellinek, E. "Phases in the Drinking History of Alcoholics: Analysis of a Survey Conducted by the Official Organ of Alcoholics Anonymous." *Quarterly Journal of Studies on Alcohol*, June 1946, 7 (1), 1–88.

Jellinek, E. "Phases of Alcohol Addiction." *Quarterly Journal of Studies on Alcohol*, 1952, 13 (1), 673–684.

Jellinek, E. *The Disease Concept of Alcoholism.* New Brunswick, N.J.: Hillhouse Press, 1960.

Johnston, L., O'Malley, P., and Bachman, J. *Use of Licit and Illicit Drugs by America's High School Students, 1975–1984.* DHHS

Publication No. (ADM) 85-1394. Washington, D.C.: U.S. Government Printing Office, 1985.

Julien, R. *A Primer of Drug Action.* (2nd ed.) New York: W. H. Freeman, 1978.

Kagan, D. "Alcoholics Not So Anonymous." *Esquire,* Feb. 1985, p. 64.

Keller, M. "The Definition of Alcoholism and the Estimation of its Prevalence." In D. J. Pittmann, and C. R. Snyder (eds.), *Society, Culture and Drinking Patterns.* New York: Wiley, 1962.

Kissin, B. "Theory and Practice in the Treatment of Alcoholism." In B. Kissin and H. Begleiter (eds.), *The Biology of Alcoholism.* Vol. 5: *Treatment and Rehabilitation of the Chronic Alcoholic.* New York: Plenum, 1977.

Knupfer, G. "The Epidemiology of Problem Drinking." *American Journal of Public Health,* 1967, *57,* 973-986.

Knupfer, G. "Ex-Problem Drinkers." In M. Roff, L. Robins, and M. Pollock (eds.), *Life History Research in Psychopathology.* Vol. 2. Minneapolis: University of Minnesota Press, 1972.

Kobler, J. *Ardent Spirits: The Rise and Fall of Prohibition.* New York: Putnam's, 1973.

Korcok, M. "A & D Certification Approved." *U.S. Journal of Drug and Alcohol Dependence,* Sept. 1985a, *9* (8), 1.

Korcok, M. "Alcoholism Treatment a Growing 'Product Line.'" *American Medical News,* Oct. 1985b, *28* (37), 29-30.

Korcok, M. "For Profit A & D Programs Expand by More Than Fifty Percent." *U.S. Journal of Drug and Alcohol Dependence,* July 1985c, *9* (7), 20.

Korcok, M. "Changes in JCAH Standards to Be Released This Summer." *U.S. Journal of Alcohol and Drug Dependence,* Mar. 1986 *10* (3), 1.

Krout, J. *The Origins of Prohibition.* New York: Knopf, 1925.

Levine, H. "The Discovery of Addiction: Changing Conceptions of Habitual Drunkenness in America." *Journal of Studies on Alcohol,* Jan. 1978, *39* 1, 143-174.

Levine, H. "Manifesto for a New Alcohol Social Science." *Drinking and Drug Practices Surveyor,* Sept. 1981a, No. 17, pp. 20-29.

Levine, H. "Spirits in America: The Birth of Demon Rum." *Public Opinion,* June/July 1981b, pp. 13-15.

Levine, H. "The Committee of Fifty and the Origins of Alcohol Control." *Journal of Drug Issues,* 1983a, *13* 1, 95–115.

Levine, H. "The Good Creature of God and the Demon Rum: Colonial American and 19th Century Ideas About Alcohol, Crime, and Accidents." In R. Room and G. Collins (eds.), *Alcohol and Disinhibition: Nature and Meaning of the Link.* Rockville, Md.: National Institute on Alcohol Abuse and Alcoholism, 1983b.

Levine, H. "The Birth of American Alcohol Control: Prohibition, the Power Elite, and the Problem of Lawlessness." *Contemporary Drug Problems,* Spring 1985, pp. 63–115.

Lewis, J. *The Alcoholism Report* (a subscription newsletter). Vols. 10 (1982) through 14 (1986). See specific dates in text.

Lewis, J. "The Federal Role in Alcoholism Research, Treatment and Prevention." In E. Gomberg, H. White, and J. Carpenter (eds.), *Alcohol, Science and Society Revisited.* Ann Arbor, Mich., and New Brunswick, N.J.: University of Michigan Press and Center of Alcohol Studies, Rutgers University, 1982a.

Lewis, J. "Washington Report." *Journal of Studies on Alcohol,* 1982b, *43* (5), 616–619.

Roy Littlejohn Associates. *Proposed National Standard for Alcoholism Counselors.* Rockville, Md.: National Institute on Alcohol Abuse and Alcoholism, 1974.

MacAndrew, C., and Edgerton, R. *Drunken Comportment: A Social Explanation.* Hawthorne, N.Y.: Aldine, 1969.

McBride, R., and Mosher, J. "Public Health Implications of the International Alcohol Industry: Issues Raised by a World Health Organization Project." *British Journal of Addiction,* 1985, *80,* 141–147.

McCrady, B., and others. "Cost Effectiveness of Alcoholism Treatment in Partial Hospital Versus Inpatient Settings After Brief Inpatient Treatment: 12-Month Outcomes." *Journal of Consulting and Clinical Psychology,* 1986, *54* (5), 708–713.

McGinley, L. "Move to Raise Drinking Age in Wisconsin Reflects Nationwide Pressure and Concern." *Wall Street Journal,* May 21, 1986, sec. 2, p. 1.

Mäkelä, K., and others. *Alcohol, Society, and the State: A Com-*

parative Study of Alcohol Control. Vol. 1. Toronto: Addiction Research Foundation, 1981.

Malin, H., Wilson, R., and Williams, G. "1983 NHIS Alcohol/ Health Practices Supplement: Preliminary Findings." In *Proceedings of the 1985 Public Health Conference on Records and Statistics*. Pub. No. (PHS) 86-1214 Hyattsville, Md.: U.S. Public Health Service, 1985.

Malzberg, B. *The Alcoholic Psychoses: Demographic Aspects at Midcentury in New York State*. New Haven, Conn.: Yale Center of Alcohol Studies, 1960.

Mandell, W. "Types and Phases of Alcohol Dependence Illness." In M. Galanter (ed.), *Recent Developments in Alcoholism*. Vol. 1. New York: Plenum, 1983.

Marlatt, A. "The Controlled-Drinking Controversy: A Commentary." *American Psychologist*, Oct. 1983, *38*, 1097-1110.

Marlatt, A. and Gordon, J. (eds.). *Relapse Prevention: Maintenance Strategies in the Treatment of Addictive Behaviors*. New York: Guilford Press, 1985.

Maxwell, M. "Alcoholics Anonymous." In E. Gomberg, H. White, and J. Carpenter (eds.), *Alcohol, Science and Society Revisited*. Ann Arbor, Mich., and New Brunswick, N.J.: University of Michigan Press and Center of Alcohol Studies, Rutgers University, 1982.

Medicine in the Public Interest. *The Effects of Alcoholic-Beverage Control Laws*. Washington, D.C.: Medicine in the Public Interest, 1979.

Miller, W. "Haunted by the *Zeitgeist:* Reflections on Contemporary Treatment Goals and Concepts of Alcoholism in Europe and the United States." *Annals of the New York Academy of Sciences*, July 11, 1986, *472*, 110-129.

Miller, W. "Behavioral Treatment Research Advances: Barriers to Utilization." In L. Sobell and M. Sobell (eds.), *Two Decades of Behavioral Research in the Alcohol Field: Change, Challenge, and Controversy*. Special issue: *Advances in Behavior Research and Therapy*. Elmsford, N.Y.: Pergamon Press, 1987.

Miller, W. "Motivation and Treatment Goals." *Drugs and Society*, 1987, *1* (2-3), 133-151.

Miller, W. and Hester, R. "Treating the Problem Drinker: Modern Approaches." In W. Miller (ed.), *The Addictive Behaviors: Treatment of Alcoholism, Drug Abuse, Smoking, and Obesity.* Oxford, England: Pergamon Press, 1980.

Miller, W., and Hester, R. "The Effectiveness of Alcoholism Treatment: What Research Reveals." In R. Miller and N. Heather (eds.), *Treating Addictive Behaviors.* New York: Plenum, 1986a.

Miller, W., and Hester, R. "Inpatient Alcoholism Treatment: Who Benefits?" *American Psychologist,* July 1986b, *41* (7), 794–805.

Miller, W., and Hester, R. "Matching Problem Drinkers with Optimal Treatments." In W. Miller and N. Heather (eds), *Treating Addictive Behaviors.* New York: Plenum, 1986c.

Morgan, P. "The Political Economy of Drugs and Alcohol: An Introduction." *Journal of Drug Issues,* Winter 1983, *13* (1), 1–7.

Mosher, J. "The Alcohol Beverage Control System in California." Unpublished draft paper. Berkeley, Calif.: Alcohol Research Group, Feb. 1979.

Mosher, J. "Tax-Deductible Alcohol: An Issue of Public Health Policy and Prevention Strategy." *Journal of Public Health Policy and Law,* Winter 1983, *7* (4), 855–888.

Mosher, J. "The Impact of Legal Provisions on Barroom Behavior: Toward an Alcohol-Problem Prevention Policy." *Alcohol,* 1984a, *1,* 205–211.

Mosher, J. *Server Intervention: A Guide to Implementing Local and State Programs.* Berkeley, Calif.: Prevention Research Center, Oct. 1984b.

Mosher, J. "Alcohol Policy and the Presidential Commission on Drunk Driving: The Paths Not Taken." *Accident Analysis and Prevention,* 1985a, *17* (3), 239–250.

Mosher, J. "The Model Alcoholic Beverage Retail Licensee Liability Act of 1985." *Western State Law Review,* Spring 1985b, *12* (2), 442–517.

Mosher, J. "Public Policies Affecting the Prevention of Alcohol-Related Problems: Options for California." In A. Mecca (ed.), *Prevention Action Plan for Alcohol-Related Problems.* San Rafael: California Health Research Foundation, 1985c.

Mosher, J., and Beauchamp, D. "Justifying Alcohol Taxes to

Public Officials." *Journal of Public Health Policy*, Dec. 1985, *4* (3), 442–439.

Mosher, J. and Mottl, J. "The Role of Nonalcohol Agencies in Federal Regulation of Drinking Behavior and Consequences." In M. Moore and D. Gerstein (eds.), *Alcohol and Public Policy: Beyond the Shadow of Prohibition*. Washington, D.C.: National Academy Press, 1981.

Mosher, J. and Wallack, L. "Government Regulation of Alcohol Advertising: Protecting Industry Profits Versus Promoting the Public Health." *Journal of Public Health Policy*, Dec. 1981, *2* (4), 333–353.

Moskowitz, D. and Pave, I. "The Sobering of America: A Push to Put Drinking in Its Place." *Business Week*, Feb. 25, 1985, pp. 112–113.

Murray, R., Clifford, C., and Gurling, H. "Twin and Adoption Studies: How Good is the Evidence for a Genetic Role?" In M. Galanter (ed.) *Recent Developments in Alcoholism*, Vol. 1. New York: Plenum, 1983.

Nathan, P. and McCrady, B. "Bases for the Use of Abstinence as a Goal in the Behavioral Treatment of Alcohol Abusers." *Drugs and Society*, 1987, *1* (2–3), 109–131.

National Advisory Committee on Alcoholism. *Interim Report to the Secretary of the Department of Health, Education and Welfare*. Washington, D.C.: National Advisory Committee on Alcoholism, 1968.

"The National Alcohol Research Centers." *Alcohol Health and Research World*, 1985, *9* (3), pp. 6–9.

National Association of State Alcohol and Drug Abuse Directors. *The BATF: "Revenooers" and Regulators*. Washington, D.C.: National Association of State Alcohol and Drug Abuse Directors, 1980.

National Association of State Alcohol and Drug Abuse Directors. *Federal Response to Alcoholism and Alcohol Abuse*. Washington, D.C.: National Association of State Alcohol and Drug Abuse Directors, 1984.

National Institute on Alcohol Abuse and Alcoholism. *First Special Report to the U.S. Congress on Alcohol and Health*. Rockville, Md.: National Institute on Alcohol Abuse and Alcoholism, 1971.

National Institute on Alcohol Abuse and Alcoholism. *Annual Report to the U.S. Congress, Fiscal Year 1972.* Rockville, Md.: National Institute of Alcohol Abuse and Alcoholism, 1972.

National Institute on Alcohol Abuse and Alcoholism. *Accomplishments and Challenges: Five Years of Progress.* Rockville, Md.: National Institute on Alcohol Abuse and Alcoholism, 1975.

National Institute on Alcohol Abuse and Alcoholism. "French Prevention Effort Takes Varied Approaches." *NIAAA Information and Feature Service,* Apr. 27, 1977a, No. 35, p. 6.

National Institute on Alcohol Abuse and Alcoholism. *6th Annual Report to the United States Congress, Fiscal Year 1977.* Rockville, Md.: National Institute on Alcohol Abuse and Alcoholism, 1977b.

National Institute on Alcohol Abuse and Alcoholism. *Report to the U.S. Congress on Federal Activities on Alcohol Abuse and Alcoholism, FY 1977.* Rockville, Md.: National Institute on Alcohol Abuse and Alcoholism, 1979.

National Institute on Alcohol Abuse and Alcoholism. *Credentialing of Alcoholism Counselors.* Rockville, Md.: National Institute on Alcohol Abuse and Alcoholism, 1980.

National Institute on Alcohol Abuse and Alcoholism. *Fifth Special Report to the U.S. Congress on Alcohol and Health.* Rockville, Md.: National Institute on Alcohol Abuse and Alcoholism, 1983.

National Institute on Alcohol Abuse and Alcoholism. "Epidemiological Bulletin 2: Changes in Alcoholism Treatment Services, 1979-1982." *Alcohol Health and Research World,* Winter 1983/84, *8,* 44-47.

National Institute on Alcohol Abuse and Alcoholism. *Prevention Strategies Plan . . . FY 1986 to FY 1991.* Rockville, Md.: National Institute on Alcohol Abuse and Alcoholism, [1986a].

National Institute on Alcohol Abuse and Alcoholism. *Towards a National Plan to Combat Alcohol Abuse and Alcoholism: A Report to the United States Congress.* Rockville, Md.: National Institute on Alcohol Abuse and Alcoholism, 1986b.

"NIAAA Announces Change in Grant Review Process." *Bulletin on Alcohol Policy,* Winter 1985, *4* (1), 8-9.

National Research Council and Institute of Medicine. *Injury in

America: A Continuing Public Health Problem. Washington,
D.C.: National Academy Press, 1985.

Nieberding, S. "The Evolution of the National Institute on Alcohol
Abuse and Alcoholism." In B. Stimmel (ed.), *Federal Priorities
in Funding Alcoholism and Drug Abuse Programs.* Advances in
Alcohol and Substance Abuse, Vol. 2, No. 3. New York: Haworth
Press, 1983.

Niven, R. G. "Alcoholism—A Problem in Perspective." *Journal of
the American Medical Association,* 1984, *252* (14), 1912-1914.

O'Briant, R., and Lennard, H. *Recovery from Alcoholism: A Social
Treatment Model.* Springfield, Ill.: Thomas, 1973.

O'Donnell, M. *Research on Drinking Locations of Alcohol-
Impaired Drivers: Implications for Prevention Policies.* Berkeley:
Alcohol and Drug Abuse Prevention Program, Student Health
Service, University of California, 1984.

Osterberg, E. "From Home Distillation to the State Alcohol Monop-
oly." *Contemporary Drug Problems,* Spring 1985, *12* (1), 31-51.

Packard, M. "DUI/DWAI Offenders Compared to Clients Seen in
an Outpatient Alcohol-Treatment Facility." *Journal of Alcohol
and Drug Education,* 1987, *32* (2), 1-12.

Pattison, E. "Rehabilitation of the Chronic Alcoholic." In B. Kissin
and H. Begleiter (eds.), *The Biology of Alcoholism.* Vol. 3:
Clinical Pathology. New York: Plenum, 1974.

Pattison, E., Sobell, M., and Sobell, L. (eds.). *Emerging Concepts
of Alcohol Dependence.* New York: Springer, 1977.

Payer, L. "U.S. Alcohol Treatment in Jeopardy." *The Journal,*
1985, *14* (4), 4.

Paz, O. "Notes on the United States." *Wilson Quarterly,* Spring
1986, *10* (2), 80-93.

Peele, S. "The Cultural Context of Psychological Approaches to
Alcoholism: Can We Control the Effects of Alcohol?" *American
Psychologist,* Dec. 1984, *39*, 337-351.

Peele, S. "The Implications and Limitations of Genetic Models of
Alcoholism and Other Addictions." *Journal of Studies on
Alcohol,* 1986, *47* (1), 63-73.

Pendery, M., Maltzman, I., and West, L. "Controlled Drinking by
Alcoholics? New Findings and a Reevaluation of a Major
Affirmative Study." *Science,* 1982, *217*, 169-175.

Petrakis, P. *Alcoholism: An Inherited Disease.* Rockville, Md.: National Institute on Alcohol Abuse and Alcoholism, 1985.

Plaut, T. *Alcohol Problems: A Report to the Nation by the Cooperative Commission on the Study of Alcoholism.* New York: Oxford University Press, 1967.

Pokorny, A. "Alcohol and Drug Abuse Education in U.S. Medical Schools." *Alcohol Health and Research World,* Fall 1983, *8* (1), 13–16.

Polich, J., Armor, D., and Braiker, H. *The Course of Alcoholism: Four Years After Treatment.* Santa Monica, Calif.: Rand, 1980.

Polich, J., and Orvis, B. *Alcohol Problems: Patterns and Prevalence in the U.S. Air Force.* Santa Monica, Calif.: Rand, 1979.

Poltz, K., and others. "Alcohol on the Rocks: The New Prohibitionists and Health-Conscious Consumers Are Sobering Up America." *Newsweek,* Dec. 31, 1984, pp. 52–54.

Prevention Research Center. *Research Issues in the Prevention of Alcohol-Related Injuries.* Vols. 1 and 2. Berkeley, Calif.: Prevention Research Center, 1986.

Reed, P., and Sanchez, D. *Characteristics of Alcoholism Services in the United States, 1984.* Rockville, Md.: National Institute on Alcohol Abuse and Alcoholism, 1986.

Reinarman, C. *Social Movements and Social Problems: "Mothers Against Drunk Drivers," Restrictive Alcohol Laws and Social Control in the 1980s.* Publication E-182. Berkeley, Calif.: Alcohol Research Group, 1985.

Reynolds, R. "Building Constituencies for Prevention of Alcohol Problems." Paper presented to Prevention Symposium, Addiction Research Foundation, Toronto, March 19, 1985.

Richman, A. "Cost/Benefit Analyses of Alcoholism and Drug Abuse Treatment Programs: The Relevance of Recidivism and Resource Absorption." Paper presented at annual meeting of the American Association for the Advancement of Science, Washington, D.C., Feb. 1978.

Roizen, R. "Comment on the 'Rand Report.'" *Journal of Studies on Alcohol,* Jan. 1977, *38* (1), 170–178.

Roizen, R. *The World Health Organization Study of Community Responses to Alcohol-Related Problems: A Review of Cross-*

Cultural Findings. Berkeley, Calif.: Alcohol Research Group, 1981.

Roizen, R. "The Great Controlled Drinking Controversy." In M. Galanter (ed.), *Recent Developments in Alcoholism.* Vol. 5. New York: Plenum, 1987.

Roizen, R., Cahalan, D., and Shanks, P. " 'Spontaneous Remission' Among Untreated Problem Drinkers." In D. Kandel (ed.), *Longitudinal Research on Drug Use: Empirical Findings and Methodological Issues.* Washington, D.C.: Hemisphere, 1978.

Roizen, R., and Weisner, C. *Fragmentation in Alcoholism Treatment Services: An Exploratory Analysis.* Berkeley, Calif.: Alcohol Research Group, 1979.

Room, R. "Governing Images and the Prevention of Alcohol Problems." *Preventive Medicine,* 1974a, *3,* 11-23.

Room, R. "Minimizing Alcohol Problems." *Alcohol Health and Research World,* Fall 1974b, pp. 12-17.

Room. R. "Priorities in Alcohol Social Science Research." *Journal of Studies on Alcohol,* Nov. 1979, Supp. No. 8, pp. 248-268.

Room, R. "New Curves in the Course: A Comment on Polich, Armor, and Braiker, 'The Course of Alcoholism.' " *British Journal of Addiction,* 1980, *75* (4), 351-360.

Room, R. "Alcohol, Science and Social Control." In E. Gomberg, H. White, and J. Carpenter (eds.), *Alcohol, Science and Society Revisited.* Ann Arbor, Mich., and New Brunswick, N.J.: University of Michigan Press and Center of Alcohol Studies, Rutgers University, 1982.

Room, R. "Alcohol Control and Public Health." *Annual Review of Public Health,* 1984a, *5,* 293-317.

Room, R. "Former NIAAA Directors Look Back: Policymakers and the Role of Research." *Drinking and Drug Practices Surveyor,* April 1984b, No. 19, pp. 38-42.

Room, R., and Day, N. "Alcohol and Mortality." In National Institute on Alcohol Abuse and Alcoholism, *Second Special Report to Congress on Alcohol and Health.* Rockville, Md.: National Institute on Alcohol Abuse and Alcoholism, 1974.

Room, R., and Mosher, J. "Out of the Shadow of Treatment: A Role for Regulatory Agencies in the Prevention of Alcohol Problems."

Alcohol Health and Research World, Winter 1979/80, *4* (2), 11–17.

Rootman, I., and Moser, J. *Community Response to Alcohol-Related Problems.* Rockville, Md.: National Institute on Alcohol Abuse and Alcoholism, 1984.

Rorabaugh, W. "The Alcoholic Republic: America, 1790-1840." Doctoral dissertation, University of California, Berkeley, 1976. Now available revised as *The Alcoholic Republic: An American Tradition.* New York: Oxford University Press, 1979.

Rosenthal, L. "Federal Funding of Research and Research Training Programs in Alcohol Abuse: Priority Areas and Mechanisms of Support." In B. Stimmel (ed.), *Federal Priorities in Funding Alcoholism and Drug Abuse Programs.* Advances in Alcohol and Substance Abuse, Vol. 2, No. 3. New York: Haworth Press, 1983.

Ross, H. L. *Deterring the Drinking Driver: Legal Policy and Social Control.* Lexington, Mass.: Lexington Books, 1982.

Rush, B. *An Inquiry into the Effects of Ardent Spirits upon Body and Mind.* Reprinted in Y. Henderson, *A New Deal in Liquor: A Plea for Dilution.* New York: Doubleday, 1934. (Originally published 1795.)

Saxe, L., and others. *The Effectiveness and Costs of Alcoholism Treatment.* Washington, D.C.: Office of Technology Assessment, U.S. Congress, 1983.

Schramm, C., and Archer, J. "Evaluation of Occupational Alcoholism Programs." In *Prevention, Intervention and Treatment: Concerns and Models.* Alcohol and Health Monograph No. 3. Washington, D.C.: National Institute on Alcohol Abuse and Alcoholism, 1982.

Schuckit, M. "Alcoholism and Sociopathy—Diagnostic Confusion." *Quarterly Journal of Studies on Alcohol,* 1973, *34,* 157–164.

Segal, B. *Drugs and Behavior: Cause, Effects, and Treatment.* New York: Gardner Press, 1987.

Shaw, J., Reuben, S., and Johnson, R. *Development of Model Professional Standards for Counselor Credentialing.* Rockville, Md.: National Institute on Alcohol Abuse and Alcoholism, 1984.

Snow, R., and Wells-Parker, E. "Drinking Reasons, Consumption

Levels, and Drinking Locations Among Drinking Drivers." *International Journal of the Addictions,* 1986, *21* (6), 671–689.

Sobell, M., and Sobell, L. *Individualized Behavior Therapy for Alcoholics: Rationale, Procedures, Preliminary Results and Appendix.* Sacramento: Department of Mental Hygiene, State of California, 1972.

Sobell, M., and Sobell, L. "Conceptual Issues Regarding Goals in the Treatment of Alcohol Problems." *Drugs and Society,* 1987, *1* (2–3), 1–37.

"Sober Prospects for Distillers." *Business Week,* Mar. 22, 1985, pp. 229–230.

Speiglman, R. "Issues in the Rise of Compulsion in California's Drinking Driver Treatment System." In M. Valverius (ed.), *Punishment and/or Treatment for Driving Under the Influence of Alcohol and Other Drugs.* Stockholm: International Committee on Alcohol, Drugs and Traffic Safety, 1985.

Spicer, J., and Owen, P. *Finding the Bottom Line: The Cost Impact of Employee Assistant and Chemical Dependency Treatment Programs.* Center City, Minn.: Hazelden Foundation, 1985.

"Spirits Advertising Down in '85 as Wine and Beer Up Spending." *Impact,* Aug. 1 and 15, 1986, *16* (14–15), pp. 1–10.

Straus, R. "Types of Alcohol Dependence." In B. Kissin and H. Begleiter (eds.), *The Biology of Alcoholism,* Vol. 6: *The Pathogenesis of Alcoholism: Psychosocial Factors.* New York: Plenum, 1983.

Straus, R. "Alcohol Studies in Social Perspective." Paper presented at meeting of the Research Society on Alcoholism and the Medical Society on Alcoholism, San Francisco, Apr. 21, 1986.

Strickland, D. "Content and Effects of Alcohol Advertising: Comments on NTIS Pub. No. PB82-123-142." *Journal of Studies on Alcohol,* 1984, *45* (1), 87–93.

Taube, C., Lee, E., and Forthofer, R. "Diagnosis-Related Groups for Mental Disorders, Alcoholism, and Drug Abuse: Evaluation and Alternatives." *Hospital and Community Psychiatry,* May 1984, *35* (5), 452–455.

Taylor, J. "Controlled Drinking Studies: Methodological Issues." *Drugs and Society,* 1987, *1* (2–3), 83–107.

Taylor, M. "Alcoholics Anonymous: How It Works: Recovery Processes in a Self-Help Group." Unpublished doctoral dissertation, University of California, Berkeley, 1977.

Thornberry, O., Wilson, R., and Golden, P. "Health Promotion and Disease Prevention: Provisional Data from the National Health Interview Survey: United States, January–June 1985." *Vital and Health Statistics of the National Center for Health Statistics*, No. 119. Washington, D.C.: U.S. Department of Health and Human Services, 1986.

Tocqueville, A. de. *Democracy in America.* (G. Lawrence, trans.; J. Mayer, ed.) New York: Doubleday, 1969. (Originally published 1835.)

Trachtenberg, R. *Report on Alcoholism Treatment.* Rockville, Md.: Alcohol, Drug, and Mental Health Administration, 1986.

Trice, H., and Roman, P. *Spirits and Demons at Work: Alcohol and Other Drugs on the Job.* Ithaca: New York State School of Industrial and Labor Relations, Cornell University, 1972.

Turkington, C. "PPOs: Friends or Foes?" *APA Monitor,* Aug. 1986, *17* (8), 13.

"U.S. Death Rates Decline Except for Ages 15 to 24." *San Francisco Examiner,* Jan. 7, 1983, p. 4.

U.S. Departments of Treasury and Health and Human Services. *Report to the President and the Congress on Health Hazards Associated with Alcohol and Methods to Inform the General Public of These Hazards.* Washington, D.C.: U.S. Government Printing Office, 1980.

Vingilis, E. "Drinking Drivers and Alcoholics: Are They from the Same Population?" In R. Smart and others (eds.), *Recent Advances in Alcohol and Drug Problems.* Vol. 7. New York: Plenum, 1983.

Wagenaar, A. "Youth, Alcohol, and Traffic Crashes." In *Research Issues in the Prevention of Alcohol-Related Injuries.* Proceedings of an NIAAA-sponsored conference on trauma. Berkeley, Calif.: Prevention Research Center, 1986.

Walcott, E., and Straus, R. "Use of a Hospital Facility in Conjunction with Outpatient Clinics in the Treatment of Alcoholics." *Quarterly Journal of Studies on Alcohol,* March 1952, *13* (1), 60–77.

Wallack, L. "Practical Issues, Ethical Concerns and Future Directions in the Prevention of Alcohol-Related Problems." *Journal
of Primary Prevention,* Summer 1984a, *4* (4), 199–224.

Wallack, L. "Television Programming, Advertising, and the
Prevention of Alcohol-Related Problems." In D. Gerstein (ed.),
*Toward the Prevention of Alcohol Problems: Government,
Business and Community Action.* Washington, D.C.: National
Academy Press, 1984b.

Wallack, L. "A Community Approach to the Prevention of Alcohol-
Related Problems: the San Francisco Experience." *International
Quarterly of Community Health Education,* 1984–85, 5 (2), 85–
102.

Wallack, L., Radcliffe, J., and Wittman, F. "Changing Perspectives
Toward a Redefinition of Alcohol-Related Problems." In A.
Mecca (ed.), *The Future of Alcohol Services in California.* San
Rafael: California Health Foundation, 1982.

Waller, J. "Alcohol and Unintentional Injury." In B. Kissin and H.
Begleiter (eds.), *The Biology of Alcoholism.* Vol. 4: *Social
Aspects of Alcoholism.* New York: Plenum, 1976.

Watson, L. "Executive Recovery in the Hills of Marin." *San
Francisco Examiner,* Feb. 26, 1986, p. 29.

Weisner, C. *Community Response to Alcohol-Related Problems: A
Study of Treatment Providers' Perceptions.* Report C-30.
Berkeley, Calif.: Alcohol Research Group, 1981.

Weisner, C. "The Changing Alcohol Treatment System: A Profile
of Clients." Paper presented at meeting of the International
Group for Comparative Alcohol Studies, Stockholm, Oct. 1984.

Weisner, C. "The Transformation of Alcohol Treatment: Access to
Care and the Response to Drinking Driving." *Journal of Public
Health Policy,* Spring 1986, 7 (1), 78–92.

Weisner, C. "The Social Ecology of Alcohol Treatment in the U.S."
In M. Galanter (ed.), *Recent Developments in Alcoholism.*
Vol. 5. New York: Plenum, 1987.

Weisner, C., and Room, R. "Financing and Ideology in Alcohol
Treatment." *Social Problems,* Dec. 1984, *32* (2), 167–184.

Weisner, C., and Speiglman, R. "Accommodation to Coercion:
Changes in Alcoholism Treatment Paradigms." Paper presented

at annual meeting of the Society for the Study of Social Problems, San Francisco, Sept. 1982.

Welch, B. "Professional Point." *APA Monitor,* Aug. 1986a, *17* (8), 15.

Welch, B. "Professional Point." *APA Monitor,* Sept. 1986b, *17* (9), p. 17.

Wiener, C. *The Politics of Alcoholism.* New Brunswick, N.J.: Transaction Books, 1981.

Williams, G., Aitken, S., and Malin, H. "Reliability of Self-Reported Alcohol Consumption in a General Population Survey." *Journal of Studies on Alcohol,* May 1985, *46* (3), 223–227.

Wittman, F. *Community Perspectives on the Prevention of Alcohol Problems.* Berkeley, Calif.: Prevention Research Group, 1982a.

Wittman, F. *Zoning Ordinances, Alcohol Outlets, and Planning Prospects for Local Control of Alcohol Problems.* Berkeley, Calif.: Alcohol Research Group,1982b.

Wittman, F., and Hilton, M. *Local Regulation of Alcohol Ability: Use of Planning and Zoning Ordinances to Regulate Alcohol Outlets in California Cities.* Berkeley, Calif.: Prevention Research Center, 1984.

Zimmerman, R. "Social Model: As Effective, Cheaper Than Hospital." *U.S. Journal of Drug and Alcohol Dependence,* Mar. 1986, *10* (3), p. 12.

Index

A

Aaron, P., 32

Accreditation, of professionals, 167–169

Addiction Research Foundation (Canada), 21, 45, 89, 138

Advertising: by alcohol industry, 84–85, 92–98; recommendations for, 187

Advocacy groups: analysis of 61–80; background on, 180–181; conclusions on, 194–197; cooperation among, 80; described, 69–80; inventory of 66–69; recommendations for 180–197; views of, 61–66

Airline Pilots Association, 49

Aitken, S., 13

Alameda County, studies in, 112

Al-Anon, 66

Alaska: consumption in, 4; treatment in, 192

Al-Ateen, 66

Albee, G., 107

Albuquerque, tertiary prevention in, 117

Alcohol: consumption of, 1–5, 82–83, 86; as drug, 5; images of, 104; love-hate for, 23–24; physical damage from, 5–6, 43; policy recommended on, 196–197

Alcohol and Drug Problems Association of North America, 66, 100, 149, 168

Alcohol dependence syndrome, 15

Alcohol, Drug, and Mental Health Administration (ADAMHA): recommendations for, 182, 184; and research, 38, 171; as umbrella agency, 47, 52, 56–57, 59

Alcohol education, and prevention, 106–107, 108–112

Alcohol industry: advertising by, 84–85, 92–98, 187; and advocacy groups, 184–186; analysis of, 81–102; defensiveness of, 98–101; history of, 81–85; incentives for cooperation by, 101–102; and labeling, 90–92, 97; and marketing conglomerates, 85–89; and marketing controls for prevention, 121–123; and National Council on Alcoholism, 74–76; subsidies from, 100–101; and taxes, 80–90, 101

Alcohol problems: and advocacy groups, 61–80; age differences in, 9–10, 11; and alcohol industry, 81–102; analysis of, 1–22; background on, 1–4; control effort failures for, 37–102; costliness of, 4–7; cross-national comparisons